A New Diplomacy for Sustainable Development

Routledge/SEI Global Environment and Development Series

1. A New Diplomacy for Sustainable Development
The Challenge of Global Change
Bo Kjellén

A New Diplomacy for Sustainable Development

The Challenge of Global Change

Bo Kjellén

Routledge
Taylor & Francis Group
New York   London

Routledge
Taylor & Francis Group
270 Madison Avenue
New York, NY 10016

Routledge
Taylor & Francis Group
2 Park Square
Milton Park, Abingdon
Oxon OX14 4RN

© 2008 by Taylor & Francis Group, LLC
Routledge is an imprint of Taylor & Francis Group, an Informa business

Printed in the United States of America on acid-free paper
10 9 8 7 6 5 4 3 2

International Standard Book Number-13: 978-0-415-95839-4 (Hardcover)

Library of Congress Cataloging-in-Publication Data

Kjellén, Bo, 1933-
    A new diplomacy for sustainable development : the challenge of global change / Bo Kjellén.
        p. cm. -- (Routledge/SEI global environment and development series ; 1)
        Includes bibliographical references.
        ISBN-13: 978-0-415-95839-4
        1. Sustainable development--Government policy. 2. Sustainable development--International cooperation. 3. Environmental policy--Economic aspects. 4. International economic relations. I. Title.

HC79.E5K54 2008
338.9'27--dc22   2007033466

Visit the Taylor & Francis Web site at
http://www.taylorandfrancis.com

and the Routledge Web site at
http://www.routledge.com

To Gia

Contents

viii   *Contents*

Foreword

Some years ago the then Minister of State of the UK Foreign Office, Peter Hain, published a small book with the title *The End of Foreign Policy*. This is quite a remarkable title for a book written by a Minister in a Foreign Office. A title without a question mark, a title as a statement. In this book Peter Hain underlines that the differentiation between foreign affairs and home affairs is more and more difficult to single out. Indeed, there is less and less chance to distinguish between "we here" and "you there."

There are more and more central challenges in a world with more than six billion people depending on influences and interrelations which are "out of the control of any individual State." More and more developments are asking for global solutions; for integrated answers beyond national boundaries, even beyond continents.

This development is particularly important in the field of the environment. The destruction of the ozone layer, the desertification process, climate change, the use of toxic chemicals — all these and quite a number of others are problems which can only be tackled at the global level. Their solution is indeed "out of the control of any individual State." Legally binding arrangements, conventions and protocols, financial mechanisms and reliable monitoring, systematically developed instruments for compliance and enforcement — all these are preconditions for the development and implementation of coordinated action programmes.

This paradigm shift requires new thinking and new negotiation skills, combining the understanding of technology and scientific findings with reliable legal regulations. There is really a need for a "New Diplomacy" to respond to dramatic global changes. It is of course needless to say that it is not only the global environment that asks for this new diplomacy. The globalization of economic activities, the multinational companies, the enormous amounts of dollars going around the world in seconds need this new type of negotiations in order to develop global solutions. The same is true for the struggle against terrorism and for the fight against new kinds of infections like the avian flu.

Nevertheless, it was the environment that first and with special urgency proved the need for a new diplomacy; the environment as part of the struggle to overcome poverty and social injustice — the environment as one of the three main components of sustainable development. The Earth Summit in Rio de Janeiro in 1992 echoed this need quite systematically. The year 1992! Only a very short time after the end of the bipolar world, after the collapse of the Eastern block, of Soviet communism and the centrally planned economy. This was a time of euphoric expectations for a world of cooperation and solidarity, a world dedicated to avoiding a new cold war between North and South, between rich and poor. It was a world determined to cease to consider environmental costs as externalities and to recognize the impact on the environment of the unprecedented consumption patterns of the people living in developed countries. It was time to recognize the effects of climate change, ozone layer destruction, waste and chemicals on the poorest people in the developing countries. The world was determined to come to an end with all kinds of ecological aggression. Rio was a great start for this new diplomacy for sustainable development.

The Earth Summit was served by some visionary and skilled personalities. Bo Kjellén was without any doubt one of those. He proved that this new diplomacy needs credibility and dedication, technical knowledge and patience. He proved the need for awareness of the medium- and long-term perspectives while tackling the urgent problems at hand. Therefore it is so essential that Bo Kjellén, who was highly influential in negotiating the most important results of the Rio Conference, and who was one of the leading personalities in developing the Convention to Combat Desertification in the years after Rio, has written this book. He proved that success mainly depends on the skill to influence developments without being in the limelight of the media. The book is of high importance for all those who have to create new institutional structures for solving global problems in the UN system and in the Bretton Woods institutions, based on the groupings of nations in the G8, the G20, and the G77 and China, in a world of regional integration, with the EU as the most important example. It is good that Bo Kjellén integrates his thinking with his personal experiences, that he goes beyond theoretical considerations to practical implementation of his thoughts. I sincerely hope that many students and dedicated actors at the national, regional and global levels will take the opportunity to read this book, to reflect on it, and to combine it with their own experiences in finding solutions to the new international challenges.

Klaus Töpfer

Preface and Acknowledgments

This book is the fruit of an almost constant reflection on multilateralism, an effort to understand the mechanisms and practice of intergovernmental economic and environmental co-operation. It started in Brussels in 1962, when as a young man I had the privilege of joining the then observer mission of Sweden to the European Communities. It has continued ever since, even though I left active negotiation work after the Swedish Presidency of the European Union in 2001. Most of the time I have been a Swedish civil servant but in the late sixties and early seventies I had the good luck to serve in the OECD as Chef de Cabinet of the then Secretary-General Emile van Lennep, who taught me more than anyone else about the workings of the international economy.

In 1985 I came back to OECD as Permanent Representative of Sweden. From this observation point I witnessed the beginning of the end of the bipolar world that had up until then conditioned our thinking on international co-operation. Old barriers were broken down, there was a new sense of opportunity. But it was not the end of history, nor the uncontested victory of a global market economy. A new world was emerging, driven by technological change, in particular the revolution in information and communication technologies. My conviction is that we have only seen the beginning of their impact.

For me, other areas of multilateral co-operation opened when the then Swedish Minister of Environment, Birgitta Dahl, in 1990 offered me the job as Chief Negotiator in the Ministry. It brought me deep into the Rio process and the negotiations on the Conventions on Climate Change and on the Combat of Desertification. The growing insight of man's impact on the global system has changed my perception of the world. It has also brought me closer to the academic community, providing new tools for analysis and — I hope — understanding. This book is mainly an effort to reflect on the avenues for multilateral diplomacy that have opened with the emergence of global threats of a new kind over the last fifteen years, and of my conviction that we have to make the long-term an integral part of policy thinking and of international negotiation. This reflection has led me to the conclusion that a New Diplomacy for Sustainable Development has been added to the traditional pattern of relations between states; my first ideas on the subject were outlined in a speech in New York in 1999.[1]

The book is dedicated to my wife Gia, who has given me more support and intellectual stimulus than anyone else, and to our children Johan, Fredrik, Jonathan and Emily.

- - - - - - - - - - - - - - -

This book could not have been written without the assistance of the Swedish International Development Agency (SIDA). The constant contact with the Agency, and in particular with Inge Gerremo, has meant that I did not only have financial support, but also a stimulating exchange of ideas. This has helped me to venture into the academic world, trying to absorb the essentials of thinking and theory in the several disciplines close to my professional activities, and to reflect on synergies between research areas, and between research and practice.

The Stockholm Environment Institute has offered me constant support in my work, both intellectually and in practical matters. Professor Roger Casperson gave me initial encouragement, and his successor as Director of the SEI, Professor Johan Rockström, has been instrumental in providing me with ideas and offering me the opportunity to join the Institute as Senior Research Fellow. I am deeply grateful to them and to other SEI staff.

The Tyndall Centre for Climate Change Research at the University of East Anglia in Norwich, UK, has offered me a visiting fellowship, which has enabled me and my wife to spend long periods at this important University. The intellectual stimulus received at the campus through a number of seminars and through the daily exchange of ideas with researchers on climate change policy and its social and economic ramifications has been of capital importance to me. In particular I wish to thank the Director of the Centre, Mike Hulme, Dr. Alex Haxeltine, and Professor Tim O'Riordan, for their constant support and encouragement.

Around the world, I have had the opportunity for discussion with former colleagues in the world of multilateral negotiation, and I wish to thank all of them for their contributions. My friends in the Swedish Government services have continued to be generous in helping me to keep in touch with developments even after I retired from active work; particular thanks to Anders Turesson, my successor as Chief Negotiator for climate. Also in Sweden, the academic world has provided many opportunities for most helpful exchanges of ideas and opinions with many researchers on sustainable development and global change. One person has been of particular importance, Professor Bert Bolin, former Chairman of the Intergovernmental

---

1   Kjellén B., 1999. Acceptance address, *Pace Environmental Law Review*, New York, Vol. 17, 1.

Panel on Climate Change, who probably knows more than anyone else about the complicated interplay between research and policy making.

Finally, two persons have played a special role in helping me to formulate my ideas through continuous dialogue of a broad-ranging nature. One is Ambassador Sverker Åström, who has been a leading official in the Swedish Ministry for Foreign Affairs since the early 1950s and who after his retirement has contributed very actively to the Swedish debate on foreign policy. As Ambassador to the United Nations, he played a decisive role in launching the Stockholm Conference on the Human Environment in 1972, which really was the beginning of the New Diplomacy for Sustainable Development.

The other is Dr. Emily Boyd. She is not only part of my family, but also a brilliant young researcher on several aspects of climate change; her academic insights have helped me greatly in organizing my ideas.

I express my warm thanks to all the many people who have taken an interest in my book: their help has been indispensable to my work. But I take, of course, the responsibility for any errors or omissions.

Introduction

In the late evening of June 13, 1992, I left the Riocentro Conference Hall at Bairra da Tijuca outside Rio de Janeiro with a sense of accomplishment. I had been chairing some of the most difficult negotiations of Agenda 21 and we had just concluded the deal in a tense negotiation to the wire. The package of Rio — with Agenda 21 and the Conventions on Biological Diversity and Climate Change as major components — was safe.

Our expectations for the future were high. An agenda for the twenty-first century had been drafted, a blueprint for a sustainable world. The new conventions on Climate Change and on Biological Diversity had been signed. Coming on top of the major political changes after the end of the cold war it seemed to us that the new millennium had already started and that the road to international co-operation on major survival issues was open.

WHO WERE WE?

We were the negotiators, at both political and official level; the representatives of civil society, who had had intense weeks of lectures, debates and panel discussions at the Global Village, close to downtown Rio de Janeiro; the journalists — all in all a total of 30,000 people, who felt that Rio was the beginning of something really new. The presence of more than one hundred heads of state or government had added to this sense of opportunity.

And yet today, we have to realize that the decade since Rio has not brought the expected results, that we are still struggling with unsustainable trends, both with regard to poverty and environmental degradation. The Johannesburg World Summit on Sustainable Development ten years after Rio had to recognize that major new efforts were needed, and there are still many doubts about the efficiency of the measures agreed upon there. At the same time, the UN is now committed to another set of goals, adopted in 2000: the Millennium Development Goals, principally dealing with world poverty.

However, my conviction is that we have entered a new era of international co-operation and that the boundaries of traditional diplomacy — concentrated on national security and economic and commercial matters — are being extended to a much broader concern for global sustainability. This is the *new* diplomacy. The questions to be addressed are why the results are slow to emerge, and what are the obstacles barring the way to more efficient action. It is also necessary to analyse the process since Rio in a nuanced way: there *have* been successes on the road to sustainable development during this period, such as the Kyoto Protocol on Climate Change or the successful negotiation of a Convention to Combat Desertification, as well as the progress made on the chemicals agenda, just to mention a few examples. One purpose of this book is to draw on my personal experiences from a number of these negotiations in order to better catch the sense of what has happened and to better understand the political, social and economic mechanisms behind the reactions of the international community to these new challenges.

But beyond this analysis hides broader issues. Some observers may argue that the period after September 11, 2001, has put in question the concept of a *new* diplomacy for sustainable development. Are we not witnessing the erosion of the multilateral system, as the United States is pursuing a clearly unilateral approach to world affairs? Is it not true that the first example of this policy line was the Bush administration's refusal to ratify the Kyoto Protocol? Is the multilateral system in its present shape really capable of taking on the survival issues of the twenty-first century?

Undoubtedly, traditional diplomacy and power politics continue to rule the world. This point was brought home very forcefully by the UN Secretary-General Kofi Annan in his speech to the General Assembly in September of 2003. But he took this state of affairs as a point of departure for proposing important changes in the United Nations system, as he also announced the creation of a High-Level Panel to give advice on these matters. On the basis of this report, a summit of world leaders was held in New York in September 2005. It seems quite obvious that structures which were established more than fifty years ago, in the immediate aftermath of World War II, are not designed to tackle unforeseen problems in a totally new global environment; and that there would be a need for a thorough overhaul of institutions.

The important point here is that it will not be enough to propose reform of the Security Council, the centrepiece of UN action of the more traditional character. The survival issues related to global change, the very concept of long-term sustainability, all this forces us to think in terms of yet more radical institutional changes, also mentioned in the Secretary-General's speech. The decade after the Rio Conference, including the World Summit on Sustainable Development in Johannesburg in 2002, and the many negotiating rounds on legally binding instruments such as the Framework

Convention on Climate Change, has given us a valuable insight into the nature of the system, its strengths and weaknesses.

Environmentalists sometimes use the expression "saving the planet." This is not the problem, the planet will survive. The problem is the human species: during the cold war, extinction by the effects of a nuclear holocaust were not ruled out. Today the risks are of a different nature, more creeping, more diffuse, more long-term, such as the effects of global warming. And even if resilience and adaptation will go a long way to avoid disaster, we have to realize that the globalized earth system will require a better capacity of global management than we have been able to craft so far. It is in this perspective that the arguments of the New Diplomacy would strengthen the forces that seek to save a multilateralism under siege, threatening the fundamental gains of the system that was established through far-sighted US leadership in the years after 1945.

All of us who are involved in these processes also know that the inertia of the system is resisting change and that there is a fear that the present state of international political will is simply not sufficient to generate a momentum of reform. Therefore, we need a vision for the future, but we cannot escape the boundaries of political realism and the need for tangible results in the short and medium term.

But such a process of reform cannot take place in a vacuum. The analysis of international events and the future of multilateral co-operation have to take into account the broader picture of national political realities, and of the still wider processes of societal change as spurred by technological development or changing values and trends. Since we are discussing here the consequences of new global risks, e.g., the greenhouse effect on long-term food security, new theories of risk and resilience enter the picture. Furthermore, globalization has underlined the essential role of the markets, and of the need to see the market forces as essential movers of a sustainable future within a well-functioning international framework.

My perspective is that of the practitioner. But my arguments will be underpinned by references to the considerable body of academic research on sustainable development. It is of course quite impossible to give justice to all this background material. Neither is it possible to cover all the issues that merit consideration. The ambition is therefore necessarily more limited: to bring my own practical experience to bear on the insights offered by the different disciplines involved, and in this way to contribute to capacity-building and to a deepening of the increasingly important dialogue between government officials, representatives of civil society, and researchers.

- - - - - - - - - -

The book is divided into three parts.

The first part exposes the essential "Concepts" that have been behind the main new international developments discussed in this book. Chapter 1 will elaborate on the subject of sustainable development itself with its three components of environmental, economic, and social sustainability.

The evolving global dimension is not just a question of scales, it signifies a qualitative step in our perception of sustainability; therefore Chapter 2 discusses the human impact on global natural systems — global change — in the perspective of the effects of our action on economic and social systems worldwide — globalization. Given the role of global markets in the world of today, the interaction between environment and the economy will be given special attention. And finally these different threads of reasoning are brought together in Chapter 3, which discusses how the sustainability paradigm has created a new perception of international relations, modifying diplomatic theory and practice, forming a New Diplomacy for Sustainable Development.

The second part of the book, "Practice," aims at giving insights into the working of the diplomacy for sustainable development, and at the same time exploring more in detail some of the central problems facing its practitioners. It is obviously impossible to be complete in treating this subject, and my ambition has therefore been to present some particularly relevant themes, drawing on my own experiences from negotiations over the last fifteen years. These experiences mainly, though not exclusively, refer to the normative Rio–Johannesburg process, and to the negotiations for the Conventions on Climate Change and on the Combat of Desertification.

A constant feature of several multilateral negotiations in the period after 1960 has been the diverging positions of the industrialized countries in the north and the developing nations in the south. Chapter 4 aims at exploring how the north–south divide has impacted on the negotiations within the new diplomacy. Chapter 5 looks into another central area of discord, namely the relations between Europe and the United States which to such a large extent have conditioned progress in the negotiations, not least in recent years.

Chapters 4 and 5 are broadly structured in the same way, beginning with a brief general background presentation of the evolution of international politics over the post-World War II period, to which will be added some comments of a more personal nature with a bearing on some of these developments. The main body of the chapters contain narratives of negotiations which in my view have been particularly illustrative. Readers might find that this part of the book gives too much room for my personal stories. However, I wished to provide the practitioner's view; I believe that fellow negotiators will recognize the situations and experiences, since they have been shared by all of us. I also think that this perspective is a useful complement to academic theory on multilateral negotiation.

The development of the new diplomacy is still in its early stages. It is not yet possible to have a clear picture of how the emergence of global threats of a new character, such as climate change, will influence international relations, nor how the complicated relationship between national policy making and international relations will develop over the next decades.

In Part III, "Global Sustainability in the Twenty-first Century," Chapter 6 aims at developing and integrating some of the concepts already discussed in order to understand better how these new challenges will influence policies and structures in the future. The point of departure is the increasing need for individuals to understand the nature of global change as a rationale for societal change, closely linked to action in the international arena. The key concept is "enabling conditions," which is the set of domestic situations, attitudes and policies that will make it possible to reach positive results in international negotiations. However, success is also dependent on the existence of well-functioning institutions, good leadership, and skilled negotiators.

Chapter 7 turns to the present situation in a number of the most important fields of the negotiations on sustainable development, developing ideas about the likely course of events in some central areas, in particular the normative work of the United Nations, and the negotiations on climate change. The concluding part of the chapter will contain some personal ideas about reform of the global institutions in order to make them more efficient in meeting the challenges of long-term global change.

The book is built on my personal experience from the public sector and from multilateral diplomacy. Increasingly, governments have to realize that actors outside these spheres will be of central importance for the future of international relations. In various parts of the book I comment on the role of non-governmental organizations and the corporate sector in developing the new diplomacy. But within the framework I have chosen it has not been possible to give full justice to their importance, nor of the dynamics they provide for the future. Just to give one example, I have no doubt that solutions to the threat of global warming cannot be found, unless the markets, through their financial and technological capacity, will be fully engaged. This would certainly warrant a book of its own. More in general, I would hope that this present effort of exploring the border-line between practice and theory in the vast and dynamic field of the new diplomacy for sustainable development will inspire more research on a number of these issues by both academic scholars and practitioners of diplomacy. Both perspectives are necessary.

Part I

Concepts

1 Reflections on Sustainable Development

WHAT IS SUSTAINABLE DEVELOPMENT?

This whole effort of negotiation has been based on the notion of sustainable development, which became a household expression with the report of the World Commission on Environment and Development (WCED 1987), chaired by the former Prime Minister of Norway, Gro Harlem Brundtland, who was later to become Director-General of WHO. The Brundtland Commission was not the first to use the term, but its report "Our Common Future," came at a favorable point in time: the relationship between economic growth and the environment had become an essential element of the discourse of development. There had been a conflict brewing between these two concepts ever since the first large UN Conference on the Human Environment, in Stockholm in 1972. At that time, Indira Gandhi, then Prime Minister of India, took the lead in stating that the main priority for developing countries was to combat poverty and deprivation. Environmental issues were seen as a distraction from this main objective, or worse, a way of the industrialized north to keep the developing countries down.

However, the very creation of the Brundtland Commission was proof that the environmental issue would not go away. In the previous decades, some of the global consequences of environmental deterioration had become more obvious: the thinning of the ozone layer, the problems of desertification and drought, the threat of climate change — all this demonstrated that the developing countries themselves might well be victims of serious environmental problems. So it was logical to look for a formula which could demonstrate that the world community could deal with environment and development at the same time. Two quotes are illustrative:

> Environment and development are not separate challenges, they are inexorably linked. Development cannot subsist upon a deteriorating resources base: the environment cannot be protected when growth leaves out of account the costs of environmental destruction. (WCED 1987, p. 37)

Sustainable development seeks to meet the needs and aspirations of the present without compromising the ability to meet those of the future. Far from requiring the cessation of economic growth, it recognizes that the problems of poverty and underdevelopment cannot be solved, unless we have a new era of growth in which developing countries play a large role and reap large benefits. (WCED 1987, p. 50)

The formula offered a convenient way out of a dilemma, in underlining the need to achieve both inter-generational equity and intra-generational equity. At the same time, the sweeping character of the expression meant that efforts of interpreting it more in detail or to make it operative would lead to difficulties. It has been pointed out that probably any attempt to move beyond Brundtland's definition would raise scientific questions and even ethical and political dilemmas. (Owens 2003).

The political attractiveness of the Brundtland formula was greatly strengthened by the preparations for the Rio Conference 1992. World Commissions generally have great difficulties in making a real impact, because there is no specific forum available to spread the message. However, here was a Conference that could take up the challenge and provide a platform for the Commission's report. Furthermore, the efficient and charismatic Brundtland became one of the stars of the Rio Conference, which also benefited from the major changes in world politics that had created new dynamics in the United Nations: there was no longer a Soviet bloc, and one could feel an opening of minds.

Nevertheless, many of us who were involved in the Rio negotiations had doubts and misgivings about the concept of sustainable development. To me it seemed more of a convenient political slogan than a basis for real action. The developing countries continued to be suspicious; and UN Secretary-General Boutros Boutros-Ghali created a certain confusion by launching, shortly after Rio, an Agenda for Development. Since Agenda 21, which was one of the main results of Rio, set out to be an agenda for sustainable development in the twenty-first century, we had in fact two parallel agendas for a certain period of time. In a way, one could say that this confusing situation persisted until the Johannesburg World Summit on Sustainable Development in 2002.

However, the problems related to definitions seem largely irrelevant today. It is more important to note that the concept of sustainable development has been generally accepted as a guideline for policy action and that it is now recognized that it rests on a triangle of economic, social and environmental sustainability. Official rhetoric in most countries uses this trinity of components, sometimes with too much enthusiasm, creating the feeling that the mantra hides a reluctance to take concrete action.

At this point, it is useful to develop two further lines of thought with regard to sustainable development: first, the need to elaborate a more nuanced analysis of the components of sustainability, and, second, the dichotomy between the general acceptance of the concept and the lack of efficient implementation. Together they form a basis for reflection on the practical value of the idea and its relationship to deep societal trends.

Figure 1.1 (the "Diamond") is an effort to go beyond the triangle, based on the idea that a practically unlimited number of factors influence policy making at all levels. The graph uses eight parameters, grouped in clusters representing the traditional three components of sustainability. On top are the closely linked environment and health, further down to the left are social components and moving up on the right side different economic aspects. These eight parameters represent a small sample of all possible elements, but they serve to demonstrate the fundamental inter-relationship between them, thus illuminating political processes which need to accommodate conflicting demands. The graph can also serve as an illustration of the need for inter-disciplinary research as a help for policy making. There are, however, a number of "exogenous" factors that influence the shape of the diamond. These are at the top demographic factors and lifestyles, and at the bottom technological development and politics/policies. To take

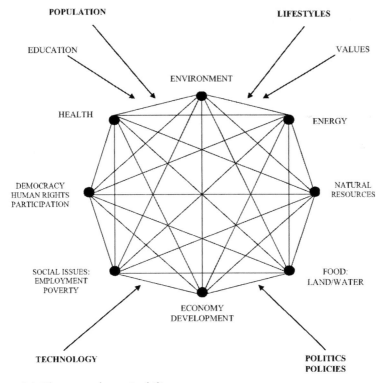

Figure 1.1 Elements of sustainability.

demography as an example, it is quite obvious that the aging population of Europe will impact on the way in which European governments will have to perceive sustainability over the coming decades. And it is also quite obvious that the issue of lifestyles and consumption patterns among the rich of this world — and they do not all live in the developed countries — will be decisive for long-term sustainability. Similarly, technological development will open new avenues for energy production, transports and industry. We know that the world of 2050 will be very different in terms of technology; but it is dangerous to believe that technology alone will be able to bail mankind out of a situation when most indicators point to unsustainable trends.

The "Diamond" is a helpful analytical and pedagogical tool in trying to understand better the nature of sustainable development. It can also serve to clarify how governments look at the environmental component of sustainability, since the economic and social elements have for a long time been essential parts of governments' policies: sustained economic growth and reasonable social conditions have been central policy objectives for almost two hundred years. The new component is environment, and it is not surprising that the ecological issues have been given emphasis in the debate of sustainability. As the discussion became more nuanced in the course of the 1990s the main attention focused on the relationship between environment and other policies, and it is highly probable that this issue will be of central importance in the coming decades.

We have thus seen that sustainable development is a complicated concept: but in its simplest and most general expression it carries an attractive political message, underlining a concern for the *unborn* and for the *unseen*. The Rio process opened the door to a political discourse which most governments found irresistible: to make general statements about the need for sustainability, while not defining the contents of action to be taken or the conflicts of interest that were inherent in the concept. At the same time, the environmental NGOs, for obvious reasons, embraced the notion of sustainability with enthusiasm. Furthermore, the Rio Declaration and Agenda 21 provided general guidance which could be used in many different ways. In domestic politics, the "mood of sustainability" provided a background against which specific national circumstances could be projected. For example, in Sweden the center/right government in office at the time of the Rio Conference, launched a forceful campaign for local implementation of Agenda 21, based on Chapter 28 of the document, which called for local Agendas 21 to be elaborated. The success was striking: within two years practically all of Sweden's 288 municipalities had adopted their local Agendas, and a large number of enthusiastic young people were employed as Agenda 21 coordinators. As Susan Owens has pointed out, "The diffusion and take up of the concept was remarkable and throughout numerous institutions, strategies began to proliferate. In this era of promise, then, sustainable development seemed to meet everyone's requirements and to offer a pragmatic way forward" (Owens 2002).[1]

Toward the end of the 1990s, however, it became obvious that an implementation deficit was appearing, both at the national and the international level. In Sweden, the municipalities became less inclined to finance the Agenda 21 coordinators, and in the UN, and other international organizations, it became increasingly difficult to move from general statements to concrete commitments. Indeed, the World Summit on Sustainable Development in Johannesburg in 2002 set as its main objective to ensure implementation of Agenda 21, not to repeat previously agreed general texts. This ambition is reflected in the Plan of Implementation agreed in Johannesburg, but it is still uncertain to what extent this document will actually be able to influence policies on a broader scale. These issues will be elaborated further in Chapter 2.

Turning once again to Susan Owens, she has offered explanations of this process, which go beyond the idea of an "implementation gap." She has pointed out that there is no singular definition of sustainable development upon which we can all agree. In this context she has quoted John Rawls, who in his "A Theory of Justice" pointed out the distinction between a concept — the broad meaning of a term — and a conception, which must include the principles required for implementation.(Rawls 1972). In this way, we can range the concept of sustainability along with such ideas as democracy, justice and liberty. Owens also quotes Bagehot (1856) who observed that the path of great principles is marked through history by trouble, anxiety and conflict.

For those of us who have observed government action at close range over the last twenty years, it is obvious that these observations are highly pertinent. Sustainability is a concept which reality is imposing upon government action, in particular against the background of global threats to the future of mankind. But since so much of the sustainability discourse deals with the long term, and the claims on government action generally relate to the short or medium term — and in this fast-moving world perhaps increasingly so — there falls a shadow between the expression of support for a principle and the concrete measures. A recurrent theme in the reflection on sustainable development has to be how to bridge this gap.

In societal terms, one important prerequisite for success in moving from the concept to its implementation is the degree of support at various levels, moving from the "man in the street" to the ruler. One example is the management (or mismanagement) of the concept of democracy. There are few countries today that would not label themselves democracies, but we all know that there are several of those which cannot properly live up to democratic standards. A striking example was of course the communist states in Eastern Europe, which, until the breakdown of the Soviet system, claimed to be "people's democracies": nobody was fooled to believe that this pleonasm described a particularly excellent form of democracy, in particular not the citizens of these countries. They knew that the concept could not be given real substance because there were no mechanisms available to implement it, and there did not exist any channels to really express the views of the majority of citizens.

When discussing international negotiations in the following chapters, I will underline the importance of the state of public opinion for the instructions given by governments to their negotiators. At this stage, it is enough to state that in our democratic societies no government can take decisions which are out of step with what the public can accept, if it wants to survive in office. On the other hand, the government has a critical responsibility to lead and not just to execute what it believes to be the views of the majority of people.

Here is a dilemma for environmental policies, since the long-term gains might be difficult to see, whereas the short-term costs often are evident. Policies to reduce the emissions of carbon dioxide are a case in point: the dangers of climate change might seem diffuse and long-term, whereas the measures to be taken would go straight into the very heart of our industrial civilization: energy and transport.

Public information campaigns and similar actions of concerned people, non-governmental organizations or the media certainly have an impact, but it is difficult for them to be heard in the loud noise of all sorts of messages that are moving around in our societies today. It would seem that the only way in which sustainability can be a real force to reckon with would be if it forms part of a new societal paradigm, a new set of values. This may seem far-fetched; but we know that beyond the daily concerns facing both governments and individuals there are profound movements that ultimately shape the realities of an era, and permeate almost all expressions of ideas, and all activities in societies. There is a German word that captures the idea: "Zeitgeist" — the mood of the time.

Can sustainability as a concept acquire a strength which will allow it to have such a societal impact, and what would be the conditions that could make this happen? This is a crucial issue, both at the national level and for international co-operation.

One way of approaching these questions would be to make a comparison with the long period of time — between 1950 and 1990 — which was characterized by the cold war. The "Zeitgeist" which influenced several generations at the level of the planet was built on a bi-polar conflictual relationship between two superpowers and two competing economic and social systems. Furthermore, the nuclear capacity of the superpowers was such that the conflict could degenerate into a nuclear exchange which could lead to mutual destruction, global environmental disaster and the end of civilization as we know it. New evidence over the last decade has shown that these risks were real: nuclear war was very close during the Cuba crisis in 1962.

This situation had deep-going consequences, not only for international relations or the role of the United Nations, or the operation of the world economy, but in terms of the fundamentals of societies, the way people perceived the world. It was not possible to escape the trauma of the nuclear threat: it was there and it influenced literature and art, philosophy and social theory. In fact it is impossible to dissociate the trends governing societies in these years from the overwhelming impact of the cold war.

Obviously, the Second World War had had still more deep-going effects on societies: but the reason why the cold war could give us lessons in reflecting on the issue of sustainability is the way in which the superpower conflict could come to an end without a nuclear disaster.

The reasoning behind the successful US policy in the face of the Soviet threat was based on the idea of containment, first presented by George F. Kennan. The basic theory behind it was that the Soviet Union should face certain opposition to all efforts of expansion but that the west should not provoke the USSR. In order to make this policy credible the strength and capacity of NATO to oppose any Soviet move could not be put in doubt. The credibility of the NATO defenses became a guarantee for peace. Therefore, billions and billions of dollars were put into weapons systems, new aircraft, missiles, bombs, troops, intelligence; there were seldom any questions whether the costs would be too high. The priority was absolute, but the ultimate purpose was that this arsenal should never be activated. And the objective was realized: the Soviet Union imploded peacefully, and large parts of the military build-up would simply be scrapped.

The real character of the Soviet threat was rarely put in doubt in the west. The economic and other sacrifices that the reaction to it forced citizens to accept were not questioned. It was part of the reality of the time, integrated in people's thinking about society and the world.

As we now struggle with the concept of sustainability and its impact on society, the lessons of the cold war seem highly relevant. Because if the threats of climate change, waning water resources, depletion of the ozone layer, disappearance of species; and all the other effects of global change, can be perceived as an overriding issue of the same character as the threats we faced during the cold war, then there would be much better preconditions for achieving the societal changes that could make sustainability move from a general concept to conceptions which could be implemented.

The argument just made is based on an interpretation of the concept of sustainability which could be called an *organizing principle* in the sense that it is part of a general pattern of how societies work and how people perceive their situation in relation to the outside world. It goes without saying that this effect of a "Zeitgeist" can be weaker or stronger depending on circumstances, and it is also clear that the dominating concept is all the time competing with other influences. In this context, the notion of the "risk society" as coined by Beck and others is highly relevant, as it could provide a bridge between the two overriding impacts I have tried to illustrate through the comparison between the period 1950–1990 and a possible time in the future when sustainable development becomes a generally accepted public concern.

In order to arrive at that stage, there is no doubt that sustainability as a *political instrument* requires attention. The very fact that world leaders, ever since the Rio Conference in 1992, have continued to give support to the concept of sustainable development in many different ways proves that they feel that the idea would strike a positive chord with voters, as long as the statements are of a general character and do not offend important groups' concrete interests. There is also a cyclical pattern in the way governments use the concept: Sweden may be taken as a good example.

In the middle of the 1990s the Prime Minister, Goran Persson, endorsed sustainability with great enthusiasm and in several speeches, both at home and internationally, gave a very strong support to the concept. He underlined in particular that the triangular notion of economic, social, and environmental sustainability fitted well into the traditional policy priorities of Swedish social democracy, focusing on a stable economy, equality and social justice. During the Swedish Presidency of the European Union in the first half of 2001, this policy line was one of the main pillars of action: and in fact several important European decisions were achieved, both in the general endorsement of a strategy for sustainable development and in the specific field of climate policy.

However, relatively soon it seemed that the enthusiasm for sustainability faded at the highest level of government, and it was only in 2004 that the concept returned to the forefront. An additional element was now added to give strengthened political visibility, based on traditions from the thirties, when the then social democratic Prime Minister, Per-Albin Hansson, coined the expression "the home for the people" (folkhemmet), based on the notion that the nation should be like a good home to all its members, leaving nobody out or badly treated. This was at the time a forceful metaphor, and had a considerable impact on Swedish politics.

Now Prime Minister Persson launched the expression "the green home for the people" (det grona folkhemmet). It is still uncertain how much effect the renewed interest in sustainability will have, but a government reshuffle in the autumn of 2004 seemed to confirm the ambitions of the Prime Minister. A new Ministry for Sustainable Development, integrating the former Ministry of the Environment, was created, and a high-profile politician, Mona Sahlin, was appointed to lead it. Sahlin has now been elected Persson's successor, leading the Social Democrats, presently in opposition.

This Swedish example is representative for the attitudes of the great majority of European political leaders. At the same time it is obvious that governments are struggling with the seeming paradox referred to by Susan Owens: it is relatively easy to make general statements about sustainability, but as concrete policies have to be developed, i.e., with regard to taxes and subsidies or other instruments of economic and regional policy, challenging established interests, the going is much harder, and difficult conflicts of goals and objectives appear. Sustainability as a political instrument will only be fully operative as its role as an organizing instrument becomes generally accepted, or to use another expression, as the enabling conditions for policy change are better fulfilled.

Nevertheless, it is interesting to note that sustainable development as an *opinion-shaping tool* is becoming more and more attractive. The concept has been embraced with enthusiasm by a great number of environmental NGOs. Organizations such as WWF (World Wildlife Fund) or IUCN (International Union for the Conservation of Nature) have given strong support to the concept, and a great number of other non-governmental organizations have also been instrumental in promoting the concept through direct actions of different kinds or through the participation in government-sponsored think-tanks or broad-based commissions at both national and international level. The Rio process became particularly instrumental in this context, since the Secretary-General of the UNCED Conference, Maurice Strong, had a particular interest in and knowledge of the potential of NGOs and actively promoted their participation in the Conference as well as in all associated meetings.

It is not easy to measure the impact of NGO's activities, but it is certainly significant, in particular, in the field of environment. At the same time it has to be recognized that the role of NGO's in supporting development has been more modest. Representatives of developing countries have sometimes complained that the northern NGOs have no real understanding for the need for growth in the developing countries as a means to combat poverty, and that they therefore tend to be supporting a northern agenda. There is some merit in this argument: and it may well be behind the apparent dichotomy between "sustainable development" and "development" that has previously been referred to.

Finally, sustainability is a concept that calls for *systemic thinking* It is difficult to analyze the concept without a continuous reference to the many complex interrelationships that appear within this set of ideas, and in fact sustainability seems to be rather meaningless if it would not have an impact on systems, be they biological or human. At the present time, with threats such as climate change being given increased attention, the very notion of global sustainability requires an approach which evaluates resilience and vulnerability in relation to these threats as parts of a global system.

In terms of research, this is a major challenge. Earth science, or global change research, requires new methods and new priorities. It requires a better understanding of the needs for inter-disciplinary approaches, and for closer contacts between natural and social sciences, humanities and law. The importance of technology in changing practices which are detrimental to the earth system makes it necessary to involve engineering better than before. Systems analysis, as developed over a relatively long period of time, will have to be adapted to the new requirements of global change. All this forms part of the moving scenery of research organization and financing, the structure of higher education and the role of universities, institutes, think-tanks, and other research institutions: and the relationship between research and political processes at the global, regional, and national levels.

This chapter has mainly dealt with the concept of sustainable development and some of the fundamental issues related to its implementation. The issues addressed in the last section underline the particular importance of globalization: in fact it may well be that the understanding of the concept must take a quantum leap as we approach it in the global dimension. The reason is that mankind has never been in this situation before: sustainability has been an issue over thousands of years, and we know that environmentally unsustainable practices have led to major disasters, bringing down civilizations in various parts of the world. But for all this time, humans and societies were small, nature and the planet large. Now a world population of six billion people, rising to more than nine billion in the next fifty years, and requiring improving living standards on a global scale, will have a decisive impact on the earth system. The notion of ecological footprints has illustrated the challenge: and the reality of a globalized earth system with risks for a dysfunctional planet dramatizes the choices to be made by this and the next generation. In fact, Paul Crutzen, who was awarded the Nobel Prize in Chemistry 1995 for his research on the ozone layer, has (together with E. Stoermer) coined the expression "the Anthropocene Era" to demonstrate that we are now living in a geological epoch when the human species has a decisive impact on the whole earth system.

The next chapter will analyze in more detail the global character of the problem and the efforts that have been made to craft the response of the international community.

2 Global Change, Globalization and the Economic Dimension

REFLECTIONS ON GLOBAL CHANGE

Sustainability has taken on a new meaning in the beginning of the twenty-first century with the realization that ours is the first generation to have an impact on the whole global system. For the main part of the existence of the human species on this planet, nature was overwhelmingly large and humans just a small group living at the mercy of natural forces. Even in the year 1800, the world population was only 900 million. Most people were still living in poverty with a limited impact on the environment. New technologies and industrialization changed this radically.

The industrial revolution in the nineteenth century introduced a period of unprecedented change, with improvements in living standards and health conditions for many millions on the planet, with revolutionary changes in energy production and transports, in agricultural and industry production, transforming living conditions in ways which had not been known before. As we are being more and more concerned about the impact of humans on the global environment, it is important not to forget what life was like for most people in the periods before the industrial revolution: a short lifespan in misery, a majority of children dying in early age, a harshness of living conditions which we can hardly visualize today. The improvement brought about by technological change, advances in medicine and hygiene, and new production methods, has led to a tremendous lengthening of the average lifespan and to opportunities in life which were denied previous generations.

These factors have contributed to the rapid increase in world population, which has taken place over the last 200 years. In the year 1900 the global population was 1.6 billion, which in 2000 had increased to 6 billion. However, the aggregates need to be nuanced through a number of additional considerations: in the course of the last decades of the twentieth century the population increase slowed down considerably through family planning, increased incomes, and better education opportunities for women. "The population explosion," with its Malthusian overtones, has lost some of its ominous character.

Of course, this does not mean that the population increase does not continue to be a driving force in the human-induced global changes we are witnessing today. The demographic dynamics are such that present projections for 2050 point to a total world population of around 9 billion. Nobody knows when, and at what level, stabilization can be achieved. Together with lifestyle expectations everywhere this will mean that there will most probably be a global escalation in both per capita demands for Earth's resources, and in the environmental consequences of production and consumption for the functioning of the Earth system.

Furthermore, we must realize that the global figures hide very important regional and structural differences. Practically all the increase from 6 to 9 billion in the world population will occur in developing countries, whereas in particular Europe will experience a stagnant and therefore aging population structure. The consequences of this situation can be quite dramatic with regard to social conditions, production and societal effects of different kinds. Already today, the organization and financing of pension systems is a major political issue in all European countries.

However, for the purposes of this analysis, the essential point is to realize that the population increase together with lifestyle expectations everywhere will most probably lead to a global escalation both in per capita demands for the Earth's resources, and in the environmental consequences of production and consumption for the functioning of the Earth system. (Steffen et al. 2004).

It is true that environmental disasters have occurred previously in history, but they have been on a local scale. There are the examples of the Babylonian culture, the Maya civilization, and the mysteries of Easter Island. Today, however, we are in a different situation: the present generation carries a responsibility stretching far into the future, since man is now for the first time in history capable of influencing the whole global system, becoming a geological force (Clark, Crutzen, Schellnhuber 2004).

A major research effort by the International Geosphere-Biosphere Programme (IGBP) together with other global change programs and involving a large number of scientists from different disciplines led to the publication in 2004 of an important contribution to our understanding of these complicated problems (W. Steffen et al., *Global change and the Earth system: A planet under pressure*, Springer Verlag Berlin/Heidelberg, 2004).

The theme of the research is expressed as "the nature of the Earth as a system, the evolving role of anthropogenic activities as an ever-increasing planetary-scale force in the System, and the consequences of rapid change for the future of the Earth's environment and for the well-being of human societies."[1]

The consequences of the human impact on the Earth system are multiple. Climate change is of course the most obvious example of a global threat: greenhouse gases emitted anywhere end up in the atmosphere, which is shared by all. But global change is much more than climate. The depletion of the ozone layer has led to serious consequences, and air pollution, including transboundary air pollution is becoming a serious problem in many parts of the world. Nearly 50% of the land surface has been transformed by direct human action, with significant consequences, i.e., biodiversity (Vitousek et al. 1986, Turner et al. 1990, Daily 1995); and more than half of all accessible freshwater is appropriated for human purposes (Postel et al. 1996), while fish stocks are being depleted at an accelerating pace.

Most of these problems are local and regional, but the very fact that they appear in many parts of the world simultaneously means that they have global significance.

IGBP has underlined that "classical analytical science in which individual variables are isolated and their separate effects determined individually cannot cope with the challenges posed by Earth System science. This is often most clearly seen where responses to environmental problems have been designed to address specific, narrowly defined problems within a framework that fails to consider the full range of consequences inherent in a complex, interactive system."

In my view, this position represents a view of the world which should be the basis for policy action. Therefore, efforts to prioritize action in the way advocated in the so-called Copenhagen Consensus (2004), when a number of economists were asked to rank the world's problem to decide which issues should be given new resources to find solutions, are bound to fail. The systemic links are simply too strong.

As an example, in northern Europe recent research seems to show that the situation with regard to the Baltic Sea is much more serious than previously considered: this means that efforts to reduce eutrophication of the sea through reduction in emissions might no longer have the desired effects, with the consequence that fish stocks will not be restored in the way expected. Some researchers talk in terms of a collapse of the whole ecosystem of the Baltic.

The clearest expression so far of the findings of Earth System science appeared at a major conference in Amsterdam in 2001, with the participation of over 1,400 people. The Conference adopted the Amsterdam Declaration on Global Change, which summarizes the scientific findings in the following succinct way:

- The Earth System behaves as a single, self-regulating system comprised of physical, chemical, biological and human components.
- Human activities are significantly influencing Earth's environment in many ways in addition to greenhouse gas emissions and climate change.
- Global change cannot be understood in terms of a simple cause-effect paradigm. Human-driven changes cause multiple effects that cascade through the Earth System in complex ways...that interact with each other...that are difficult to understand and even more difficult to predict. Surprises abound.

- Earth System dynamics are characterized by critical thresholds and abrupt changes. The probability of a human-driven abrupt change in Earth's environment has yet to be quantified but is not negligible.
- The nature of changes now occurring simultaneously in the Earth System, their magnitudes and rates of change are unprecedented. The Earth is currently operating in a no-analogue state.

These far-reaching conclusions by the Amsterdam meeting give reason for very deep reflection, at all levels: personal, societal, and global. For both research and political processes questions have to be raised whether structures are now appropriate to meet these extraordinary challenges, in particular since they have to be approached in a world which seems to prioritize the short term rather than the long term, and the spectacular rather than the important.

In the previously mentioned book by Clark, Crutzen and Schellnhuber (2004) the question of the role of research was raised. It is pointed out that efforts were being made in the 1990s to reconsider how science could better help in achieving the goals of sustainable development. At the World Summit in Johannesburg in 2002, there was an important effort to bring together researchers to consider these issues, with ICSU (International Council of Scientific Unions) deeply involved. Clark and colleagues note that "one immediate outcome of this activity was the realization that the range of organized, disciplined, reflective activity needed for intelligently and effectively guiding a sustainability transition was much broader than what is conventionally subsumed under the term of 'science'." Of course, the earth sciences have a role in promoting the transition, but so would technology, innovation and tacit knowledge of practice: "Even more broadly, there was clearly a need to mobilize the humanistic perspectives that would help us to understand where ideas about environment, development, and sustainability interacted with other dimensions of human thought about what we think we are and what we want to be." At this point, the authors struggle with terminology: they feel that the closest term in the English language to embrace this wide range of activities would be "knowledge." But they find that still more appropriate would be to use the German idea of *Wissenschaft*, which would embrace the systematic pursuit of all knowledge, learning, and scholarship. (It might be worth noting that the Swedish language has the word *vetenskap* which carries more or less the same connotation as the German word.)

Based on my own experience as Chairman of the Swedish Research Council for Environment, Agricultural Sciences and Spatial Planning (Formas), I believe that the analysis above is important for all who reflect on the role of research in promoting sustainability. It points to the need for advanced systemic thinking and inter-disciplinary reflection, but it also underlines the importance of the humanities and a generally broad approach to the role of research. Given the existing university structures and the deeply embedded trenches between disciplines, as well as the relative lack of systems-embracing expertise, the effort will require considerable patience, staying power and resources. It is also necessary that governments see the need to support these efforts in a sustained way through adequate financing and institutional structures.

This is all the more important, since the efforts of sustainability science have to be matched by corresponding attention to the broad system of education. A great deal of work has already been devoted to the issue of environmental education, i.e., through an important programme of the OECD Centre for Educational Research and Innovation (CERI). At the same time, we have to realize that environment is only part of the sustainability paradigm, and that broad systemic issues are difficult to teach. In fact, we are also talking here of existential problems which raise complicated ethical questions, going beyond most curricula. Furthermore, it is a moving target: for every year we learn more about the operation of the global system, and there has to be a constant revision of the facts involved.

Nevertheless, we all realize that no real progress can be made on the sustainability agenda, unless there is a broad public support for such measures. In the previous chapter, I was underlining the need for a new societal paradigm. How can that be achieved? Science and research — and diffusion of scientific findings — are important components. Education must play a key role, but the question is if our educational systems at present are well designed for this task. Again, the German language offers a good term to illustrate the objective. In German, the word *Bildung* conveys the idea of something more than just education (which in German would be *Ausbildung*). The concept of *Bildung* means a capacity to have an overview, to be able to set observations, experience and knowledge in a coherent framework, in short to understand better the world and world events. It also contains cultural elements, which would echo the previously quoted reference to "other dimensions of human thought about what we think we are and want to be" (Clark et al. 2004).

This is the reason why it could be tempting to try to define such ideas in the form of a new humanism or another renaissance in order to activate new layers of human reflection on the world. The Australian scholar Andrew Brennan has explored ideas of this kind in a chapter in *Environmental Values in a Globalising World* (edited by J. Paavola and Ian Lowe, 2004), entitled "Globalisation and the Environment: Endgame or a New Renaissance" (pp 17–37). You don't need to share Brennan's rather dim view of the world of today to appreciate the interest of an argument which uses quotes from Shakespeare to illuminate thinking about sustainability. Brennan points out that *King Lear* provides an example of the rehabilitation of wisdom, which is accompanied by a constant invocation of folly and stupidity in the guise of cleverness. "In Shakespeare wisdom — unlike cleverness — derives from respect for balance and hierarchy, the avoidance of excess and the cultivation of a moral intelligence that embraces compassion" (Op.cit p. 27).

Is the world of today too prone to embrace cleverness rather than wisdom as an ideal? Maybe. But above all I believe that it is essential today to reflect on the importance of cultural dimensions in better understanding the world and the actions of humans in relation to the planet and the long-term perspectives for mankind, since global change forces us to face dimensions of problems which we had never reflected on before There is a parallel here with the sixteenth century: at the time not only new ideas, but new perceptions of the world geography and the place of the planet in the universe created new forms of awareness. As we consider globalization and the phenomenal advances of the natural sciences, we need not only bold new thinking but a new form of wisdom, which will serve as a compass to enable us to realize that our action to tackle global environmental issues must be based on a strong sense of equity and fairness; because otherwise it will neither be effective nor accepted.

GLOBALIZATION

If global change is the consequence of human activities on the natural system, globalization affects the world's economic and social systems. The term "globalization" only became well-known in the last decades of the twentieth century; it is interesting to note that it coincides in time with the realization that there were global threats to the world environment. Nevertheless, it has long been maintained that capitalism was global in character, whether its origins are traced to the seventeenth century Eurocentric world, or to more ancient civilizations — global in vocation if not in geographic extent. (Cox 1996). The theory of international division of labour, with origins in Adam Smith's *An inquiry into the Wealth of Nations*, has dominated economic thinking and practice for a long time, even if the quantity of products traded internationally was rather limited until the end of the nineteenth century. However, with the second industrial revolution around 1900 and with the colonial system, the expansion of international trade became an essential feature of the global economy, but it turned into an increasingly unbalanced system. Because of differences in terms of trade, the countries in the south became agricultural producers; in the case of the United Kingdom the imperial preference system contributed greatly to this development. The relative specialization on a limited number of export crops also made these countries extremely dependent on the swings of the business cycle, with corresponding effects on demand and prices for primary commodities.

The Great Depression of the 1930s had disastrous effects on the world economic system. It led to a general contraction of world trade and to a breakdown in payments systems. It paved the way for strong protectionist measures — protective tariffs and quantitative restrictions, and competitive devaluations of currencies. The economic consequences of the depression with unemployment and deteriorating social conditions led to political unrest and the success of dictators in Europe. The thirties demonstrated the weakness of the democracies, which ultimately led to the Second World War.

This is a very succinct description of an extremely complex period in the history of Europe. It has to pass over important nuances. But it serves to illustrate one factor which for the people in policy-making positions during and after the war had a decisive influence in the crafting of the postwar system: "never more the thirties." Never more protectionism, economic nationalism, competitive devaluations. Never more war between European countries.

Against this background, the end-phase of the second world war and the immediate post-war years were extremely creative in terms of multilateral co-operation. A large part of Europe was in ruins, economic prospects were dim, Soviet communism expanded in eastern and central Europe. Nevertheless, forward-looking US policies, a supportive environment in Europe, and the personal commitment of some extraordinary personalities, managed to turn the tide. The effort of containment of Soviet expansionism was supported by visionary ideas in the economic field, which led to the establishment of the multilateral system for economic co-operation which is still in place.

During the war the plans had already been drawn up for the Bretton Woods institutions: the International Bank for Reconstruction and Development (World Bank), and the International Monetary Fund, which were established in 1944. They aimed at creating a stable world economic order which would prevent governments to embark on the destructive policies of the 1930s and still permit considerable freedom in pursuing national economic objectives within an orderly framework. This system, which was based on stable exchange rates and an American commitment to keep the dollar convertible into gold at $35 an ounce operated reasonably well until increasing US balance of payments deficits in August 1971 forced President Nixon to suspend gold convertibility and introduce what became a dollar standard, until in 1973 the Bretton Woods system came to an end with a decision to let currencies float (Gilpin 1987).

The international monetary system has been subject to many crises during the period after 1973. Now in 2007 it continues to inspire periodic concern, not least because of the enormous amounts of money now in the markets and the continuing imbalances between the main actors, the United States, Europe, and Asia. However, no one can deny that the structures that were set in place after the Second World War and the management of the world economy ever since have succeeded in creating unprecedented wealth and opportunity, though unfortunately not everywhere.

This development had not been possible without the other initiatives taken in the 1940s and 50s.

There was the general effort of trade liberalization through the General Agreement on Tariffs and Trade (GATT) in 1948, Through a number of rounds of successive liberalization agreements, GATT came to provide a stable framework for world trade, with a corresponding tremendous expansion of the volume of trade.

This system has since developed into the World Trade Organisation with a number of new features, including trade in services and special rules for developing countries.

There were also the efforts of European integration, which were actually launched through the Marshall Plan in 1948. This plan remains an outstanding example of what can be achieved through imaginative policies and a firm political will to make the policies work. The Truman Administration was rightly concerned with the slow pace of reconstruction in Europe after the war, a situation which risked playing into the hands of communism. Initially, the United States sent aid to Western Europe at a rate which amounted to 4.5% of US GNP between 1949 and 1952. (*New York Times*, quoted in Gilpin 1987). But this aid was not unconditional: it required corresponding efforts on the part of the recipients, and in particular that they would be able to cooperate between themselves to make aid efficient. That meant the creation of the Organization for European Economic Cooperation (OEEC), established in 1948, which became a great success.

These initiatives led to a rapid improvement in the European economies, which soon entered a period of rapid growth. The bold visions of Truman and Marshall were matched at the European side by personalities such as Jean Monnet, Robert Schuman, and Konrad Adenauer. They quickly realized that economic inter-state cooperation was not enough, but that one needed to create a new framework, an integrated Europe. And in this endeavor, they were strongly supported by the United States.

The European adventure started when Belgium, France, Germany, Italy, Luxemburg and the Netherlands in 1950 launched the negotiation for the European Coal and Steel Community (ECSC). It was a courageous move, aiming at putting the destinies of some of Europe's most important industries in the hands of a supranational body, the High Authority. Jean Monnet became its first President, when the ECSC Treaty came into force in 1952.

Various plans for intensified European integration, including the establishment of a European Defence Community, were tried in the following years, but did not succeed until negotiations between the six ECSC countries in 1956 led to the establishment of a much broader framework for economic integration, The European Economic Community (EEC), which started working in 1957, covering all areas of economic cooperation. In the meantime, other European countries also intensified their cooperation, leading to the establishment of the European Free Trade Area (EFTA), in 1960.

At the level of cooperation between industrialized countries, the end of the phase of European reconstruction led to the transformation of OEEC into OECD (Organization of Economic Cooperation and Development) in 1960. All Western European countries except Finland became members together with the United States and Canada. Later on Japan, Finland, Australia and New Zealand joined the OECD to bring the membership to twenty-four in the 1980's. Today, thirty countries, including Mexico and South Korea, are members of OECD.

After this creative phase in the 1950s and early 1960s no major new global multilateral economic institutions were established, with the exception of the UN Conference on Trade and Development, which held its first meeting in 1964, and became an organization taking particular interest in promoting the trade interests of developing countries. It is also noteworthy that UNCTAD from its inception gave an important contribution to the advancement of thinking around north-south issues, mainly because of the role of the Argentine economist Raul Prebisch, who prepared the influential background report to UNCTAD I in Geneva, "Towards a New Trade Policy for Development". Prebisch, who became the first Secretary-General of UNCTAD, based his analysis on the theory of center/periphery, and maintained that developing countries needed to participate fully in world trade. He saw trade as an "engine of growth" and recommended active export policies and an end to import substitution as a guideline for trade policy.

It should also be noted that in many parts of the developing world, regional and sub-regional cooperative institutions were created; this development will be further commented upon in Chapter 4.

With regard to regional co-operation, the story of the European Union is particularly important, with a sustained effort of integration leading to a significant change in the structure and conditions of international cooperation. The attraction of the EEC on other European countries proved irresistible, and in 1972 the community welcomed Denmark, Ireland and the United Kingdom as members. Ten years later, the extension to the south became reality with the entry of Greece, Portugal, and Spain. With the arrival of the former Prime Minister of France, the dynamic Jacques Delors as President of the Commission in 1985, the EU embarked on an ambitious program of finalizing the internal market; and the dramatic changes in the political balance of Europe brought about by the demise of the Soviet Union opened two new rounds of enlargement, first in 1995 with Austria, Finland and Sweden, and then in 2004 with Estonia, Latvia, Lithuania, Poland, Czech Republic, Slovakia, Hungary, Slovenia, Malta and Cyprus. In 2007, Bulgaria and Romania also joined the Union. The European Union certainly experiences difficulties in accommodating all these new members, but the enlargement to twenty-seven countries and a union of almost 500 million people has given EU an enhanced role in international affairs. The special role of the European Union will be further elaborated on in Chapter 5.

It is legitimate to ask what the role of the central institutions of the United Nations has been in this development. In the structure of the UN, three Councils were established to carry the main tasks under the general supervision of the General Assembly: the Security Council, the Economic and Social Council (ECOSOC), and the Trusteeship Council. The Security Council continues to be the central political body of the UN; and the Trusteeship Council had concluded its work when there were no longer any UN Mandate territories to manage. The ECOSOC generates much activity, but it has never achieved real political influence. However, the specialized agencies, which formally report to ECOSOC (FAO, ILO, UNESCO, WHO, etc.), are important components of the multilateral framework today.

This brief overview of the evolution of multilateral institutions serves to underline that globalization as we perceive it today, in terms of free movement of goods, capital and labour, is really the dream of a generation come true. There is no way back, and when anti-globalization protesters line up today, it seems that their argument is not against globalization *per se*, but against the lack of effective international control of big market operators, against the lack of empathy for those disadvantaged by globalization, against the incapacity to marry the effects of economic globalization with legitimate social and environmental concerns.

There are, of course, many reasons why the notion of a globalized world has become particularly pervasive at the present point in time. I just want to highlight two elements which have contributed to intensify the transformation of international economic relations into a world market with strong corporate actors operating rather independently.

The first is the breakdown of the Soviet Empire in 1991. As Eric Hobshawn has pointed out, during the "Short Twentieth Century" (1914–1991), capitalism was challenged by another potentially global force, "real socialism," or "world communism." In fact, for those of us who experienced the period 1948–1991, it was a strictly divided world, with societies that had few similarities. This divide was obviously most graphically felt in Berlin. The cold war enabled this semi-globalization to proceed within the two worlds; the break-down of communism in the Soviet Union meant that their socialist model had proved unworkable, and that globalization from that moment would proceed in line with the principles of the market economy. It was not the "end of history" as Francis Fukuyama stated in 1989, but it was the beginning of a drive towards complete globalization at a world-wide scale, based on the market economy system.

The second point is linked to technological development. The acceleration of history, as the then President of the European Union, Jacques Delors, called the political process just referred to, was further strengthened by the rapid development of information and communication technology, and the expansion of air transport, to a certain extent comparable with the impact of the spectacular downturn of ocean freights towards the end of the nineteenth century (Lewis 1977). The capacity to operate a global economy in real time was greatly enhanced; financial and other markets were able to operate around the clock.

We are in the middle of an often confusing and disorganized reorganization of the world system, creating new tensions and new opportunities. Contradicting tendencies are manifest in the new patterns of international migration or in the effects of capital seeking maximum returns by moving production to countries with lower wages. Globalization at the present stage tends to increase inequality and reduce the power of national governments, in particular in developing countries. Some observers conclude that large corporations rule the world. Since most of these actors on the global scene are based in the United States, and since the United States today wields an overwhelming power in world politics, globalization is seen as an instrument of US dominance. According to this analysis, intensified European integration is seen as a necessary contribution to a more balanced international system.

It is clear that these formidable forces driving globalization present a real problem to governments of most countries. Sovereignty is being challenged at a scale never experienced before. Since the process has been moved by conscious political decisions, aiming at the setting up of a robust multilateral system under the control of governments, the answer should be a strengthening of that system, thus recognizing that anarchistic globalization must be controlled.

To a certain extent this is happening. The World Trade Organization continues to have strong influence over trade practices and trade policy through its different institutions, not least the panels which are set up to examine complaints. The Bretton Woods institutions, IMF and the World Bank, continue to recommend economic policies and serve as important reference points for economic policy. Regional institutions in different parts of the world are increasing their influence.

Nevertheless, serious concerns are voiced over the potential instability of the system, its vulnerability to different kinds of shocks, and in particular to the perceived risks of a uniform world culture, copied on the American way of life. Such concerns have been strengthened by tendencies for market values to permeate broader sectors of human life. As the former French Prime Minister Lionel Jospin put it: "We have to accept a market economy, but we should not accept a market society".

The present neo-classical economic policy paradigm offers solutions to many problems, but some fundamental issues cannot be solved by the market. The break-down of the Soviet Union meant that the attraction of the centrally planned economy was gone. But how can the market economy at a global level deal with issues such as fairness, justice, and the environment? The Secretary-General of the Rio Conference, Maurice Strong, put the problem very succinctly in a speech at the UN Headquarters in the middle of the 1990s: "If the market economy cannot solve the problems of social injustice and environmental deterioration, then it will not last" (Author's recollection). It seems probable that an important part of the continuing future debate on globalization will turn around this kind of problems.

These diverging views on globalization prompted the International Labour Organization to establish a World Commission on the Social Dimension of Globalization, which published its report in early 2004. The Commission was co-chaired by President Tarja Halonen of Finland and President William Mkapa of Tanzania.

Against the background of a generally favorable attitude towards globalization, the Commission concluded that "the current process of globalization is generating unbalanced outcomes, both between and within countries. Wealth is being created, but too many countries and people are not sharing in its benefits."

The report underlines the elements of uncertainty engendered by rapid change and globalization, and it quotes a participant from Costa Rica, who says "There is a growing feeling that we live in a world highly vulnerable to changes we cannot control." However, the Commission feels that there are glimmers of hope: "a truly global conscience is beginning to emerge, sensitive to the inequities of poverty, gender discrimination, child labour and environmental degradation, wherever these may occur."

Furthermore, the globalized world economy itself is a dynamic concept, with power relations changing all the time. A group of economists linked to Goldman Sachs in 2003 projected that the economies of Brazil, Russia, India and China were now developing so fast that by 2050 only the United States and Japan would join them among the world's six largest economies, with China becoming the biggest economy in the world by 2050. Given the fact that China and India today represent almost 40% of the world's total population, and that Europe and Japan will have a stagnant, ageing population over the next several years, it is evident that demographic factors will lead to important changes in the globalized world.

At this point, this short elaboration on globalization needs to be linked to the previous section on global change, since unacceptable effects of global change, such as dangerous anthropogenic climate change or depletion of the ozone layer, set absolute boundaries which have to be respected. One additional problem is of course that science cannot tell with absolute certainty what these boundaries are, which has led to the adoption by the Rio Conference of the precautionary approach (Rio Declaration) or precautionary principle.

It would also be worthwhile to recall the report of the so-called Club of Rome from the early 1970s, entitled "Limits to Growth". A team of researchers of the Massachusetts Institute of Technology had developed models that indicated that continued growth patterns would place the world system in an unsustainable situation within one hundred years, because of environmental pressures and scarcity of important raw materials. For a long time, this report fell into oblivion, or ridicule, as its conclusions seemed exaggerated; however, for the present generation it is important to remember that the message remains valid: important changes have to be made within the next decades; and business as usual is not a viable option.

THE ECONOMIC DIMENSION

In considering the possibilities for the world to have a sustainable global development in the long term, the economic dimension is essential. The question of costs always comes up in political discussions and in negotiations: cost/benefit analysis is seen as a logical and objective way of creating a basis for action. This is in the logics of neo-classical economic general equilibrium models.

But economics is not only a mathematically-based science, it is also a behavioral science, built on expectations and human perceptions of reality, be it short-term or long-term. The calculation of costs of action to safeguard the environment, as compared to the costs of cleaning up a deteriorated environment, cannot really answer the questions of policy-makers. If you take an issue such as climate change, and if you try to calculate the total costs of mitigation over a very long period of time, say 100 years, it is not difficult to arrive at staggering figures. But if you look at the expected growth of the world economy over this long period, based on even a rather modest rate of growth, these figures become part of a dynamic framework, indicating that the cost of combating climate change might simply delay an expected world output of X by a few years.

The last twenty-five years have also seen the development of a different setting for the use of the neo-classical theory, because of the demise of Keynesian economics and the politically driven adoption of supply-side economics, giving new life to reduced state intervention, increasing independence of Central Banks and credit policy, signaling an end to fine-tuning of demand management. It can indeed be argued that these policies have been successful in reining in inflationary tendencies and promoting stable economic growth. But they have also meant that income differentials have generally increased and raised new questions about the welfare implications of economic policy.

It is against this background that some economists are questioning the relevance of neo-classical theory in relation to sustainable development. Their fundamental point is that it is false to see the environment as part of the economy instead of the other way round: if the economy creates conditions that are not sustainable in the long term many will suffer. As Lester Brown has pointed out, ecologists worry about limits, while economists tend not to recognize any such constraints. (Lester Brown 2001).

Even if the Stern review (see below) might influence thinking in mainstream economics, it has to be recognized that a paradigm shift in economic thinking does not seem particularly probable in the short term At the same time, political signals do matter; and value issues always count in social research. The Swedish economist Gunnar Myrdal underlined this on several occasions, as in the following quotation:

"Our valuations determine our approaches to a problem, the definition of our concepts, the choice of models, the selection of observations, the presentation of our conclusions – in fact the whole pursuit of a study from beginning to end." (Myrdal 1978, quoted in Soderbaum 2000).

This means that if an increasing number of people become convinced that the long term environmental consequences of present policies could be disastrous, then there will be adaptation of values long before a full-fledged paradigm shift is in sight, with a corresponding effect on the execution of economic policy, both at the national and international levels.

What would that imply for the perception of costs?

One element could be to recognize that the costs of non-action or postponed action might well by much higher than action now. It is a question of applying discount rates to a model over a very long time. It would also mean a greater recognition of the dynamic qualities of our economies in a period of rapid structural change: costs of environmental action will be part of a broader pattern.

> In fact, it seems recognized that because of the extreme difficulty of assessing costs, especially over the long term, in reality cost distribution and effects on competitiveness are more important parameters than absolute costs in terms of political and public acceptance of environmental policies. (Riggs ed., Aspen Institute 2004)

Finally, the question of technology and the structural impact of technological change on economic growth is part of this pattern of change. If increased environmental awareness and concern for global threats of the kind we are discussing here would lead to more rapid development and more general acceptance of new technologies, e.g., in energy production, building methods or transport systems, then the time-span over which these new technologies, say solar energy, become competitive would be shortened.

The main point of my reasoning on the economic dimension is to argue that economic arguments are generally relative and open to interpretation, and that the simple call for cost/benefit analysis to solve problems in negotiation and policy-making is not sufficient. In a world of scarcity, cost effectiveness will always be essential. But it is also important to consider different time scales, and the character of the threats which need to be addressed.

By the end of 2006, this discussion was set in a new framework through the so-called Stern Review, commissioned by the UK Government.[2] Sir Nicholas Stern has been Chief Economist in the World Bank and Chief Economist in the UK Treasury. He is well anchored in the mainstream of traditional economic theory, and it is no doubt that the Stern review will have an impact on thinking in Ministries of Finance and in Central Banks worldwide.

The main message of the Stern Review is that the costs of no-action on climate change would be extremely high in terms of loss of GNP; the report compares these costs to the effect of the Great Depression in the 1930s or the economic consequences of the Second World War. On the other hand,

Stern argues that the cost of preventive action aiming at maintaining the global concentration of CO_2 equivalent in the atmosphere at 550 parts per million in 2050 could be achieved at a cost of 1% of world output, provided that early measures can be set in motion. The models put the cost of no-action at a level 5 to 20 times higher.

Stern underlines the role of the markets and the efforts to develop new technologies as essential elements in the common effort to combat climate change. He also emphasizes the need for adaptation measures, since climate change is already happening.

The methods and thinking of the report can and will of course be challenged. Some have already maintained that the models are biased in their description of the consequences of climate change, and that this is unnecessary alarmist. But the report is a well-documented and serious piece of work, and its conclusions cannot be wiped away. In the discussion about the economic consequences of global change, and more generally, of action to protect the environment, it provides an essential input into the thinking of governments. It is also to be expected that the academic discussion of the economic aspects of policies to achieve global sustainability will benefit from this new contribution.

3 The New Diplomacy for Sustainable Development

In previous chapters, I have tried to demonstrate that human-induced global change combined with globalization has created a new perspective in the approach to world developments. It is indeed sobering to reflect on the responsibility of the present generation and to realize that our capacity to meet these challenges is limited: global change does not dispense us from managing the short-term problems facing us, both as individuals and as parts of society. However, there is no way to avoid facing this situation; and since we are talking about global threats, they have to be tackled through international cooperation. It is also natural that the United Nations' system has had a special role to play and that sustainable development has become a major issue for the world organization.

In this chapter, I will demonstrate why I believe that international diplomacy for sustainable development contains a number of special features, which justify the expression "a new diplomacy." Of course this does not mean that its procedures and tools are different from traditional diplomacy or that it is not part of a broader pattern of international relations. But we are dealing with global problems of a different nature than those which frame traditional diplomacy. With a fair degree of simplification we could maintain that on these issues of global survival — climate, ozone layer, state of the oceans, land degradation — we are all on the same side: traditional diplomatic bargaining, of course, goes on, but if we fail in the endgame, there will not be any winners anywhere.

The first part of the chapter will give an account of the roots of this new diplomacy and its history, as reflected mainly in the big global conferences dealing with sustainable development. Since I have been lucky enough to participate intensely in many of these negotiations over the last fifteen years, I will also make some personal reflections on these events. However, as I am still dealing with concepts, details will be saved for the presentation in later chapters.

The second part of this chapter will deal more systematically with the characteristics of the new diplomacy.

For a long time I have been quite fascinated with the practice of multilateral diplomacy. My initial experience was the first Conference on Trade and Development (UNCTAD), held in Geneva in 1964. The magnificent Palais des Nations, with its dimensions, its white marble, and its setting, overlooking Lac Leman with Mont Blanc majestically in the background, gave me a sense of solemn harmony that had a lasting impact on the young, inexperienced diplomat. I soon realized that the debates in the meeting rooms were mostly not at a level which would match the setting; and I have probably spent more time than most people would find healthy in never-ending drafting sessions, exchanging the same arguments over and over again, seeking words that would paper over difficulties in order to move the negotiation forward. Nevertheless it happens that I sneak into empty half-dark conference halls when the day's meetings are over, to listen to the silence, still somehow vibrating with the arguments of the day. I may be forgiven for comparing my feelings on such occasions with those of entering a church: in multilateral meeting rooms women and men from many different backgrounds worship reason, and capacity to settle conflicts in a non-violent way.

My continued multilateral work was mainly on economic co-operation, with long postings to the European institutions in Brussels and to OECD in Paris. As Head of the Multilateral Department on Development Co-operation in the Foreign Ministry, I got to know the world of multilateral financial institutions, participating in a number of replenishment exercises of the soft funds of regional development banks (ADB, AsDB and IDB) and of the World Bank's International Development Association (IDA). In most of these negotiations there was of course always a certain background of broad ideas to consider: the future of the multilateral system; the need to ensure sufficient development financing, the stability of the world economy. But most of the time national interests, as expressed in your instructions, were there to condition and guide the negotiation, and set the boundaries for what could be achieved.

As a negotiator, I was also well aware of the impact of the cold war. Power politics and military strength set the limits for much that could be achieved in other fields. Traditional diplomacy at high level and of high quality was needed to steer the world through these dangerous years. For Sweden, as a neutral country, support for the United Nations, and initiatives in the field of disarmament, were priority areas.

However, as we have seen already, other forces were at work also during this period. The environmental problems were slowly edging their way into the structures of the multilateral system, with the 1972 Stockholm Conference as a landmark. My own contacts with this development were rather limited during the 1970s and the 80s, though I met some of these new issues as Permanent Representative to OECD and UNESCO. But it was only when I was offered the job as Chief Negotiator in the Ministry of Environment in 1990 that I become fully aware of the strength of these new trends in international affairs. This was probably not surprising, since I think that most Ministries of Foreign Affairs, being rather traditional and conservative institutions, were quite reluctant to take on the new challenges of multilateral environmental policy.

So, beginning in Stockholm in 1972, the elements of a new diplomacy were slowly emerging, with the new United Nations Environment Programme (UNEP) as an important driver on many of the central issues, such as biological diversity, climate, or desertification, and with regional problems in Europe, linked to acid rain or to eutrophication of seas, given increasing political attention. And of course, we are still in a gradual process of change. Still I believe that it is the Brundtland Report and the Rio-Johannesburg process as well as the global Rio Conventions which give substance to the claim that there is such a thing as a new diplomacy for sustainable development.

It was only in the 1960s that environment became part of the international agenda, as public opinion had become alerted to the new threats through Rachel Carson's *Silent Spring*, published in 1964. In 1968, the Swedish Government took the initiative for a major UN Conference on the Environment. At the time, it was logical for Sweden to take the lead since there was a strong support in public opinion for action on environmental matters, further strengthened by the country's traditional commitment to the United Nations. After many difficult preparatory negotiations, initially led by the then Swedish Permanent Representative to UN, Sverker Åström, one of Sweden's top diplomats, the UN Conference on the Human Environment was finally convened in Stockholm in 1972. The Canadian businessman and diplomat Maurice Strong became the efficient Secretary-General of the Conference, a post he was to hold also twenty years later, at the UN Conference on Environment and Development, in Rio de Janeiro. The Stockholm Conference was the first global meeting on environmental matters, and it had a lasting impact, even though the Soviet bloc boycotted the meeting in order to protest the non-recognition of the German Democratic Republic, (East Germany) by the Western powers. There were also important conflicts between north and south, which will be further commented upon in Chapter 4. However, agreement was reached on an important Declaration, containing a set of twenty-six principles, and a number of other documents.[1] It might be interesting to note that the main architect behind the agreements was Hans Blix, Chief Expert on international law in the Ministry for Foreign Affairs at the time.

At the time, global environmental threats were not yet top of the agenda, but the Conference made important recommendations on regional environmental problems, one of them later leading to the path-breaking agreement on trans-boundary air pollution in Europe, under the auspices of the UN Economic Commission for Europe (ECE). The Conference's recommendations for domestic environmental policies also led to the creation of Ministries of Environment in many countries. And finally, at the UN level, the Conference decided to establish a UN Environment Programme (UNEP). The United Nations later on decided that the new program should have its

Headquarters in Nairobi, the first UN centre in a developing country. Maurice Strong became UNEP's first Executive Secretary, to be succeeded a few years later by the Egyptian politician and scientist Mostafa Tolba.

Environment had entered the international agenda by the front door, and it is fair to say that Stockholm represented the first step towards the new diplomacy for sustainable development.

Part of the background was the previously mentioned report of the Club of Rome. Furthermore, in 1969, the new Secretary-General of OECD, Emile van Lennep, former Treasurer-General of the Ministry of Finance of the Netherlands, prepared a report, which gave a number of good reasons for OECD as an organization for economic cooperation to take environment seriously. This recognition was important and led to the creation in 1970 of an Environment Committee in OECD. This organization with its strong constituency in Ministries of Finance and Central Banks has ever since been a voice for forward-looking environmental policies in developed countries, not least because of its detailed reviews of national environmental policies.

At the time, I was Chef de Cabinet to the Secretary-General and I recall vividly the way in which Mr. van Lennep pleaded the cause of the environment in conversations with Prime Ministers and Ministers of Finance of the Member countries. His arguments were based on the notion of quality of growth, a concept which comes rather close to the way in which the Brundtland Commission later defined sustainable development. The work in OECD these years led to the adoption by the organization in 1974 of the polluter-pays principle (PPP).

Though multilateral work on the environment continued in various fora over the coming years, the 1970s were characterized by the first oil crisis and the severe concerns for oil shortages; this situation also forced the industrial countries to review their policies towards the south. It was the time of the north-south dialogue which is presented more in detail in Chapter 4. The developing countries were pressing for a New International Economic Order, but nothing came out of these negotiations, and after a new oil scare in 1980 everything seemed to return to status quo in the north-south relations. Nothing really indicated that anything new would happen in multilateral negotiations, still marred by the continuous East-West tensions, which in 1980 looked more serious than ever. And with regard to environment, the interest in renewable sources of energy and energy saving, which had been a positive result of the oil crisis, quickly subsided as the world edged toward the reverse oil shock in 1986–87, when oil prices sank below $10 a barrel. As Swedish Permanent representative to OECD at that time, I recall that I tried to argue with my own Government for increasing energy tax levels in order to compensate for the dramatic reduction in oil prices, thus improving prospects for renewable sources of energy. But there was no interest in such proposals: the reverse oil shock opened too good prospects for non-inflationary economic growth. I have no doubts that we would be better off today if there had been a forward-looking international response at the time, aimed at supporting research in renewable energy sources with appropriate measures.

In terms of the operation of the world economy, the 1980s proved to be a period of turbulence, particularly in financial markets. It was also a decade of much uncertainty about the future of international economic cooperation and of concern over US deficits, both in the budget and on the current account. There were continued worries about slow growth in Europe and in the United States.

Towards the end of the decade, however, concerns for the world economy were overshadowed by the dramatic events within the Soviet Union and its effects on the international situation. The cold war came to an end with the implosion of the Soviet empire and the establishment of a totally new world balance. For many people in my generation, living for decades with the bi-polar world and the concrete threat of a nuclear war between the super-powers, this was an almost incredible development. It falls outside the scope of this book to go into the details of these events, but I have to reaffirm that for many people in the world this was a demonstration that even the most established structures can crumble, that change for the better is possible.

It carries a lesson for us all today, when we struggle with the resistance to change of sometimes petrified structures, which contribute to global environmental damage.

In this context, it is also worth noting that the beginning of change in the Soviet Union was linked to an environmental disaster, the catastrophe at the Tchernobyl nuclear power plant in 1986. Early efforts by the Soviet authorities to cover up what had happened (it was Sweden that first reported increased levels of radioactivity in the atmosphere) backfired and demonstrated that the secrecy of the Soviet system had had its day; and that the leaders had to gain the trust of their people by more openness. Mikhail Gorbachev promised to open the system with his perestroika policy, but ultimately the whole edifice crumbled. As the process moved on, environmental issues of different kinds became part of the story of the break-down of the Soviet empire: one example was the Baltic states (Estonia, Latvia and Lithuania) where environmental movements played an active role in the opposition to continued Soviet rule.

More generally, as we came to know more about the so far closely guarded details of the Soviet economy, the full extent of environmental damage became clear. The system had operated with production results as a central feature in the five year plans, the backbone of medium-term planning. But in this struggle to fulfill plans, everything that could limit production results was considered secondary, including environmental consequences. The cleaning-up is still under way. In a number of cases the damage was irreversible, one example being the Aral Sea in Central Asia. This was once the fourth largest inland lake in the world, but Soviet irrigation systems to support intensive production of cotton in the region from 1960 onwards has led to the virtual disappearance of the lake, now divided into three smaller lakes, creating an environmental disaster and difficult living conditions for five million people living near the former shores, in present Uzbekistan and Kazakhstan.

The tidal change in the Soviet Union also had environmental links; and it is an ironic twist of history that Mikhail Gorbachev after retiring from politics has taken on a new role as Chairman of the Green Cross movement, which he has started to promote environmental information and action.

So, events in the Soviet Union opened up new perspectives for international environmental cooperation. The decade of the 80's also saw the concerns of anthropogenic global environmental change beginning to gain public attention, leading to actions by governments. The main results were achieved with regard to the atmosphere. Research on the negative effects of chloro-fluoro-carbons (CFCs) on the protective atmospheric ozone layer led to the adoption in 1981 of the Vienna Convention. This was a framework convention with very limited substantive contents, but it paved the way for continued negotiations, ultimately leading to agreement on the Montreal Protocol in 1989, which was a decisive step in restoring the ozone layer (even if this process will take a very long time).

The broader concerns of climate change also took a new direction in the 1980s. Researchers had long worked on the relationship between concentrations of carbon dioxide (CO_2) and other so-called greenhouse gases in the atmosphere and the average global temperature. Now it became clearer that the increase in CO_2 concentration from 280 ppm (parts per million) in pre-industrial times to about 360 ppm in the 1980's could lead to a significant increase in world temperature with potentially disastrous consequences. There were several international conferences, and in 1988 the World Meteorological Organization (WMO) and the United Nations Environment Programme (UNEP) jointly set up the Intergovernmental Panel on Climate Change (IPCC), which has since played a central role in serving multilateral negotiations on climate change.

Hence, environmental change at a global scale became a subject of concern. The international community realized that since most of these problems had been created by the industrialized countries and since the poorer countries had the right to development, it would be necessary to tackle environment and development together. A well-known method of approaching an international problem of this kind is to establish a commission of eminent persons, equipped with a good secretariat, and mandated to produce a report. These commissions generally produce very interesting results, but very often the link between the recommendations and changes in policy is rather weak. However, in this case, things were different, as has been pointed out in Chapter 1. The Brundtland report, issued in 1987, served as backstopping for the Rio Conference, thereby launching the concept of sustainable development and providing concrete justification for action. Many of the Brundtland suggestions were taken up in the negotiations of the Rio documents, in particular Agenda 21.

The UN Conference on Environment and Development, which met in Rio de Janeiro in 1992 was the largest international meeting that had ever been convened. The initiative for a new environmental meeting, twenty years after Stockholm, once again came from the Swedish Government, which originally had wished the Conference to be held in Stockholm once again. However, when Brazil launched its candidature, it seemed logical that an important developing country would host the Conference. Arrangements were also very satisfactory. The preparatory process and the Conference itself benefited from an excellent Secretariat, once again headed by Maurice Strong, and an extraordinary Chairman, the former Chairman of the Law of the Sea Conference, Tommy Koh of Singapore.

A Preparatory Committee was established by the General Assembly; this Committee met four times between August 1990 and May 1992 for three- or four-weeks meetings. The Conference itself was held June 3–14, 1992. The Preparatory Committee had three plenary working groups, dealing with all the various elements contained in Agenda 21, and the other Rio documents. I was chairing WG 1, which was responsible for Chapters 9–16 in Agenda 21, dealing with atmosphere, land management (including agriculture, forests, desertification and drought, and mountains), biological diversity and biotechnology.

The complexity of the issues facing the Conference was staggering; and it was only the good preparation of meetings that made it possible to reach a successful outcome.

During all the sessions, Tommy Koh would hold a one-hour meeting every morning with a small group of people, including the Working Group Chairmen, coordinators of special negotiations, and leading people in the Secretariat. Exchanges were frank, sometimes rather heated, as negotiating problems and logistical issues were discussed in detail. These meetings served as the main management instrument for Koh and Strong.

In Rio de Janeiro, Tommy Koh asked me to coordinate and chair negotiations for Chapter 9 of Agenda 21, dealing with atmosphere. This was a difficult subject, highlighting some of the most contentious problems related to the position of the OPEC countries; in fact our negotiations mirrored those of the Climate Convention. It was also the very last negotiation to be concluded, long after the rest of the texts had been adopted.

The Rio documents were adopted by consensus, but with a number of formal reservations; the latter have not had any real impact on future negotiations, and were never given much attention. These documents are:

- Agenda 21, an action program for the twenty-first century, divided into forty chapters, dealing with general issues related to development, the most important environmental problems, the role of "major groups" (NGOs, young people, women, indigenous people etc), and financing, research, institutions etc. This is a rather impressive document, negotiated in detail, of lasting importance.

- The Rio Declaration, containing twenty-seven principles, some of which were carried over from the Stockholm principles. The text opens with a principle that underlines that human beings are at the centre of attention; and follows up with a reference to the right to development. Among the new principles, it is essential to highlight the polluter-pays principle (PPP), and the precautionary approach.

- The Forest Principles. It might seem surprising that forests would be given this particular attention, but it is understandable, given their economic importance and political sensitivity. The document was the first global consensus on forests and thus served as a background for further efforts to tackle forests and deforestation in an international framework.

The Rio Conference was attended by more than 100 heads of state or government, which contributed to an impressive media attention. It was also the first major UN conference after the end of the cold war, and expectations were running high. With hindsight, it is clear that UNCED led to an increased awareness of the links between environment and development, but that some of its promises were not fulfilled. However, both at the national and international level, Rio set important new processes in motion.

The central follow-up mechanism in the United Nations was the Commission on Sustainable Development (CSD) which meets every year. It is difficult to evaluate the importance of this body, which is formally a sub-committee to ECOSOC, but has proved able to attract quite a lot of Ministers for its meetings. It operates with a thematic approach with specific sets of problems highlighted every year and it has no doubt kept the Rio results alive over the years. But it has not (yet?) become a major policy forum for periodic discussions on sustainable development.

Five years after Rio, in 1997, a Special Session of the General Assembly considered the follow-up to Rio. It was hoped that this session would give a new political impetus to the process, but the results were rather disappointing. On the contrary, ten years after Rio, the World Summit on Sustainable Development (WSSD) in Johannesburg in 2002, boosted interest in the problems of sustainability. It was made clear from the beginning that the purpose would not be a renegotiation of the Rio documents, but a major effort to speed up implementation. Therefore, the main result was an agreed Plan of Implementation, which is now operative, with more attention than before on action at the regional level, and a special section on Africa. There was also a specific effort to design cooperative projects with the private sector. It is also worth noting that since Johannesburg came after the adoption by the UN General Assembly of the Millennium Development Goals (2000), important efforts were made to harmonize the outcome of Johannesburg with these goals.

It was felt after Johannesburg that the UN system had now probably reached a threshold with regard to the productivity of large Conferences on sustainable development. The Johannesburg Plan of Implementation should now really be implemented, and of course monitored, but there was a certain sense of fatigue which would militate in favor of using existing mechanisms over the next decade; maybe a period of twenty years — as between Stockholm and Rio — before the next major Conference would serve the process best.

Be that as it may, I am convinced that the normative process, best represented by the CSD, is gathering speed, becoming an important fixture in the UN agenda. Having served as Sweden's chief delegate at a number of CSD meetings, I think that the Commission has potential to keep the concept of sustainable development well alive in the UN framework. The weaknesses of UN procedures are difficult to avoid, and far too much time is spent on detailed drafting of texts, a time-consuming activity which does not always yield satisfactory results. However, I will return to these and other institutional aspects in Chapter 7.

The normative Rio-Johannesburg process is one important part of the present negotiating pattern on sustainable development. The second branch is constituted by the new global conventions, linked to Rio: they are sometimes called the Rio Conventions. The Convention on Biological Diversity (CBD) and the Framework Convention on Climate Change (FCCC) were negotiated in parallel with the preparations for Rio, and signed at the Conference. The Convention to combat Desertification (CCD) was negotiated in 1993–94 on the basis of an agreement reached at the Conference. A previously mentioned text, the Vienna Convention on the Ozone Layer with its Montreal Protocol belong to the same category of global, legally binding instruments; some other later Conventions should also be added, in particular the Stockholm Convention on Persistent Organic Pollutants (2001).

It should also be added that some of these various instruments are now supplemented with protocols which strengthen them considerably. Within the Convention on Biological Diversity, the Cartagena Protocol on Biological Safety (2002) has sharpened commitments in an important way, and the adoption of the Kyoto Protocol to the FCCC (1997) for the first time committed a group of countries (industrialized countries in Annex I) to quantitative reduction targets. Both these protocols have now entered into force.

At this point, I wish to recall that these major global conventions only constitute a part of the pattern of environmental agreements which are in force today. There are about 200 others, some of them with a global bearing, that cover more limited segments of the environmental agenda

Finally, in considering the issue of sustainability as reflected in UN work since 1990, it is worth mentioning that the decade of the 1990s saw an important number of major global Conferences on a number of central subjects: there was the Conference on Women in Beijing in 1993, the Population Conference in Cairo in 1994, the Social Summit in Copenhagen in 1995, and the Habitat Conference in Istanbul, in 1996. Since all these worldwide Conferences, gathering thousands of delegates, came after Rio, they were all considering their specific themes in the light of the results of Rio, in particular with regard to sustainability.

I have defined four different tracks which over the last decades have come to be part of the international sustainability agenda:

- The normative Rio-Johannesburg process;
- The major global, legally binding Conventions ("Rio Conventions");
- The large number of other, legally binding agreements;
- The major UN Conferences on different subjects, with sustainability as an important component.

The negotiations in these different processes add up to a new body of diplomatic practice, involving new types of thinking, new types of preparation, new groups of negotiators, new government agencies; a different atmosphere from other multilateral negotiations I have known in a long working life experience.

I have participated actively in a large number of these negotiations, with particular emphasis on the Rio process, and the Conventions on Climate change and on Combating Desertification. Beyond my role as head of the Swedish delegations in these processes, I have also served as an officer in various posts, which have enabled me to see the negotiations from inside: Chairman of Working Group I in the Rio Preparatory Committee; Chairman of the Negotiating Committee for the Convention to combat Desertification; Chairman of the central negotiating committee for the so-called Berlin Mandate in the Climate convention, as well as a number of other positions in that Convention and in the Kyoto Protocol. These experiences have convinced me that there are specific aspects of these negotiations which warrant the expression "A New Diplomacy for Sustainable Development." Section II of the book aims at giving some insights into the practices of this new diplomacy by discussing a number of specific issues relating to the problematic, in particular linked to the relations between major actors.

But first I wish to conclude this chapter with a more complete exploration of the various elements which in my view constitute the building blocks of this new diplomacy.

At the time of the Rio Conference, it was logical to think boldly about the future. The cold war had ended, there was a new sense of movement and opportunity in world politics. The traditional discourse of diplomacy certainly maintained its force, but within a new setting. It was not surprising that the new awareness of global environmental problems would be translated into efforts within an additional discourse of international relations.

With hindsight, we know that the co-existence of traditional and "new" diplomacy has been uneasy. But a central point in my reasoning is that the recognition of a different kind of international relations is a useful tool in analyzing what is really happening in the international arena today.

On the one hand, we have the old, power-based diplomacy, which is today specifically illustrated by the military discourse of the present US administration, underlining the need for support in the war on terrorism; and a fundamental lack of confidence in the multilateral system. The tensions between Europe and the United States, or between the US and the UN Secretary-General, arising out of this state of affairs need to be settled within a framework of distributive bargaining, and the stakes are high.

On the other hand, the Rio process has laid the basis for a framework of negotiation which is more integrative, where bargaining positions and the underlying interests are more varied and where the bottom line is the concern for long-term human survival of a different nature than that constituted by military supremacy. As all negotiators of the Rio process know, this does not mean that solutions are easy to find; powerful interests of economic and social nature are challenged, and progress is slow. But the underlying purpose of negotiation is different.

What are then the central features in this new diplomacy? I wish to distinguish between a set of fundamental parameters and some other elements which are of a more specific and organizational character. The structure is summarized as follows:

Fundamental Parameters

- The existence of absolute limits/threats
- The need for a broad vision
- The primacy of the long term

Specific Elements

- The emergence of new international actors
- The impact of civil society and non-governmental organizations
- The role of science and research

I will deal with these one by one.

The existence of absolute limits/threats

Chapter 2 dealt with the many disturbing elements of global change, underlining that we are living in an era when humans have a distinct effect on the whole global system. This gives a new dimension to the definition of the risk to society as outlined by Beck and others: the dangers of a global disaster caused by a major nuclear war have subsided, but instead man's impact on climate, for example, can lead to consequences with catastrophic global effects. For the individual it is extremely difficult to visualize disasters of this kind, they fall outside our normal frames of mind. But responsible governments have to calculate different courses of action in order to avoid these dangers ever becoming a reality. During the cold war, the superpowers handled the threat of nuclear war with great caution, within the boundaries of traditional diplomacy. Established patterns of thought could be applied; in the academic discourse on negotiations, game theory was highly relevant.

In the new diplomacy, the threats are of a different character. They are long-term, and sometimes diffuse. The American scientist Michael Glantz has coined the expression "creeping disasters." There is no concrete enemy, the threat is nowhere and everywhere. The threat is also within the very fabric of our societies and lifestyles, often linked to material progress. In all countries, it is difficult to make this kind of threat credible in order to create a state of public opinion that permits funds to flow and action to be taken.

If we now consider the international arena, it becomes clear that new dimensions are added to traditional diplomacy. The threat is absolute: there is no adversary on the other side of the table who can be bullied or subtly convinced to postpone the execution of the threat or accept the terms of a compromise: global change will happen unless the negotiating parties can agree among themselves on global action to modify certain actions, such as excessive emissions of carbon dioxide. To make things still more complicated, we are uncertain about the terms of the threat: we are facing absolute limits of a kind, but we do not know where these limits are. Furthermore, we are dealing with systemic effects of a tremendously complicated nature: where and when will the sensitive fabric of global resilience tear apart?

The policy-makers in capitals and the negotiators — middlemen between the desirable and the possible — are caught in a dilemma: on the one hand they are operating within the boundaries of traditional methods of multilateral negotiation, and on the other hand they are negotiating about problems of a totally new kind. The long-term threats are real though diffuse; but in the short term very important economic and other interests are challenged, if efficient action should be taken. My distinct impression is that we are all on a learning curve, trying to understand better how the international negotiating framework could be better adapted to the new kind of problems and at the same time facilitate that action in capitals which is decisive for all international negotiations: how can the many national interests and the state of public opinion enable governments to take sufficiently advanced and forward-looking negotiating positions in this new situation?

The broad vision

At this stage, my conviction is that the way forward must be to recognize that we need to base international action on a broader vision than in other types of international negotiations, be they of a political or economical nature. The reason is that both instructions and negotiations need to recognize an extremely complex reality, which involves a reasonable understanding of the forces that are at play in global change as well as the many social and economic consequences of action to promote sustainability at the global level.

My experience as a negotiator has given me a fair amount of admiration for my colleagues as persons and as professionals, not least considering the representatives of developing countries. Neither have I felt much difference between colleagues from different Ministries: whether they come from Foreign Affairs, Environment or Industry they share the same qualities.

But as I look back I also sense that most of us from the beginning were ill equipped to grasp the inter-linkages between the many different forces that operate in the field. We all had a basic training of some kind, mostly university degrees in economics, political science, law, sociology; but very few had a background in the natural sciences. Given the existing divides between disciplines in all our countries this has created a sense of uncertainty, as problems became increasingly complex. How much do I really understand? Do I have the competence and the information to try to find new solutions in tricky negotiating situations? Or is it safer to stick to a narrow interpretation of my instructions? And do I really have the background to discuss with my masters in the capital possible new ideas or new avenues of compromise?

A recognition of the specific character of negotiations on sustainable development should lead to proposals for the training of negotiators, and should generally be part of projects for capacity-building in the south. But what would this approach contain? In Chapter 1, I have already developed some ideas relating to the need for a broad overview of the world, what the Germans would call "Bildung." It is not easily achievable, but in my view it is necessary to try to promote this broad vision, meaning that people working in the field of sustainable development would have the capacity to set events in a broad global framework.

The question of climate change could serve as an illustration of my line of thought. The fact that climate change is occurring and that there is a connection between concentrations of carbon dioxide and climate change is straight-forward. But how do you interpret conflicting academic views about the seriousness of this situation? How do you see climate change as part of broader phenomena of global change? What are the consequences for different parts of the world? What about the responsibilities for this situation? If we are convinced that important reductions of GHG emissions are necessary, how should they be achieved, and who should bear the burden? Are there winners and losers in the process? Is the globalized world economy capable of taking the strains of reducing GHG emissions? What is the relationship between the price of oil and economic conjunctures? Will significant action to cut emissions cause civil unrest? How can we ensure fairness and justice as central components of climate change action?

These random examples show the kind of questions that need to be addressed and that would have to be part of the curriculum in training negotiators. Some might argue that the broad vision cannot be neither taught nor learned; it is a matter of personality and personal choices. I do not agree: I think it is perfectly possible to formulate the right sets of questions that will stimulate interest and improve the capacity of the international community to pursue realistic and constructive negotiations on sustainable development.

There is another aspect of the broad view that needs to be addressed, and that is the link between this new diplomacy and traditional international relations. Negotiators have to well understand the impact of international relations in general; they also need to understand how different countries function in formulating positions and instructions. As the quest for sustainability moves up the ladder of international priorities, these aspects will become increasingly important. One example will be an increasing tendency to take up essential and controversial issues, such as climate change, at summit meetings. The G-8 meeting at Gleneagles, in July 2005, with its emphasis on aid to Africa, and its serious discussions on climate change, offer a good example. It is now becoming clear that successive European Chairmanships of the G-8 will continue this process, including the effort to associate important developing countries, such as China, India, Brazil and South Africa with the discussions on global environmental issues, the most recent example being the G-8 meeting in Germany in 2007.

Ultimately, it is not primarily a question of the competence of officials and negotiators. Governments need to recognize that the broad vision will be a necessary element of political action, nationally and internationally. The interdependence of nations has been growing all through the last decades, and globalization has political, economic, social, and cultural consequences. Increasingly, Governments have had to act within the limits of interdependence. But the sustainability imperative takes the reasoning into yet another dimension: international action has to contribute to global sustainability in many different ways. The new diplomacy is a complicated arena, where most Government departments have to be engaged in one or the other way.

The primacy of the long term

The very influential British economist John Maynard Keynes coined the expression "In the long run we are all dead." Probably the purpose was to discourage speculation of what could happen in a distant future and to focus on practical policy. Many people have also laughed at the quip of Groucho Marx: "Why should I do anything for the future? The future hasn't done anything for me."

However, the Anthropocene era changes the perspective. If humans are now influencing the entire world system, then we have a responsibility towards future generations, not just children and grandchildren, but all future generations. This is a daunting responsibility in a world with so many, and so difficult, short-term problems. .

Politicians are often accused of lacking interest in long-term issues. A common charge is that "they don't look further than the next election." In my view this is unfair, since in the day-to-day operation of governments there are issues that cannot simply be postponed and where action has to be taken straight-away. A former British Foreign Minister, Douglas-Home, once famously complained that "foreign policy is just one damned thing after another."

The importance of the long-term has to be explained to public opinion. One obvious example is the ozone hole; people are in general now quite aware of the fact that the ban on CFC's is in force, but that the effects on the atmospheric ozone layer will be with us for a very long time. The climate issue raises more complicated problems, related to the slow reactions of the atmosphere. The various models for Co_2 concentrations in the future do not give clear-cut answers to questions related to the time-scales and reduction levels needed to achieve sustainable concentrations of GHGs towards 2050s. Indeed, the 2006 Stern Review stated that developed countries would need to achieve a 60–80% reduction by 2050. Such precise policy objectives, stretching over more than one generation are normally not required in politics. It may be argued that this is a very graphic illustration of the unusual nature of global environmental threats. But there is not yet much public debate about the implications for political theory and practice, even though it must be considered very unusual that a body such as the council of the European Union, composed of heats of states and governments in March 2007 state that "developed countries should continue to take the lead by continuing to reduce their emissions of greenhouse gases in the order of 30% by 2020 compared to 1990. They should do so with a view to collectively reducing their emission by 60% to 80% by 2050 compared to 1990" (Council of the European Union, March 9, 2007).

In no other negotiations, outside the field of sustainable development this kind of long-term precision is in use. The UN Millennium Development Goals adopted in 2000 use the target year of 2015, or in one case (improvement in life of slum dwellers) by 2020. But it is unavoidable that we will see more of such long –term objectives, as the implications of global change become more generally understood, and as the international community realizes still more clearly that time is short if humanity is to avoid disasters of different kinds, linked to the environment.

At the same time, previously expressed concerns about the reserves of certain non-renewable resources, reappear. A case in point is oil. Some experts maintain that the world's oil production may well peak during the next ten to fifteen years, but all seem to agree that easily available resources might well be depleted before the end of the twenty-first century. Perspectives of this kind also mean that a world, which has become so dependent on oil, needs to carefully consider different energy futures, once again in a long-term perspective.

We are here very much at the heart of the new diplomacy, and the primacy of the long-term is one of its most salient features.

So, the absolute character of the threats, the need for a broad vision, and the primacy of the long-term are defining elements for the very concept of the new diplomacy for sustainable development. But there are also a number of other aspects of a more concrete nature, which have emerged over the last decade:

New international actors

In my experience of multilateral negotiations on economic and development matters, the pattern of participation and influence did not change much in the period 1960–1985. The superpowers had their dominating role, the permanent members of the Security Council were heavy-weights, the EU became more and more important, and the developing countries defended their interests through the Group of 77. A number of smaller developed countries carried weight as firm supporters of the United Nations or as important donors of development aid.

The new realities of the 1990s changed this situation radically. China emerged as a major player on the international stage, and other large developing countries followed. India and Brazil are now major forces in international negotiations. In negotiations within the WTO, these countries are now taking their logical role as major economic units, and in the discussions about reform of the Security Council India and Brazil are claiming permanent seats. This is natural, since their economies are really not comparable to those of any other developing countries: there are still large pockets of poverty, but at the same time their economic structure is extremely diversified, they have sophisticated industrial production, and their participation in the global economy is intense, both with regard to trade and services. Economic growth is rapid and has permitted the emergence of large middle classes, in the case of China and India numbering at least in each country, two hundred million people. These countries are also major players in the globalized world economy.

This pattern has been reflected in the negotiations on sustainable development, though with some nuances. The cohesion of the G 77 has been considered essential for the group of developing countries, reflecting the fact that development of the new diplomacy has been rooted in the United Nations and that developing countries continue to be concerned about the risk that environmental policy will be detrimental to their growth and struggle against poverty. At the same time, it has become increasingly clear that China, India, and Brazil are ready to go it alone, if they feel that it is important for their national interests. (China is formally not a member of G 77, but is normally associated to all positions expressed by the group).

There are, however, other groups of countries, that normally do not play a major role in the UN, which have held a high profile in the various negotiations on sustainable development, initiated in 1990. They will be presented here very briefly, since Chapter 4 will deal in more detail with their participation in the negotiations.

One is the group of OPEC countries, in particular Saudi Arabia. This is not the first time that Saudi Arabia has played this leading role: in the north-south dialogue in the 1970's Saudi Arabia's Oil minister Sheik Yamani was in the center of attention. The whole dialogue had in fact been initiated as a response to the increase in oil prices and the risks for disruption of oil supplies that caused so much concern among the industrialized countries. In a way this negotiation, which however did not lead to concrete results, was a precursor of the new diplomacy.

Both in the Rio process and in the climate negotiations Saudi Arabia and some other OPEC countries have been taking very strong positions, trying to avoid decisions that might in any way limit the expected demand for oil. The Chief Negotiator of Saudi Arabia, Muhammed Saban, has been a central actor in all the major negotiations.

If OPEC has been trying to hold back the negotiations, another group of countries, the Association of Small Island States (AOSIS) has constantly pushed for more action on emissions control. They obviously have very good reasons: if sea level will actually rise up to 1 meter by 2100, some of the countries will literally disappear: this is the ultimate link between environment policy and security policy. The role of AOSIS has given some small islands leading roles in the negotiations; so have representatives such as Ambassador Slade of Samoa and Ambassador John Ashe of Antigua and Barbuda been among the central actors in many negotiations.

Finally, the Group of Least Developed Countries (LDCs) has been able to defend its interests with skill and perseverance, even if the results have not always been up to expectations. However, this group has been present for a long time in the UN. What has been striking is that certain countries, or certain subgroups of countries, have been particularly active in different negotiations on sustainable development. One example is the major role played by West African francophone countries in the negotiation of the Convention to Combat Desertification, or the important contribution by some smaller Latin American countries with regard to the Convention on Biological Diversity.

In this way, these negotiations may have contributed to show that there are areas in which small countries, when their interests are at stake, have a real possibility to make their voices heard in the UN. To a large extent, this is also due to the quality of their representatives.

The impact of civil society and non-governmental organizations (NGOs)

The Rio process represented a break-through for the participation of NGOs in the United Nations. Of course, non-governmental organizations had been represented in the UN before 1990, but it had been a limited group of well established, large organizations that had a long-standing agreement with ECOSOC. As the preparatory committee for Rio assembled in August 1990, it became clear that there would now be an effort to enlarge this participation. The Secretary-General of the Conference, Maurice Strong, had many linkages to civil society, and more generally it was felt that it was necessary to anchor action to promote sustainability firmly in society, and not just rely on the action of governments.

There was a fair amount of suspicion, as many developing countries feared that Northern environmental NGOs were not very sympathetic to the development aspects of sustainability. This led to a difficult negotiation at the first Prepcom, but the result was in my view very satisfactory. The decision taken meant that NGOs that had been admitted to a body of the Conference would not be considered negotiating parties; but that, on the other hand, NGOs would be admitted to participate in open meetings if the Chairman, with the consent of the meeting, so decided. This decision, which to my knowledge never has been challenged, clearly shows where the responsibility lies for the results of the negotiation, namely with the Governments. On the other hand, it gives NGOs a very significant right to be present in the negotiations, while the Chairman in any meeting could decide to close the meeting if this was necessary for the negotiation.

The practice has shown that NGOs have been admitted to practically all meetings, with the exception of sensitive final negotiations, and this has been applied both in the normative Rio/Johannesburg process and in the Conventions. The formal approval enabling NGOs to enter sessions of the various bodies has normally been a low-key and routine business. In the case of the desertification convention, a large number of grass-root NGOs from Africa participated actively. Their presence was financed through a special fund with contributions from developed countries.

The presence of NGOs at the various meetings has given a considerable contribution to the negotiations. In all sessions they have been invited to make statements, sometimes strongly critical of governments. In many of the larger conferences, such as Rio or Johannesburg, special NGO villages have been centers for side events of different kinds, meetings and manifestations. The development of side events is generally an interesting feature of the new diplomacy. These are organized with the help of the Secretariat of the Conference and cover a broad area of subjects, ranging from academic seminars to rallies aimed at directly influencing negotiations. It is a colorful part of the meetings, as is the traditional NGO party at climate negotiations, which assembles delegates and NGO representatives in a very relaxed atmosphere. With the support of some governments, some NGOs also produce regular reports on proceedings in the sessions, keeping an eye on how delegations tackle the various points on the agenda.

In general terms, the active participation of NGOs reflect an important feature of sustainability policies: the need to keep the general public informed of the issues at stake, so that everybody can have a considered judgment of the policies to be pursued. It is easy to say that paradigm shifts are needed, but in democratic countries these can only come about if there is a general support for action. The role of the NGOs in international negotiations therefore becomes particularly important; they help to provide more bridges between the negotiation reality and the reality of everyday life than those that government action can provide.

The role of science and research

When the then Chairman of the Intergovernmental Panel on Climate Change (IPCC), professor Bert Bolin, addressed meetings of the negotiating committee for the Framework Convention on Climate Change, there was a palpable silence in the room. Here came the facts, the certainties and the uncertainties; and the negotiators got a clearer picture of their responsibilities. Tactical finesse and national interests for once became secondary. Of course the moment passed, but it was a visible expression of the impact of the natural sciences on negotiations on global sustainability.

It is fair to say that natural sciences have driven these negotiations. Climate is one example, with the creation of the IPCC as a major contribution. It was a bold initiative, establishing a first link between research and political action by inviting both researchers and policy-makers to the same panel. At the same time, the major effect of IPCC on the negotiations has come through its work on modeling and impacts of global warming. The four assessment reports prepared so far — 1990, 1995, 2001, and 2007 — have greatly contributed to an improved understanding of the climate problems at the political level. The careful management of the IPCC processes, involving more than 2000 researchers, and the sober assessments contained in the short "summaries for policy-makers," has created a climate of confidence, which has been very beneficial to the negotiations.

As the preparations now begin for the post-2012 climate regime, the role of the IPCC will inevitably come up for scrutiny. As time passes, should some of the elements of structures and procedures be revised? It is too early to tell, but the fundamental need for a scientific body of this kind certainly remains. In my view, there are also other sectors which could benefit from an IPCC-style approach: water, oceans, and forests are some of the subjects which come to mind.

This does not mean that other methods of ensuring scientific backstopping could not be quite as effective. Natural research is central to the new diplomacy, but there are many ways to ensure this necessary input. One of the first examples was the research initiated by researchers from Stockholm University, in particular Svante Odén, on acid rain, which ultimately led to the European regional agreement on trans-boundary air pollution, already in 1983.

Another fascinating story is the research carried out by Paul Crutzen and his colleagues on the impact of certain chemical substances on the ozone layer. As the results became more and more certain, the issue finally surfaced at the political level, which led to the Vienna Convention in 1985, providing a framework for continued negotiation, as and when time was ripe. It took some years, but in 1987 the Vienna Convention was supplemented with a strong legally binding document, the Montreal Protocol, which many observers, such as Scott Barrett, consider one of the best examples of a really efficient environmental treaty. And in 1995, Paul Crutzen and his colleagues were awarded the Nobel Prize in Chemistry for their research.

Chemicals in the atmosphere are central to the problems we face in climate and in the thinning of the ozone layer. But chemicals are also responsible for pollution of soils, water and oceans; and there are now so many chemicals in use that it is difficult to control them. A global convention on persistent organic pollutants (POPs) was concluded in Stockholm in 2001; also here research was instrumental in moving the process forward, finally leading to a successful result. And, as research on chemicals moves on, there is no doubt that the input will be transformed into new instruments through the processes of the new diplomacy.

A broad range of natural scientists are today involved in research of high relevance for sustainability. But as it becomes clearer that we are dealing with global systemic problems, it is necessary to broaden the scope of research. Among existing institutions, such as the IIASA (International Institute for Applied Systems Analysis), consider the International Geosphere-Biosphere Programme to be of particular importance. The programme is built on inter-disciplinarity, networking and integration. In 2004, the results so far were presented in a major book *Global Change and the Earth System: A Planet Under Pressure*. The findings have already been referred to in Chapter 2; there is no doubt in my mind that international negotiations increasingly will have to take into account the fact that we live in an integrated Earth System.

Another salient feature of the present situation is that the social sciences need to be more involved in the role of research as an essential component in the new diplomacy. This means that not only economic research, so central to modeling and calculation of costs, has an essential part to play, but also that we need the full involvement of political science, sociology and social psychology. These are all essential components in preparing negotiations and understanding better the societal conditions which will be fundamental to the preparations of negotiations on sustainability. They will also be instrumental in understanding better how the relationship between global, national, and local scales will evolve, as the tackling of global problems will have effects on living conditions and lifestyles in many parts of the world. How will political structures cope with these new demands? What will be the psychological mechanisms that will permit acceptance of new kinds of constraints put on citizens in order to respond to the new requirements of intra-generational and inter-generational equity? And a recurrent theme has to be the quest for fairness and justice, as important changes in life-styles and consumption patterns will have to take place.

I have presented here some central features of the New diplomacy for sustainable development, highlighting elements which permit us to distinguish it from traditional international relations. It is obvious that there are no distinct border-lines that can be drawn; nevertheless there are good reasons to maintain that we are facing problems of a new character, problems of human survival; and that this very fact has a growing impact on how international negotiations will be conducted. In the following chapters, some of the experiences from this early period of the new diplomacy will be examined in greater detail.

Part II
Practice

4   The North-South Divide

THE BACKGROUND

It would fall outside the scope of this book to elaborate on the reasons for the large inequalities in terms of wealth and resources in the world of today. The organization of world production and world markets that developed with industrialization is one reason. Another is colonialism. In the world after 1945 which marked the beginning of decolonization it became more and more obvious that political independence for the former colonies did not mean economic independence; nor did it prove possible for the new rulers to establish stable democracies. Decolonization proceeded at great speed; and the cold war stalemate meant that east and west were competing for influence in the new independent states in the south. This was not a situation that worked in favor of carefully considered long-term strategies; and the early efforts of development assistance were not well coordinated. It was also a fact that in the first decade after the war, the European countries were not in a position to grant assistance. The United States had the resources, and the Truman administration launched the Point 4 initiative, which provided significant resources for development assistance.

As the economic situation in Europe and Japan improved, the north-south divide became more and more obvious. Towards the end of the 1950s the need to change this state of affairs led the new organization for cooperation between industrialized countries to be given the name Organization for Economic Co-operation and Development (OECD), with one of its principal objectives to coordinate and stimulate support for development. The Development Assistance Committee (DAC) was established within the organization with the purpose of promoting increased flows of development assistance to developing countries.

Institutions which originally had been designed to promote the economic recovery of Europe now became involved in north-south assistance, with the World Bank (IBRD – International Bank for Reconstruction and Development) as the most important one. Aid agencies were established in many countries in the north, and there was genuine, though not very focused, support for reducing international inequalities.

53

However, many countries in the south felt that their problems were not given sufficient attention in the bipolar world that became the consequence of the east-west conflict. One response was political: the creation of the Group of Non-aligned countries with rulers such as Nehru of India, Sukarno of Indonesia, and Tito of Yugoslavia as leaders. This group played an important role in world politics over a long period of time; but it had no real clout in the economic field, where it was felt by many that the prevailing system of world trade — controlled by the General Agreement on Tariffs and Trade (GATT) — was biased against the developing countries.

All through this period of time, the UN Economic and Social Council struggled to establish itself as a forum for economic cooperation between north and south, without great success. In the early 1960s a new initiative was launched, the UN Conference on Trade and Development (UNCTAD), which was held in Geneva in 1964. This Conference was a major new departure, with a broad and high-level participation from both north and south. The negotiations were long and laborious, stretching out over more than two months, but the concrete results were limited. However, it was decided that a new UNCTAD should be held in New Delhi in 1968; and after that regular UNCTAD Conferences became a permanent feature on the multilateral agenda. It also became a symbol for increased south participation in the world economy, with its Geneva Secretariat widely regarded as a "secretariat for the south." (From the very beginning, the Secretary–General of UNCTAD has always come from the developing countries.)

UNCTAD I also had another important result: the Conference led to the creation of the Group of 77, which has ever since played a major role in multilateral economic and trade negotiations within the UN framework. In Geneva in 1964, the countries belonging to the UN geographical groups from Africa, Asia, and Latin America established a close cooperation; at the time these countries numbered 77, hence the name of the Group. Today, there are around 135 developing countries represented. It is quite obvious that this quite heterogeneous group sometimes has great difficulties of arriving at coordinated positions. Nevertheless, its size and the strengths of the arguments of the countries of the south have given G 77 a quite unique position in the UN system.

In the early years, UNCTAD also provided important intellectual leadership through its first Secretary-General, the Argentine economist Raul Prebisch. His report to the first UNCTAD, entitled "Towards a New Trade Policy for Development," had a deep impact. It structured the discussions on the international economy in ways which are still felt today. Prebisch spoke up in favor of a more active participation of the countries in "the periphery" in the world economy, thereby attacking the policies of import substitution, which had so far guided the trade policies of many developing countries. He saw exports as an "engine of growth," and called on the developed countries to help developing countries through a system of general tariff preferences; and he also proposed a systematic effort of nego-

tiating commodity agreements in order to stabilize export earnings for producers of primary products.

To a certain extent, these proposals led to concrete action, and the economic success of a number of Asian countries, based on a tremendous
expansion of exports, seem to confirm the theories of Raul Prebisch. Nevertheless, overall the north-south divide continued to grow. However, in
the 1970s, the debate took another turn with the great oil scare and the
negotiations on a New International Economic Order. The dramatic rise
in oil prices gave the OPEC countries clout in negotiating with the west;
and they wanted to use this newfound power to promote the interests of
developing countries in general, calling for debt forgiveness and a significant increase in development assistance. At that time, the economies of
the OECD countries were in bad shape with high rates of inflation already
before the oil price hikes; and the United States was deep in the trauma
following the Vietnam war. US Secretary of State Henry Kissinger promoted the idea of a major north-south Conference to discuss these matters,
and the Conference on International Economic Co-operation (CIEC) was
established in Paris, with intense technical work carried out among the
twenty-five participating countries.[1] Ministerial conferences were held in
1975 and 1977, but finally no substantive results came out of this effort. As
the fear of oil shortages subsided and levels of oil prices stabilized, interest
for broad north-south negotiations waned in the West, and the election
of Ronald Reagan to the US Presidency in 1980 heralded new attitudes to
economic policy. The very notion of a new international economic order
disappeared, and it is fair to say that CIEC remains one of the most forgotten episodes of north-south relations over the last fifty years.

During the decade of the 1980s, official development aid did not increase,
and the interests of economic policy-makers went into other directions. Oil
prices crumbled; the "reverse oil shock" in 1986 sent prices down below $10
a barrel for a while; and towards the end of the decade, the implosion of the
Soviet empire created a new world equilibrium, with new strategic priorities.

It was in this situation that the Brundtland Commission report and the preparations for the Rio Conference opened up new perspectives for north-south
discussions as part of the new diplomacy for sustainable development.

SOME PERSONAL NOTES

As I entered the Ministry of Environment in 1990 as Chief Negotiator, I
had spent considerable time on issues related to development. As a young
diplomat I had been posted to Brazil at the time of the move of the capital
to Brasilia in 1960; and I had taken a special interest in the activities of the
development agency for the extremely poor north-eastern region of Brazil,
called "the pentagon of drought." The then President Juscelino Kubitschek
had appointed the brilliant economist Celso Furtado to head this agency,

called "Superintendencia para o desenvolvimento de Nordeste (SUDENE)." However, in the elections of 1960, Janio Quadros was elected President, and a year later he resigned in a rather bizarre episode. His successor Joao Goulart had limited powers and was finally ousted in a military coup in 1964. SUDENE was dismantled and Celso Furtado exiled for a long period of time, until democracy was finally restored in the 1980s. However, the study of SUDENE had convinced me of the importance both of social reform and of the careful management of water in dry-land areas.

Between 1974 and 1977, I was Swedish Ambassador to Hanoi. The Vietnam war ended in 1975, and Sweden was at the time deeply involved in reconstruction and development assistance through one major industry project, the Bai Bang paper mill, and through the construction of two hospitals. At the time, I got deep respect for the nuts and bolts of development cooperation, i.e., the patient and difficult work on the ground with the many strains put on all people involved, both at the giving and the receiving end. In my multilateral work, I have constantly tried to underline the importance of this action in the real world, which is in my view too often forgotten when multilateral negotiators try to hammer out compromises through creative drafting of texts. Sometimes, in later years, I believe that my collaborators have felt that I slightly overstated this case in insisting on the fact that the real agents of development were the women planting rice in the fields, or the men driving trucks on dusty roads, or the teachers in village schools.... But I think it is an important point to make, since multilateral negotiators risk becoming absorbed by the negotiation as a game and tend to be isolated from reality by their comfortable conference premises. The role of the multilateral system is to provide the people on the ground with the instruments and the tools to create development.

After Vietnam, I became Head of the Department for Multilateral Development Cooperation in the Swedish Ministry for Foreign Affairs, and I served in this function between 1977 and 1981. A large part of Swedish Development aid is channeled through multilateral institutions; one example is that Sweden traditionally has been one of the largest donors in absolute terms to the UN Development Program (UNDP). This meant that we also had a not negligible role to play in the replenishment exercises for the "soft windows" of international financial institutions, such as the World Bank's International Development Association (IDA) or the African Development Fund. These negotiations brought me into contact with another type of multilateral work than the UN framework. Here very large sums of money were pledged as a result of negotiations that often stretched out over years, but where the negotiators only met a couple of days at a time, whereas the main work was done in capitals, principally to convince treasuries to release the necessary funds. The preparations by the institutions themselves were very thorough.

It was also through this work that I got my first professional contacts with Africa. As a deputy governor of the African Development Fund, I was asked in 1979 to chair negotiations between donor countries for a possible extension of the African Development Bank to also include non-regional countries. It was the then Managing Director of the Bank, Kwame Ford-wor of Ghana, who had launched this project, which was not immediately accepted by the Africans themselves. However, the negotiations finally succeeded, and the Bank membership was enlarged in 1981. For various reasons however, Fordwor had been forced to resign in a boardroom revolution one year earlier.

The enlargement increased the Bank's resources; nevertheless, the AfDB still has much smaller capital than other comparable financial institutions, which reflects the continuing deterioration of Africa's position in comparison with other parts of the world.

My knowledge of realities in Africa has continued to be limited and I have not had the opportunity to spend longer periods on the African continent. However, I have become deeply influenced by the continuous plight of Africa and the seeming impossibility to make development happen on a continent which possesses a wealth of natural and human resources. I remain convinced that Africa has the potential to change this state of affairs, and that the rest of the world has a deep responsibility to support development in Africa.

This was some of the baggage I had accumulated as I left the job as Permanent Representative to OECD and UNESCO in 1990 to take up the function of Chief Negotiator at the Ministry of Environment. I welcomed this opportunity to work more continuously on a subject which I had met on various occasions, in particular during my two stints at the OECD, and which I felt was of central importance. However, I did not envisage that various circumstances would get me so deeply involved in processes which in my view are central to the future. Perhaps I had a certain feeling of this, as I concluded my final report from the first meeting of the Preparatory Committee for the Rio Conference in August 1990 with the words: "This is the beginning of a great adventure."

THE NORTH-SOUTH DIVIDE AND THE NEW DIPLOMACY FOR SUSTAINABLE DEVELOPMENT

The Rio/Johannesburg process

There had been a lot of difficult negotiations in the General Assembly on the organization of the preparatory work for UNCED. The results of these negotiations were encapsulated in General Assembly Resolution 44/228. Together with the texts coming out of the first organizational meeting of the Preparatory Committee there was now a basis for serious negotiations. The Group of 77 approached these with some apprehension, mirroring their concerns that environment would detract from their main objective of development and combat of poverty. However, the G 77 obtained the Chairmanship of the Preparatory Committee, known as the Prepcom, and important positions in the different Bureaus that were created within the framework of this Committee. In particular, the choice of Chairman of the Committee was of crucial importance, and the appointment of Ambassador Tommy Koh of Singapore turned out to be decisive for the success of the process.

Koh was still young, but he had already a long and distinguished career behind him, having been UN Ambassador of Singapore and most recently his country's Ambassador to Washington. In 1990 he was Ambassador at large while keeping a number of important functions in Singapore, ranging from the university world to Chairmanship of the Arts Council.

Tommy Koh had chaired the difficult negotiations for the Convention of the Law of the Sea (UNCLOS) in the United Nations. His personal contacts with several of the main actors in the negotiation turned out to be an invaluable asset. He was rational and efficient, and his mixture of gentleness and toughness made you recall the expression "an iron fist in a velvet glove." Tommy Koh was an excellent representative of the south, and his many qualities were also to be found with several other leading negotiators coming from the Group of 77.

With Tommy Koh as Chairman, the Preparatory Committee was organized in three plenary working groups, where most of the elaboration of Agenda 21 was carried out. I chaired Working Group I, which dealt with atmosphere, land management, forests, desertification, biological diversity and biotechnology, whereas Working Group II, chaired by Bukhar Shaib of Nigeria, negotiated such issues as water management, oceans, chemicals and waste, including radioactive waste. Working Group III, led by Bedrich Moldan of Czechoslovakia dealt with a number of general issues, including the negotiation of a set of principles, later known as the Rio Declaration. In the final stages, Tommy Koh himself took responsibility for the Declaration; a number of cross-cutting issues were also dealt with by the Plenary itself. It was a complicated structure, but because of the leadership of Tommy Koh, and the skills of the Secretary-General of the Conference, Maurice Strong of Canada, the process ran fairly smoothly. The main management tool of Tommy Koh was morning meetings with the so-called "Collegium," a group of around twenty people, including the Working Group Chairs, special coordinators and leading people in the Secretariat. These meetings discussed all central issues, both related to substance and organization. On the contrary, the elected Bureau of the Prepcom, which for reasons of regional balance counted more than fifty people, met very seldom and had no real influence on the running of the negotiation.

The Preparatory committee held four long sessions between August 1990 and April 1992. During this process, divergences were narrowed down successively, but at the end of the fourth session, with the UNCED only two months away, a considerable number of outstanding issues remained on the table. In the context of this chapter, it is interesting to note that practically all of these points were part of the north-south divide. Furthermore, they look like a list of issues which have held centre stage ever since as part of the core agenda of the new diplomacy:

- magnitude and means of transferring financial resources to developing countries to enable them to improve their environment and adhere to new environmental norms;
- transfer of environmentally appropriate technology to the developing world;
- climate change and other issues in the Agenda 21 chapter on atmosphere, including energy;
- a statement on forest principles;
- institutional arrangements.

These outstanding points reflected serious concerns by members of the Group of 77 in facing the new reality of global environmental threats, in a changed world situation characterized by the breakdown of the Soviet empire and difficult conditions in the world economy. While the 1980s had seen a steady growth in the world economy, unemployment had remained too high. At the turn of the decade conditions worsened and confidence fell, causing turmoil on financial markets. The new requirements of the new market economies in the East made heavy demands on capital in a situation when world savings were already low. All OECD countries faced heavy budgetary restraints, and the much-heralded "peace dividend," i.e., the reduction in military spending, failed to make a real impact. The new diplomacy was maturing under difficult conditions, and traditional north-south problems were carried over into all negotiations that were to follow. The best summing-up of the G 77 position was probably made by one of the leading negotiators of the south, Ambassador Chandrasekhar Dasgupta of India, who was the main author of Article 4.7 of the Framework Convention on Climate Change (negotiated in parallel with the preparations for Rio) which stated:

The extent to which developing country Parties will effectively implement their commitments under the Convention will depend on the effective implementation by developed country Parties of their commitments under the Convention related to financial resources and transfer of technology, and will take fully into account that economic and social development and poverty eradication are the first and overriding priorities of the developing country Parties.

Here is, in short, the main controversy between north and south that has transcended the normative Rio/Johannesburg process and the associated negotiations far into the twenty-first century: the problem of transfer of resources and technology. The rationale is the conviction that the present international economic order is unfair, based on colonialism and neo-colonialism and the dominance of large multi-national enterprises, most of them based in the United States. The hopes of the south for a new order were dashed when the CIEC negotiation collapsed. In the new atmosphere of the 1980s with the victory of Reagan/Thatcher supply-side economics, even the carefully worded Brundtland report arouse suspicions that had already surfaced in Stockholm in 1972. Was the environmental agenda another effort of the north to keep the south down?

The response of G 77 in the Rio process was to lay emphasis on the intra-generational equity and the combat of poverty; and to use the numerical majority in the UN and the considerable skill of southern negotiators to promote these interests. Among northern negotiators, this line of action, continuously pursued by the G 77 — and in particular their New York-based diplomats — on many occasions led to frustration and irritation. But it has to be recognized that this overall strategy has been generally successful and that often few other options than skillful tactical management of procedures existed.

However, there are two caveats: first, in every negotiation there comes a time when you have to make a deal; and there is no doubt that the strategy of the south has been most successful when the G 77 leadership has been strong enough to grasp the opportunity, one typical example being the UNCED negotiation of Agenda 21, Chapter 12, which led to the Convention to Combat Desertification. The second caveat is linked to the very size of the G 77: if the G 77 Chair is not strong enough (the Chairmanship changes every year), the very size of the Group means that strongly focused minority interests can use the formidable political weight of the G 77 to promote their own interests. Undoubtedly, the OPEC countries have managed particularly well in this game.

Before embarking on a more detailed description of the main negotiating positions of the south in the Rio/Johannesburg process, there is one more remark on the operation of the UN Group system that needs to be done. I mentioned before that northern negotiators were sometimes frustrated by the tactics of G 77: there was then a certain temptation to try to play out different groups within the G 77 against each other; but such action was not frequent. In my own view, this kind of tactical game would immediately backfire: no one from outside should try to upset the delicate balance within the G 77.

We have now highlighted the main interests of the south and touched on the tactical instruments to promote these interests. Let us now consider more in detail the central objectives of the south in the Rio negotiations.

The main issues raised by G 77 in all negotiations on sustainable development over the last fifteen years have been the following:

- the need for increased flows of capital, in particular Official Development Assistance (ODA);
- the need for increased transfer of technology;
- the need for assistance in capacity-building;
- the eradication of poverty;
- the promotion of human health;
- the improvement of livelihoods and human settlements;
- the particular importance of agricultural production;
- the questions related to deforestation;
- the dismantling of agricultural subsidies in the north;
- the change of lifestyles and consumption patterns in the north;
- the change of production patterns in the north;
- the negative impacts of present rules for international trade.

All north-south controversies that have appeared in the negotiations may in one way or another be derived from the various points mentioned here. The compromises reached are reflected in the texts agreed in Rio de Janeiro and in various later instruments, including decisions by the Rio follow-up Commission on Sustainable Development (CSD), the Johannesburg World Summit on Sustainable Development 2002 (WSSD), and the UN Millennium Development Goals (2000).

It is not surprising that the issue of *capital flows* has been at the heart of many of the negotiations. The inflow of capital is essential to finance investment, and they are fundamental to economic performance and to macroeconomic management. At the same time, statistics show that capital flows from the north to the south have been volatile over the last thirty years, in particular to low-income countries.[2] Relative to GDP in the north, it is also obvious that private capital flows to these countries represent a only a very small part of outward investment. Nevertheless, they are important for the receiving countries and their volatility therefore constitutes a serious problem. Thus, it is understandable that the question of Official Development Assistance (ODA) continues to be at the centre of the discussions in international institutions.

In 1970, the United Nations established the ODA target of 0.7% of GNP. This target was accepted by all OECD countries except the United States and Switzerland, but it has never led to universal implementation. In fact, over long periods aid levels have actually been reduced, mainly as a reaction to budgetary problems in the north. Only a limited number of small European countries have reached and over long periods surpassed the target: Denmark, Netherlands, Norway and Sweden, recently joined by Luxemburg. At the time of the Rio Conference, the ODA issue as part of the more general financial package not surprisingly turned out to be one of the most difficult stumbling blocks for a final agreement.

From the beginning of the Rio process, the financing issues, including of course the 0.7% target, thus occupied centre stage. The south was pressing for "new and additional resources," but the industrialized countries continued to avoid concrete commitments. The end of the cold war did not lead to the much discussed "peace dividend" being turned into increased flows of resources to the south. UNCED Secretary-General Maurice Strong coined a phrase which illustrated the grim reality: "Seldom have the rich seemed so poor as to-day." This meant that the discussion on financing dealt more with institutions and mechanisms than with concrete resources.

Everybody realized of course that UNCED was not a pledging conference, but part of a process of a normative character. Nevertheless, the Secretariat had in their draft for Agenda 21 suggested that implementation of Agenda 21 would require $125 billion annually in additional money, which would have implied a doubling of ODA — a target which still seems unattainable. In the Rio negotiations, in the final stages chaired by the Brazilian Ambassador to Washington, Rubens Ricupero, later to become Environment Minister of Brazil and Secretary-General of UNCTAD, there was agreement that the $125 billion figure would just be considered an "estimate."

As the Rio Conference drew to its end, twenty-four hours after the conclusion of the impressive gathering of more than 100 heads of state and government in the first ever "Earth summit," two coordinators were still toiling with the final deals, Rubens Ricupero and myself. While mine was a limited issue in the Chapter 9 on Atmosphere, to be dealt with later in this book, the financial problem was right in the centre of concerns: the language on ODA.

The final text in Chapter 33 of Agenda 21 is worth quoting: "Developed countries reaffirm their commitments to reach the accepted UN target of 0.7% of GNP for ODA and to the extent that they have not yet achieved that target, agree to augment their aid programs in order to reach that target as soon as possible and to ensure a prompt and effective implementation of Agenda 21. Some countries agreed or had agreed to reach the target by the year 2000. It was decided that the Commission on Sustainable Development will regularly review and monitor progress toward this target. This review process should systematically combine the monitoring of the implementation of Agenda 21 with a review of the financial resources available. Those which have already reached the target are to be recommended and encouraged etc...."

This is a highly negotiated text, but at the time it was generally seen as a strengthening of the commitment to reach the 0.7% target, which would mean a very considerable increase in concessional resources for development.

Alas, this was not to be. The world recession turned into sustained growth, and more investment in developing countries; the globalized world market economy seemed to offer new possibilities which would make increased ODA redundant; aid levels stagnated.

In my view, the inability of the OECD countries to live up to what was perceived as ODA promises contributed to complicate many international negotiations over this period. I could feel it both in desertification and climate negotiations, when the north was constantly on the defensive, having to react to accusations of lacking political will. However, it has to be recognized that towards the end of the 1990s new effort were being made with some promising results. In 1998, meetings were held for the first time between delegates to the ECOSOC and high-level officials of the World Bank and the IMF, and the same year the UN General Assembly adopted a resolution which led to the convening, in 2002, of a High-level International Conference on Financing for Development. This meeting adopted the so-called Monterrey Consensus, which urged developed countries to make concrete efforts towards the 0.7% target, while underlining the need for more effective ODA, sound national policies and improved governance. This consensus was difficult to negotiate, but its broad economic scope, which recalled the origins of UNCTAD, pointed the way for agreement also in the WSSD in Johannesburg later in 2002. The language of the Plan of Action, contained in Articles 81 to 99, provides a very full account of the kind of general consensus that has been established with regard to national economic policies, transfers of financial resources, increase in ODA, foreign direct investment, debt relief, and trade measures. It is also worth mentioning that Article 82 contains some of the words which have been subject to most wrangling in negotiations ever since Rio, coming after a reference to the Monterrey consensus, namely "including through new and additional financial resources."

Nevertheless, the question of transfer of resources to developing countries remains highly controversial. However, I have a feeling that the international community begins to understand better the crucial role of ODA, in particular in relation to the least developed countries, and more specifically with regard to Africa. Recent developments might open up interesting avenues: but the fundamental problem remains, unless the OECD countries will really as a group move decisively towards the 0.7% target. If this would occur, the effects of both multilateral and bilateral transfers would be greatly enhanced, benefiting global sustainable development. In recent years, there have been interesting developments, including within the G-8 Group of the largest industrialized countries. A new approach was appearing at the Gleneagles summit in July 2005, when new action on Africa was agreed, and when there was agreement on a major effort of debt reduction in favor of least developed countries. The G-8 is now also regularly inviting countries like China, India, South Africa, and Brazil to attend part of its summit meetings.

If the ODA target has been controversial, this is also true of the question of transfer of technology: I must admit that I have sometimes found the exchanges on this issue in the framework of the United Nations to be too general and too distant from the real world. Since most technology is transferred in connection with commercial transactions, it has seemed somewhat strange that so much time has been spent on discussions whether such transfers should take place on commercial, non-commercial, preferential or concessional terms. A lot of energy has been used in successive meetings to find language which would satisfy everybody; and that has generally succeeded, but the concrete impact of these agreements has been limited. The compromise text in Agenda 21 (paragraph 34.11) addressing the issue of transfers through commercial channels states that "while concepts and modalities for assured access to environmentally sound technologies...continue to be explored, enhanced access" to such technologies should be "promoted, facilitated and financed, as appropriate."

Another problem of wide importance has also appeared in the negotiations on technology transfer: the question of property rights. This question has surfaced on various occasions in the normative discussions, but the decisive negotiations have taken place elsewhere, in the Convention on Biological Diversity, the WTO or the WIPO (World Intellectual Property Organization). In Rio the compromise solution was the following text (paragraph 34.18 (e)(iv): "In compliance with and under the specific circumstances recognized by the relevant international conventions adhered to by states" countries should undertake "measures to prevent the abuse of intellectual property rights, including rules with respect to their acquisition through compulsory licensing, with the provision of equitable and adequate compensation."

It may seem surprising that there has been relatively limited attention on issues related to the technology actually owned by public authorities at various scales. On the Swedish side, we have tried to raise this issue in different negotiations within the UN system, but without much success. These suggestions have dealt with technologies for water and sanitation, or various types of technology and planning for urban transport, where many local authorities command both technology and know-how. Some of these points have been given attention at specialized conferences, e.g., HABITAT, but not at the CSD level or at the Johannesburg Summit. However, I think it is worth insisting, since these are problems of high importance for people at the local level. Furthermore, this is an area where the Millennium Development Goals, in particular those related to water and sanitation are very relevant; I believe that both bilateral and multilateral development cooperation practice will be more focused on these basic problems in the years to come.

Another central area connected to technology transfer is the management of technology, linked to a concept which at one stage seemed promising, namely "appropriate technology" or "adapted technology," the idea being that in developing countries the whole framework for using technology is different from that of the industrialized countries, and that one could not simply export technology without adapting it to the boundary conditions at the receiving end. The ideas are sound; however, the north never managed to explain to developing countries that the purpose was not to export out-dated of inferior technology, thus perpetuating the inferiority of the south, but to give a real contribution to development.

Within the context of the new diplomacy, focus has shifted over time to specific technologies for improving environmental performance, based on the rationale that mistakes inadvertently made by today's industrialized countries in their process of development should not be repeated. One obvious example is climate change; where the north has built so much growth on low priced fossil fuels; shouldn't the south be given the opportunity to exploit such assets as solar energy or wind energy more fully? Or shouldn't specific solutions to city and transport planning in the south be different from those in the old urban areas in the north? Ideas of this kind have been slow in the making.

However, everybody agrees that technology use needs to be based on a firm ground of knowledge, and therefore the issue of *capacity-building* in developing countries has been much less controversial than technology transfer. Sometimes you could get the feeling that capacity-building negotiations served as a sort of safety valve to demonstrate that both north and south were ready and capable to make deals, even if progress was very difficult elsewhere. Of course, this does not mean that capacity-building texts have not given rise to controversies, not least when the issue of financing has been raised, but my impression is that we have been witnessing a common learning process, as all parties have begun to understand better the needs of countries as they embark on environmental policies and on policies to achieve sustainable development.

The present status of these discussions was summed up in the WSSD Plan of Action, Articles 125–127. The text is a product of negotiation and it is therefore very general. However, it underlines some important points:

- Human, institutional and infrastructure capacity-building should be enhanced and partnerships should be established, with the purpose of meeting the specific needs of developing countries in the context of sustainable development.
- Initiatives at all scales to this end should be supported with mobilization from all sources of adequate financial and other resources.
- Capacity-building efforts, such as the UNDP Capacity 21 program, should be strengthened in order to assess capacity development needs, design programs for capacity-building to meet the challenges of globalization and to attain internationally agreed development goals, develop the capacity of civil society, and to build and strengthen national capacity for carrying out the implementation of Agenda 21.

I have highlighted here a number of north-south issues which have been at the center of attention from the very beginning of the Rio process until the present day. Some others will be given particular attention in the following sections of this chapter. But at the general level, it is worth mentioning two sets of questions, which have become successively more important as the process has moved ahead. These are trade, and consumption and production patterns.

The failed negotiations on a New International Economic Order in the 1970s had left the old structures and institutional arrangements unchanged, as the preparations for Rio began. Trade issues continued to be negotiated in the GATT, while the more general aspects of trade and payments were part of the UNCTAD agenda. There was no real wish, neither in the north nor in the south, to open up new negotiating structures on these issues, even if G 77 went quite far to try to incorporate conclusions of UNCTAD VII, held in Cartagena, Colombia, in 1991, in Agenda 21. The discussions on the creation of a World Trade Organization had not yet begun, and the increasing commercial strength of countries like China and India was still not felt. Furthermore, the breakdown of the Soviet Empire had increased uncertainty about future global institutional arrangements, while the EU was still struggling to establish its internal market. Among the controversial points as the Rio Conference approached were agricultural protectionism, the use of subsidies, and the opening of markets. But they were not major issues in the negotiations, and in Agenda 21 they become part of a broader range of problems addressed in Chapter 2, entitled "International Economic Cooperation to accelerate Sustainable Development in Developing Countries and Related Policies."

It is not easy to pinpoint exactly to what extent the normative discussions and negotiations post-Rio have contributed to create a broader approach to trade policy issues than in the past. However, it is reasonable to assume that the continuous attention given to the three pillars of sustainable development (environment, economy, social aspects), both in CSD negotiations and in the corresponding national preparations, have helped to bring representatives of various Ministries in capitals together to discuss general issues of policy. The results are yet inconclusive, but they are reflected in the work of the WTO, particularly the Doha Ministerial Declaration 2001 as well as in the Monterrey Consensus 2002 and in the Plan of Implementation of the World Summit on Sustainable Development the same year.

It is interesting to compare the WSSD document 2002 with Agenda 21 ten years earlier. The way of looking at trade is now more inclusive, and the reference to sustainable development of a different character. Agenda 21 states in Chapter 2, paragraph 2.5: "An open, equitable, secure, non-discriminatory and predictable multilateral trading system is consistent with the goals of sustainable development etc." The tone is different in the Plan of Implementation, where the opening paragraph on trade (paragraph 90) begins: "Recognizing the major role that trade can play in achieving sustainable development and in eradicating poverty, we encourage members of the World Trade Organization (WTO) to pursue the work programme agreed at their Fourth Ministerial Conference."

The Ministerial Conference referred to above was the Conference that launched the Doha Round of negotiations in the WTO. Because of serious disagreements on a number of issues, mainly related to agricultural subsidies in the EU and in the United States, the negotiations were suspended in July 2006, but efforts are under way to restart the process. And here the linkage between trade and sustainable development can be a useful tool. Trade liberalization was from the early days of GATT seen in the perspective of the need for governments to provide social protection and domestic stability. In today's world, the concept of sustainable development provides further guidance: the Doha Ministerial Declaration pledges to "continue to make positive efforts designed to ensure that developing countries, and especially the least developed among them, secure a share in the growth of world trade commensurate with the needs of economic development". Trade liberalization and non-discrimination must be seen in the service of a broader social purpose: the goal of economic development, qualified by the need to respect the environment.[3]

These are important developments. They reflect changes in attitudes and in structures of national coordination. People dealing with trade policy recognize that there is a need for coordination with environment ministries. The suspicion that UN processes on sustainable development would disturb the work in WTO has been dampened, and it is recognized that trade policy and policies on sustainable development need to be mutually supportive. This is all the more important, since concrete problems tend to surface, in particular as rules in legally binding instruments such as the Convention on Biological Diversity or the Framework Convention on Climate Change will have trade policy impacts.

Of course, this does not mean that sustainable development is fully integrated in trade policy thinking. The previously noted dichotomy between "development" and "sustainable development" can still be felt in such documents as a recent policy statement of UNCTAD, the Sao Paulo Consensus of 2004 (UNCTAD XI). However, the references to sustainable development and environment are correctly formulated and testify to a movement in an organization which from the beginning was designed to try to accommodate trade and development.

Similar tendencies in the direction of more integrated thinking could be noted with regard to consumption and production patterns. In fact, in the early negotiations in the Rio process, G 77 members pointed out that it was unfair to ask them to take costly action to safeguard the environment, when the industrialized countries ever since the early nineteenth century had developed without reflecting on negative consequences for their environment. This meant that it was also logical to establish a link to the combat of poverty in the south: the parallel was often drawn between environmental damage caused by excessive consumption patterns in the north, while poverty and over-population forced people in developing countries to damage their environment and their resource base just in order to survive.

These positions were stated with force in the UNCED negotiations, but the issue never became a make-or-break problem. The language in Chapter 4 of Agenda 21 on "Changing consumption patterns" is rather neutral in its presentation of the problem and of the suggested action, which was presented with the following two broad objectives:

- to promote patterns of consumption and production that reduce environmental stress and will meet the basic needs of humanity;
- to develop a better understanding of the role of consumption and how to bring more sustainable consumption patterns.

The continued work has been rather intense with several separate conferences, seminars and workshops. It is therefore not surprising that the Johannesburg Plan of Implementation gives the question of unsustainable patterns of consumption and production a much more prominent place, devoting a main section to the issue, and proposing a ten-year framework of programs "in support of regional and national initiatives to accelerate the shift toward sustainable production and consumption to promote social and economic development within the carrying capacity of ecosystems...."

This long chapter opens with the following sentence: "Fundamental changes in the way societies produce and consume are indispensable for achieving global sustainable development." This important statement is thus a determinant for a detailed elaboration of the various elements of consumption and production patterns, which also includes sections on energy, transport, resource efficiency and chemicals. The evolution of thinking since Rio is quite obvious, even if the practical consequences yet remain limited.

We have now followed a number of the central negotiations within the Rio process, which have all indicated that there have been conflicts between the industrialized and the developing countries on a number of issues. On practically all of these points, the G 77 has appeared as a strong cohesive unit; even though the large number of developing countries obviously has diverging views on matters of detail, they have found that their overriding common interest is to maintain unity and try to get the maximum out of their numerical overweight. This is obviously facilitated by the normative character of the discussions and the method of work, seeking consensus and avoiding votes. It is probably also fair to say that the group of industrialized countries has felt a need to compensate their lack of concrete action, e.g., on the 0.7%-target, with an accommodating attitude on general statements without immediate concrete content.

As I now move to present some other central north-south issues as they have appeared in the negotiations on Desertification and on Climate, it is still true that on most issues the G 77 cohesion remains; but I will also focus on points where the tensions within the group of developing countries became too strong and changed the "normal" course of events. These were also moments when I had the responsibility as Chairman to deal with the problems arising out of the discord.

THE CONVENTION TO COMBAT DESERTIFICATION

Desertification and drought had become a major problem for the international community in the 1970s as a consequence of the disastrous drought in the Sahel region 1968–1973. At the time, developing countries maintained that desertification could not be solved nationally or regionally but that the problem required a global response. The industrialized countries, on the other hand, felt that there was no need for new institutions or instruments, but that the existing UN and aid structures could deal with the disaster.

However, the spectacular aspect of the Sahel drought and the unbearable images of hunger suffering on the world's TV screens created the political momentum for the convocation of a major UN Conference on Desertification. The General Assembly decided in 1974 that such a Conference should be held, and appointed the UNEP Executive Director Mostafa Tolba to be Secretary-General of the Conference, known as UNCOD.

After extensive preparatory work, UNCOD convened in Nairobi, Kenya, from August 29 to September 9, 1977 with the participation of ninety-five states and a number of NGO observers. The objectives of the Conference were to increase awareness of the problems of the dry-lands and to collect scientific information of problems related to desertification and drought. These objectives were largely achieved, but the third objective, to initiate a program to combat desertification, did not lead to major results. Certainly, a Plan of Action to Combat Desertification (PACD) was agreed, but its results became rather ephemeral: The Plan of Action did not lead to major changes in the international support for countries suffering from drought and desertification; it never achieved the status of an international agreement that would be really implemented. In particular, the necessary levels of funding were never achieved.

One reason for the disappearance of desertification from the international media's radar screens was obviously that the eighties saw a more normal situation in the Sahel countries. Of course, poverty was still rampant and conditions were very difficult: but it was no longer an unbearable disaster, and the span of attention in a world beset with many catastrophes is rather short.

As work got under way in the Preparatory Committee for the Rio Conference, the lack of results of the Plan of Action was already apparent, and many

African delegates felt that the issue would need renewed attention in Rio de Janeiro. At the organizational meeting of the Prepcom it had been decided that desertification and drought would be negotiated in Working Group I, which I chaired. It soon became apparent that the failure of PACD had affected the willingness and capacity of countries to take far-reaching initiatives, and the first sessions of the Working Group did not achieve much.

For the third Prepcom session in New York in September 1991, the Secretariat had prepared a background paper on what was to become Chapter 12 of Agenda 21. One of the leading Secretariat officials in this process was Arba Diallo, former Foreign Minister of Burkina Faso, who was responsible for relations with Africa in the UNCED Secretariat. The African countries were now quite fed up with the lack of interest in a problem which they felt was of capital importance to them; my feeling was that they were also disappointed at the lack of support from the Group of 77. One could feel that a south-south problem was brewing. The African Group also complained about the lack of interest in the NGO community, which otherwise followed discussions in Working Group I quite intensely, in particular when we discussed forests They were right, the NGO benches were empty as we discussed desertification.

At this stage I felt that the African concerns needed to be taken seriously. At the Prepcom III session I decided that drought and desertification would be given priority at the final Prepcom meeting in New York in March 1992, and that I would make a visit to some of the worst affected countries in Africa before that session, in order to gain some first-hand knowledge of the problems on the ground. These decisions were well received by the African Group, and in the first days of January 1992, I traveled to Mauritania and Mali accompanied by Arba Diallo and my Swedish collaborator Gunilla Bjorklund. The visits were very interesting, demonstrating the full impact of desertification as we were traveling in Mauritania during severe sandstorms, with the capital Nouakchott on the immediate desert border.

This visit to Africa would not have had much impact on events if other initiatives had not been taken. In November 1991 African Ministers of Environment met in Abidjan for an UNCED preparatory meeting, and adopted a common position and a declaration. Among the central points was the call for a convention to combat desertification.

As my delegation traveled to Bamako in Mali, we were informed of these proposals of African Ministers, and I made some rather positive remarks at a meeting at the UNDP office. I felt that it could be worthwhile to make this additional effort, even though we had no illusions about the difficulty of the task.

When Prepcom IV assembled in New York a few weeks later the perspectives did not seem particularly bright. Desertification was to be given priority, both in substance and in procedure, but the African group had not had time to agree on any proposals, and other parties still seemed indifferent. There were new Secretariat proposals on the table, but I had to tell the

African Group that they needed to develop some constructive suggestions of their own if they would hope for success.

An able negotiator from the Gambia, Bolong Sonko, took up the challenge, and in short time, an African proposal was put on the table. This proposal aimed at underlining the importance of desertification as a problem of development, and it was designed to facilitate consensus. The OECD countries were initially suspicious, but when the American delegate declared that the African proposal was something that the United States could basically live with, I felt that we were on our way to an agreement. In fact, the whole of Chapter 12 could be agreed at Prepcom IV, with the exception of the paragraphs on a Convention. This issue was left to negotiations in Rio, for a certain time also linked to a preference in some OECD countries for a Convention on Forestry.

In Rio de Janeiro the difficult issue of a Desertification Convention was handled in a negotiating Group chaired by Tommy Koh himself. At this stage, the African countries had the support of the whole G 77, led by the very able Pakistani Ambassador Jamsheed Marker. Negotiations were complicated, but ultimately the US accepted the idea of a Convention, and at that stage also EU gave in. The General Assembly was invited to establish an Intergovernmental Negotiating Committee to elaborate a Convention to combat desertification, "by June 1994". This decision was finally taken by the General Assembly in December 1992.

In political terms, the agreement on a Desertification Convention was seen by the African countries as the main result of UNCED; several other G 77 countries saw the decision as a good thing but were relatively indifferent. Many industrialized countries were concerned about the financial consequences of a Convention which by its very nature would be a multilateral development cooperation instrument rather than an environmental treaty. All these elements were later to impact on the conduct of the negotiations.

At the first organizational meeting of the INC, I was elected Chairman of the Committee. In fact there was some feeling that the negotiation would be a continuation of the Working Group I, and therefore this decision seemed rather logical. As for a general account of the course of the negotiation, particularly with regard to the role of science and research, I refer to E. Corell, *The Negotiable Desert* (1999). Here I wish to concentrate on the particular tensions that appeared within the G 77, particularly in the initial part of the negotiation, and some more general aspects of the Convention.

An important part of the whole background to this Convention was the role of Africa. It was an African disaster that had triggered the 1977 Conference, and it was African Ministers that had launched the idea of a Convention. The Convention title itself recognized the particular role of Africa in its cumbersome and highly negotiated title: "International Convention to combat Desertification in those Countries experiencing serious Drought and/or Desertification, particularly in Africa." All countries recognized that there should be priority for Africa, but at the first substantial session of the INCD there were problems with the implementation of this principle. I proposed that the special concern for Africa should be expressed through the negotiation of a special Annex for Africa, containing more specific provisions than those in the main body of the Convention, and that similar instruments for other regions should be negotiated later.

This proposal was not well received by representatives of other regions: in particular Latin American countries with Brazil in the lead, opposed my proposal. I was told that the atmosphere in G 77 was very irritated, and informal consultations on my part did not lead to any results. At one stage it looked as if the G 77 might be torn apart and the whole negotiation be jeopardized. I had serious doubts that the INC would have the time to negotiate implementation annexes for Africa, Latin America, and Asia, in the time available, which was extremely short, since we had to complete the negotiation in a little more than one year. This first substantive session ended on a sour note, without much progress made, and the sticky issue of the Annexes unresolved. The only satisfaction I could derive from events was a firm support by the African countries.

We now had a few months to prepare for INCD 2, which was held in September in Geneva. I tried to hold consultations with interested parties, and I am sure that there were a lot of contacts between G 77 members in New York and elsewhere. When we met for INCD-2 it seemed obvious that there was a willingness to consider a compromise, which would mean the simultaneous negotiation of the three annexes, but with the understanding that the Annex on Africa would be the most elaborated and detailed one. Furthermore, the priority for Africa would be recognized in the Convention itself. However, the INCD-2 session met other types of difficulties, more closely related to traditional north-south issues, and it also turned out to be a cliff-hanger, with central questions solved at the very end. At that time, however, it was agreed that a final decision on three Annexes would be taken at INCD-3, which was to be held in New York in January 1994.

That agreement was achieved, and the intra-G 77 controversy on the annexes was brought to a successful conclusion. The Asian and Latin American groups helped the process by taking a flexible and constructive line on the drafting of their respective annexes. Another problem related to annexes surfaced towards the very end of the negotiating process, as the European countries on the northern Mediterranean proposed that a fourth Annex should be negotiated. Initially, this proposal was not well received by the G 77, but after a number of formal and informal consultations we found a consensus on the issue, and the four Annexes were all adopted simultaneously at the last negotiating session.

By that time, more traditional north-south issues had turned out to be the main stumbling blocks on the road to agreement on the Convention. In particular the financing arrangements were extremely controversial; since the Convention actually aimed at covering the borderline between environment and development, the restrictive attitude of the OECD countries created

severe tensions. As Chairman, I tried to overcome these and other difficulties at a meeting with key delegates in Stockholm in March 1994. The
atmosphere was good, but there was no breakthrough on the substantive
points. These were left to the final negotiations (INC-5) which were held at
UNESCO Headquarters in Paris in June 1994. At the end there were problems with the organization of the Committee on Science and Technology,
which I tried to deal with myself, and finally managed to sort out, while the
financial issues were left to special high-level negotiations that were conducted by Bolong Sonko of Gambia and Pierre-Marc Johnson of Canada.

At an early stage of the negotiations, the G 77 had suggested the creation
of a special desertification fund, which was rejected by the industrialized
countries. At the very least the developing countries then wanted a financial mechanism for the Convention of the same kind that had already been
established for the Conventions on Biodiversity and Climate, with possibilities for financing by the Global Environment Facility, linked to the World
Bank. These proposals were not acceptable for developed countries, and
there was a serious deadlock during the last days and nights; at that stage
a complete failure of the negotiation was a distinct possibility as worn-out
negotiators tried to find some way out. A US proposal for a new kind of
institution, called the Global Mechanism, which would promote the mobilization and channeling of resources for measures to combat desertification, was finally accepted during a long night session, closely followed on
the spot by a number of Ministers from African affected countries.

At the time, I was much concerned by the lack of concrete funding for the
Global Mechanism; and I believe that experience has shown that a straight
decision to create a traditional Financial Mechanism had been preferable.
However, the compromise was necessary to save the Convention; and during that last night I argued forcefully for acceptance of the financial package as a lesser evil than a complete breakdown of the negotiation.

With its special features of National Action Programmes, based on a
bottom-up approach and its particular emphasis on Africa I believe that the
Convention to Combat Desertification is one of the essential instruments
to promote global sustainability. Innovative additions to the structure of
the Convention, such as the establishment of an implementation committee, have also increased its efficiency. After the first Conference of Parties,
held in Rome in 1997, I have only followed the work of the Convention at
a distance, but continuity has been ensured by the untiring efforts of the
Executive Secretary of the Convention, Arba Diallo.

The year 2006, ten years after the Convention entered into force, was proclaimed as the UN Year on Desertification and Drought. A number of events
have taken place which all serve to underline that these problems continue
to be essential issues on the development/environment agenda. The Convention has not delivered major changes in the dry-lands, and the problems
related to financial resources continue to complicate its implementation. But
there is progress with the establishment of national action programs, and the

bottom-up approach of the Convention is appreciated. Today, the linkages to the climate issue, in particular the need for adaptation to climate change, help strengthening the support for the Convention. Efforts are under way to carry out reforms which would make it more efficient.

THE FRAMEWORK CONVENTION
ON CLIMATE CHANGE

Whereas the Convention to combat Desertification has a very distinct north-south focus, the Framework Convention on Climate Change addresses a broad range of issues of a global nature, with significant consequences for the long-term development of the world economy and the very future of the human species.

Furthermore, the climate issue is — together with the question of the ozone layer — one of the clearest examples of the impact of natural science on the new diplomacy. A long history of research on the relationship between the earth's climate and the concentration of carbon dioxide and other greenhouse gases in the atmosphere led to the establishment in 1987 of the Intergovernmental Panel on Climate Change (IPCC), a large network of researchers and government officials. The greatest effect of IPCC work has undoubtedly been its forecasts on the effects of present and future emissions of greenhouse gases, presented in the so-called "summaries for policy-makers," a central feature of the IPCC Assessment Reports, presented in 1990, 1995, 2001, and 2007. A more detailed account of the scientific background to the climate negotiations will be made in Chapter 5.

The international community has overall adopted the view that human impact on the climate is happening and that the precautionary principle requires action on a global level. But from the point of view of the south — with its emphasis on economic development — it has been felt that more researchers from developing countries should be involved in IPCC work in order to bring the development perspective to bear on the reports of the Panel.

In the negotiations which followed the presentation of the First IPCC Assessment Report in 1990 and led to the adoption in 1992 of the Framework Convention on Climate Change (FCCC), the south also took a strong line with respect to the responsibility of the northern industrialized countries for the present concentrations of greenhouse gases, particularly carbon dioxide, in the atmosphere. The notion of *common but differentiated responsibilities* has become a cornerstone of the G 77 position, reflected in the differentiated commitments of developed and developing countries in both the Framework Convention on Climate Change (in force 1994) and the Kyoto Protocol (in force 2005). The phrase itself appears in Article 3.1 and 4.1 of the FCCC and in Article 10 of the Kyoto Protocol. Furthermore, in Article 3.1 of the FCCC it is stated that "the developed country Parties should take the lead in combating climate change and the adverse effects thereof."

As previously mentioned, G 77 also managed to include in the Convention Article 4.7, which states that implementation of commitments by developing countries is dependent upon the effective implementation by developed country Parties of their commitments related to financial resources and transfer of technology. In concrete terms, the clear distinction between developed and developing countries in the Convention was established through the list of countries in Annexes I and II of the Convention and Annex B of the Protocol. During the negotiations, proposals have been made from time to time to make the system more flexible through the establishment of differentiated commitments for various sub-groups of countries, but these efforts proved unsuccessful.

However, in Article 4.9 of the Convention the least developed countries are recognized as a group with specific needs for finance and transfer of technology. The effects of this recognition is somewhat reduced by Article 4.8, which lists a large number of categories of countries with specific needs and concerns, as well as Article 4.10 which speaks about particular consideration for countries "which are vulnerable to the adverse effects of the implementation of measures to respond to climate change." In Articles 4.8 and 4.10 there are also direct references to countries which are highly dependent on income generated from exports of fossil fuels.

The OPEC countries, in particular Saudi Arabia, have played a consistent role in the negotiations from 1991 until today; concerns for the development of future oil markets have led to a continuous, some would say disturbing, opposition to positive action to limit emissions of carbon dioxide. This policy choice was not necessarily obvious: at the time of the first oil shock in the 1970s, when Saudi Arabia played a leading role in the north-south dialogue, the then Saudi oil minister Sheikh Yamani took the line that since oil was bound to be more and more valuable, it was in the interest of the country to keep the oil in the ground as long as possible. However, the political rhetoric linking the Saudi position to that of the G 77 has remained. At times it has permitted Saudi Arabia to be close to mainstream G 77 positions, on other occasions their line has led to some of the few moments when G 77 solidarity has been broken. The final sections of this chapter will detail some highlights of this story.

In the negotiations for the Framework Convention, the Saudi position was set out with considerable strength, which is reflected in the texts referred to above. However, Saudi Arabia also flexed its muscles in the negotiations of Chapter 9 of Agenda 21, dealing with atmosphere. They insisted that every reference to energy or technology should be preceded with the expression *safe and sound*, the rationale being that nuclear power would then be excluded, which was unacceptable to a number of developed countries. As coordinator for Chapter 9, I had to find a solution. This became the ultimate negotiation of the whole Rio Conference: the Brazilian Under-Secretary, Ambassador Azambuja and myself negotiating a generic text of a foot-note to the introductory Chapter 1 of Agenda 21 with the Chief Negotiators of Saudi Arabia and Kuwait. At the very end, the text was submitted to a Saudi Minister present in Rio de Janeiro, who accepted it and permitted an agreement.[4] This did not preclude Saudi Arabia to introduce several reservations to the text of Agenda 21 in the Final Act of the Conference. However, like other reservations, to my knowledge these have never been referred to in subsequent negotiations.

As the FCCC entered into force in 1994 and preparations began for the First Conference of Parties (COP 1) to be held in Berlin in March-April 1995, it became clear that the rather soft commitments in the Convention itself needed to be sharpened. The Association of Small Island States (AOSIS) took the lead in calling for a Berlin Protocol with specific, time-bound, reduction commitments by developed countries. Informal preparatory meetings showed that such an outcome of the Berlin Conference would be unreachable, but that on the other hand a negotiating mandate for a later Protocol would be necessary. This set the stage for a most serious conflict within the G 77.

The Chairperson of the Conference was the newly appointed German Minister of Environment, Angela Merkel. As the negotiation of a Berlin Mandate became the obvious centerpiece of the whole meeting, she managed to establish a small negotiating group with representatives of key countries, and I was appointed Chairman of this group.

The negotiation started off along rather traditional lines, but very soon the dynamics changed, as G 77 solidarity broke as a result of the tension between the OPEC countries and the AOSIS group. A new group emerged with India, Brazil and China in the lead and T.P. Shrinivasan of India as the main spokesman. The group became known as the Green group; it numbered initially around 40 countries, but finally counted about seventy or eighty members. Normal G 77 action continued on other negotiating issues, but in the Berlin Mandate group, the G 77 Chair, Philippines, took a minor role with Shrinivasan and his Brazilian and Chinese colleagues representing the interests of developing countries.

It was a difficult negotiation, with two issues in the center: a) the question of targets and timetables, reflecting divisions between Europe and the United States, and b) the issue of commitments by developing countries, where in particular the United States insisted on quantified commitments also outside the Annex I group. However, the existence of the Green group, and the pressure of the AOSIS countries, facilitated an agreement. Nevertheless, at the level of high officials, we did not manage to reach full consensus on the question of commitments by developing countries, but the options were fairly clear-cut as I reported to the Group of Ministers chaired by Angela Merkel. During a long night of negotiation, she managed to settle the remaining difficulties, and the Berlin Mandate was adopted. This deal became the basis for the Kyoto Protocol.

The efficiency of the AOSIS countries in Berlin had reduced the impact of OPEC on G 77 and paved the way for the emergence of the Green group.

It soon became clear, however, that this was a unique situation, and that things were to change as the Kyoto COP-3 drew closer. This evolution was also influenced by the US Senate Byrd-Hagel resolution, voted 95–0 in the summer of 1997. In this resolution, it was stated that the United States would not agree to undertake commitments, unless the developing countries would also be ready to take on similar commitments. Since the Berlin Mandate, in its Article 2. b had explicitly stated that the negotiating process would not introduce any new commitments for non-annex I Parties, it was easy for negative G 77 members, such as OPEC, to point out that Annex I had broken against one of those points that made the Mandate possible, and that G 77 should stick strongly to the position of no new commitments. It was a general radicalization of the G 77, which offered new opportunities for the Saudis to slow down the process and permitted G 77 to rally to a tough line in the negotiations.[5]

From Kyoto onwards, the skilled Saudi negotiators, led by the brilliant and stubborn Mohammed Al-Sabban, have played a central role in the north-south negotiations, sometimes to the despair of AOSIS countries and a number of the least-developed countries, who want to see rapid action to reduce emissions of greenhouse gases. The sometimes filibustering tactics of the Saudis have irritated Annex I negotiators and undoubtedly slowed down negotiations. Nevertheless, all countries are trying to defend their interests, and the OPEC countries have skillfully explored the opportunities that have been open to them. It is also notable that Saudi Arabia has always been very keen to operate within a G 77 consensus; in the many difficult negotiations on issues of high interest to Saudi Arabia, which I chaired, [6] it was striking that Dr. Al-Sabban could change his position very rapidly, if G 77 consensus risked being jeopardized. Maybe this has something to do with the lessons from Berlin: after that there has never been an open rift within G 77 in the climate negotiations.

One reason is obviously the previously noted joint interest of G 77 to use their numbers (135 countries) and political clout in the UN framework to promote their main interests on transfers of financial resources and technology. Another has been the cautious position taken by major G 77 countries, such as China and India, which have strongly defended their rights to increase emissions in order to promote their rapid economic growth. They have been leading a coherent G 77 opposition to any mentioning of quantitative commitments by developing countries. In Kyoto, the OECD group, led by the United States but with New Zealand as the proponent, tried to propose that if the developed countries fulfilled their commitments in the first phase of Kyoto, developing countries should accept such quantified commitments in a subsequent period. This proposal caused uproar in the G 77; angry statements followed which extended over a whole day in the plenary.

The resourceful and imaginative Chairman of the negotiations in Kyoto, Raul Estrada from Argentina, then tried to introduce the notion of "Voluntary commitments", which seemed to be acceptable to a number of G 77 countries. It was included in the final package which Estrada tried to gavel through during a long night session at the very end. But as China, India and Brazil rejected the idea and G 77 solidarity was at a premium, Estrada dropped his proposal.

The idea of voluntary commitments resurfaced at COP-4 in Buenos Aires in 1998, but was rapidly killed by the G 77 majority.

At this point it is important to recall that the absence of quantitative commitments for non-annex I Parties, as an expression of the principle of common but differentiated responsibilities, does not mean that developing countries have no commitments at all. In fact, Article 4.1 of the FCCC outlined a number of commitments by all Parties, including the preparation of national programs to limit emissions, communication of statistics, and regional cooperation. Within the logic of the Kyoto negotiations, it would seem reasonable to make these points somewhat more precise, even though the G 77 took a rather negative view on this approach. I was coordinating a small negotiation group on the subject, with representatives from the United States, the EU and G 77. It was a frustrating experience with very slow progress and very little enthusiasm. At the same time, it was clear to all of us that some carrying over of the very idea of commitments for all Parties from the Convention to the Kyoto Protocol would be a precondition for a successful agreement in Kyoto.

As the final night started, there was still no agreement, and I had no choice but to try to make a proposal of my own, in my view rather favorable to the G 77 position. Nevertheless, OECD countries were ready to go along, but at this very late stage of the negotiation, G 77 was not ready to reconsider its position. I could only report the failure to agree: two proposals were on the table, the G 77 text and my own. At this point, Estrada overruled G 77 and my text was adopted as Article 10 of the Protocol. Estrada took a risk, but since G 77 had by then already obtained the deletion of the article on voluntary commitments, they did not raise objections.[7] Since the extremely difficult final negotiations on the Kyoto Mechanisms, in particular the question of emissions trading, originally strongly resisted by G 77, had by then already been concluded, there remained only some more procedural issues, and the conviction by all Parties that they could not take the responsibility for sinking the Kyoto Protocol. Ambassador Estrada could declare the Kyoto Protocol unanimously agreed in the late morning of December 11, 1997.

Today we know that the Kyoto Protocol had a long and bumpy road to travel on the way to entry into force. Since this story has mainly been part of the uneasy relationship between Europe and the United States, it will be told in Chapter 5. It is important to remember, however, that the north-south controversies have been part and parcel of the process all along, and that all the questions raised in this Chapter will resurface as the Parties will move into serious discussions and negotiations on the Post-2012 climate regime. The concluding Chapter 7 will explore these issues further.

5 The Uneasy Friendship
United States/Europe

THE BACKGROUND

The twentieth century has been called the American Century. The reason is, of course, the US position as the major superpower in the more than fifty years after the end of the Second World War, for a long time seriously challenged by the Soviet Union, but at the beginning of the twenty-first century the sole superpower, with military, political and economic resources that never existed before for a single state. In the time of the cold war, the United States was the uncontested leader of the coalition opposing Soviet expansion, with the North Atlantic Treaty Organization (NATO) as the main military instrument. It was also the leading economy, using its supremacy in an intelligent way, instrumental in rebuilding war devastated Western Europe through the Marshall Plan (1948), and paving the way for European economic cooperation.

Since the United States had also been instrumental in the establishment of the United Nations and the Bretton Woods institutions (International Monetary Fund – IMF, and International Bank for Reconstruction and Development/World Bank – IBRD) it is fair to say that the existing system for multilateral economic cooperation is deeply indebted to the United States for its existence.

There were, of course, tensions in the transatlantic alliance already in the first decades after World War II, but it was only in the 1970's that more serious problems arose, caused by the increasing economic strength of the European Economic Community and its corresponding political clout. The Vietnam war weakened the US position and the first oil shock created serious problems on both sides of the Atlantic. At the same time, Japan emerged as a serious competitor in the world economy. The dollar that had served as the basis for the world's monetary system had to cut its links to gold in the early seventies, and the world entered a phase of floating currencies.

The dramatic breakdown of the Soviet system in the late 1980s radically changed the face of the world, and increased the confidence of the Western democracies. The superpower position of the United States was now uncontested, and it was generally recognized that the main credit for the successful end of the cold war should be attributed to the United States. At the same time, the EU, which had had a rather lackluster performance in the 1980's, started a period of dynamic consolidation and enlargement, finalizing the internal market and increasing its membership from twelve to twenty-seven in twelve years.

All through this long period, normally characterized by close cooperation and friendship between Europe and the United States, the two societies had maintained important structural differences. Western Europe had built its new-found prosperity on a social model which was mainly represented by Scandinavian social democracy, German principles of a social market economy (Soziale Marktwirtschaft), and French state intervention in central economic sectors. The United States, on the other hand, has developed a market economy with minimal state intervention, low taxes and a general acceptance of important wage differentials.

It is obvious that this picture is far too simplistic, particularly today, when the European systems have gone far in the direction of economic liberalization. It is also true that the European countries show important differences. Nevertheless, the discussion about the future of the "European Model" shows that the differences between Europe and the United States on such issues as the role of public policy, taxation or more generally the functions of the state, still have an impact and influence policy-making well outside the economic and social sectors.

This background picture is important to keep in mind as we reflect on the Europe/USA relationship in the framework of the new diplomacy for sustainable development. Because many of the issues between these parties in the Rio process or in the climate negotiations can only be understood in the light of the competition/cooperation characteristic of the political and economic relationship on the one hand, and on the other, the differing perceptions of domestic policies.

Let me add one additional thought, of particular importance for issues related to sustainability. The United States was created — initially by European immigrants — through the extension of the territory. There was always a new frontier, always new resources to find and to exploit. As we slowly begin to realize that globalization, increasing population and global change, mean that we live on a finite planet and that lifestyles and structures have to be adapted to this new reality, it is not surprising that this understanding and its political and economic consequences are particularly painful in the United States. But Europe also has to realize that the US economy is more flexible and dynamic than the European one, more capable of adapting to new conditions. As the requirements of sustainable development, i.e., in the field of climate change, will unfold over the coming decades, Europe must be ready for new American initiatives, based on technological and economic strength.

SOME PERSONAL NOTES

In the autumn of 1969, I became Head of the Private Office of the newly appointed Secretary-General of OECD, Emile van Lennep of the Netherlands. For me, it was an unexpected new job. The role of Chef de Cabinet, as my job was mostly labeled according to French practice in a bilingual organization, gave me a good insight into the practice of an organization with its roots in the early years of post-war cooperation. As OEEC turned into OECD in 1960, the United States and Canada formally joined the organization (they had been observers in OEEC). Since Japan joined in 1964 and Finland in 1967, whereas Australia and New Zealand participated in certain activities and later became members, by this time OECD was a manageable club of like-minded countries. The main rationale of OECD was (and is) economic policy in a broad sense with macro-economic policy in the centre. One of its main working methods consists of country reviews, lucid and careful peer reviews of economic policy and other policies, which sometimes carry considerable weight.

The transatlantic relationship has always been, and continues to be, at the heart of OECD work. The organization grew out of the Marshall Plan, and all through the 1960s and onwards, as globalization changed the pattern of the world economy, the analyses of the OECD provided guidance to policy-makers on macro-economic policies and structural adjustment, with Europe, the United States and Japan as main actors. It should not be forgotten however, that the establishment of the Development Assistance Committee (DAC) also underlined the importance of sound development cooperation policies. DAC has helped define the concept of Official Development Assistance (ODA); and it has provided essential statistics on aid flows, as an important measure of the performance of OECD countries in this field. Furthermore, OECD established its Committee on Environment already in 1970, and the fundamental Polluters Pay Principle (PPP) was agreed in 1974.

EEC as an organization from the beginning had an observer mission to the OECD, led by the Commission, but the Community never played a central role in the negotiations. In fact, as the years went by, my own impression was that member states of the EEC were quite comfortable with OECD as a multilateral forum for contacts with the United States, also on controversial issues, such as trade policy or agricultural policy. To a certain extent this role continues to this day; one important example being climate policy, where experts can meet to discuss central issues in the non-political, detached atmosphere of the Annex I Experts Group.

After the end of the cold war and the enlargement of the EU, OECD operated in a different context, and my feeling is that the organization needs to redefine its role according to the new circumstances. As shown by the example of climate policy, it is possible that global change and the need for common action on issues of sustainability might provide a new impetus. As energy issues are so central to these discussions, it is also worth noting that the associated International Energy Agency (IEA) is an important actor in its field.

In the OECD I had been able to measure the importance of the transatlantic relationship for the world economy. After three years as bilateral Ambassador to Hanoi, I moved back to the multilateral arena in 1977 as Head of the Multilateral Department for Development Cooperation of the Ministry for Foreign Affairs. This gave me another perspective on policy-making in the United States and on US/Europe relations, as I became involved in replenishment exercises of the "soft" windows of different international financial institutions, including the World Bank.[1]

These replenishment negotiations aimed at raising money for several fiscal years. Since the US administration cannot formally engage funds beyond one fiscal year, complicated schemes had to be drawn up to ensure that other donors would not be bound by their long-term commitments, if the United States as the largest contributor did not comply for years two or three. As far as I know, these procedures have never needed to be put in motion, but the problem illustrates one difficulty in transatlantic relations: the difference between the European parliamentary systems, and the US Constitution with its strict division between the executive and Congress.

Because of the decision-making system in the United States, in many negotiations Congress maintains a strong physical presence, and has a strong influence on the negotiating stance. This is a constant element of uncertainty: will a deal struck with the United States be ratified by Congress? And we know that there have been critical moments when such fears have been well founded: the non-ratification by Congress of the International Trade Organization in 1946, which was partly remedied by the General Agreement on Tariffs and Trade (GATT), is an example.

These are personal experiences of US/Europe differences that have complicated negotiations. Of course broader political, security, and economic considerations have played a much larger role in framing the general transatlantic relationship. This is an example of the sometimes very strong impact of traditional international relations on the diplomacy for sustainable development. But examples like these illustrate concrete elements which have a bearing on specific negotiations and will continue to do so in the future.

Before moving to the main story of this chapter, which is centered on the climate negotiations, I wish to add another personal point: even though negotiations with the Americans are often difficult and delicate, there is generally an easy-going relationship between delegations. This reflects a set of common values and traditions, also underlined by the extreme diversity of views held in the United States on most issues, and reflected in delegates' personal opinions. The friendship is certainly sometimes uneasy at the government level, but at the personal level it is mostly very confident and agreeable.

This section will in its main part be built on my experiences from the negotiations within the framework of the Climate Convention, but I will also make some references to the Rio/Johannesburg process. Since these various processes were overlapping, I will move rather freely between them, but the climate negotiations are in the centre. The section will begin with a brief account of the scientific research and the academic discussions that led up to the negotiations of the UN Framework Convention on Climate Change.

THE SCIENCE OF CLIMATE CHANGE

There is a long history of research on the effects of carbon dioxide emissions on the world's climate, starting with John Tyndall (UK) in the 1840s and Svante Arrhenius (Sweden) at the end of the nineteenth century, but it was only after the UN Conference on the Human Environment in Stockholm in 1972, leading to the creation of UNEP, that the potential consequences of climate change began to be addressed. In 1979, the World Meteorological Organization (WMO) established the World Climate Programme (WCP), which in 1985 organized a Conference in Villach, Austria, which came close to a scientific consensus with a rather confident statement that "the most advanced experiments....show increases of the global mean surface temperature for a doubling of the atmospheric CO_2 concentration or equivalent, of between 1.5 and 4.5 degrees C." The ozone scare and the adoption of the Montreal Protocol in 1987 demonstrated that the human impact on the planet's atmosphere could have disastrous consequences. Furthermore, these problems were set in a broader context of sustainability through the Brundtland Commission Report "Our Common Future" in 1987.[2]

In 1988, climate change definitely surfaced as a political issue, being addressed at the highest levels of government, and it is interesting to note that the United States took an active role, possibly under the impact of the serious drought in the country that year, and climatic disasters around the world. John Hansen, Chief climate scientist at NASA's Goddard Institute for Space Studies stated at a Congress hearing that "the evidence is pretty strong that the greenhouse effect is here." George Bush made climate change an issue in his election campaign that year, and other world leaders, including the UK Premier Margaret Thatcher, warned about the dangers of global warming. At this time the Intergovernmental Panel on Climate Change (IPCC) was established, electing the senior Swedish climate scientist Bert Bolin as its Chairman. An important conference was held in Ottawa in early 1989 on the invitation of the Canadian government, which made a statement including several elements that should be included in a Framework Convention on the protection of the atmosphere, including a

World Atmosphere Trust Fund. A conference in New Delhi underlined the need to set global warming in a north-south context. The G 7 summit in Paris in July 1989 called for "common efforts to limit emissions of carbon dioxide" and supported the idea of a framework convention. Later that year, a Ministerial Conference was held at Nordwijk, Netherlands, with the participation of seventy-two countries, which recommended that emissions should be stabilized at levels to be recommended by the IPCC.

President Bush had committed himself to call a climate conference in Washington. Such a conference was held in April 1990, attended by seventeen countries. But now the different perceptions of the United States and other industrialized countries began to emerge clearly. According to Bush no action should be taken until scientific evidence was more certain: "What we need are facts, the stuff that science is made of." On the other hand, the German Minister of Environment Klaus Töpfer declared that "gaps in knowledge must not be used as an excuse for world-wide inaction." Töpfer, later to be head of UNEP, soon emerged as one of the most influential politicians in Europe on environmental matters.

The stage was set for the controversies between the United States and Europe on the climate issue, which ultimately led to the US refusal to ratify the Kyoto Protocol. And the question of scientific evidence of global warming, as well as the research on costs, would continue to be in the center of concern.

THE NEGOTIATIONS OF THE FRAMEWORK CONVENTION ON CLIMATE CHANGE AND THE RIO CONFERENCE ON ENVIRONMENT AND DEVELOPMENT

As previously mentioned, I became Chief Negotiator of the Ministry of Environment in 1990, while still maintaining my position as Permanent representative to OECD and UNESCO for a few months. As a recognition of Sweden's role in international environment negotiations ever since the Stockholm Conference in 1972, I was elected Chairman of plenary Working Group I of the Preparatory Committee. This included the negotiation of Chapter 9, dealing with Atmosphere, of Agenda 21. This Chapter includes climate change, the depletion of the ozone layer, trans-boundary air pollution and some other issues related to the world's atmosphere. It has an interesting structure, since it is the only chapter in Agenda 21 that deals specifically with economic sectors: energy, industry, agriculture.

Because of the existing agreements on trans-boundary air pollution and the ozone layer, and the ongoing negotiations on climate change, it contains relatively few specific recommendations: there was however a clear interface between the climate negotiations and the work on Chapter 9, particularly since the tight timetable for the two processes forced meetings to follow each other closely in time, and since the negotiators to a large extent were the same people. It became a tough agenda for all involved, with long sessions, long absences from the home base, and tiring negotiations, often stretching far into the night. For me, who at this stage was a newcomer to the atmosphere issues, it provided however an invaluable opportunity to come to know people and to learn more about the substance of the issues.

The United States had so far played a leading role in the work on climate change. At the same time, the George Bush administration had not made up its mind on the political reaction. Furthermore, as an IPCC meeting in Sundsvall, Sweden, at the end of August, 1990, managed to agree on its First Assessment Report, the administration in Washington and the rest of the world were forced to address a different kind of threat: Saddam Hussein's invasion of Kuwait. This was a foreign policy crisis that put all other issues in the background.

Nevertheless, as the UN General Assembly in the autumn of 1990 agreed to establish an Intergovernmental Negotiating Committee (INC) for a Framework Convention on Climate Change,[3] the US government invited the first negotiating session to take place in Westlands Conference Center outside Washington. The session was held in February 1991, while the first Gulf War was fought in Iraq and commanded the attention of the media.

The negotiations were mainly about the organization of the process, but behind the procedural issues broader problems appeared. It was already at this stage clear that the United States would not be ready to consider binding targets and time-tables for emission reductions. The European positions were not yet firmly established, and many of the negotiators were still relatively unacquainted with the substance of the problems to be addressed: it is not surprising that the session was characterized by considerable uncertainty. The NGO community was not slow to criticize the negotiators for failing to address the real issues.

As often is the case, the negotiators on the floor did not really share this sense of frustration, even if some of us would have liked to see more rapid progress. The election of the highly respected Frenchman Jean Ripert to chair the INC and the appointment of Michael Zammit Cutajar of Malta to head the Secretariat helped establish confidence in the possible success of the process; and decisions to establish two plenary Working Groups, one on commitments, and one on mechanisms and institutions, meant that the organization was in place for the future negotiations. As Ripert and his collaborator Delphine Borione later pointed out, these difficult procedural negotiations also served to define the scope and content of the Convention.[4]

The dynamics of the Rio process, with the agreed objective that the Climate Convention would be signed in Rio de Janeiro in June 1992, also introduced a sense of urgency, which served the negotiations well. Nevertheless, the magnitude of the task, the uncertainties surrounding the climate issue, and the difficult political choices that had to be made, on several occasions made weary negotiators doubt if success was really within reach.

The INC held four further formal sessions: INC-2 in Geneva in June 1991, INC-3 in Nairobi in September, INC-4 in Geneva in December, and INC-5 in New York in February 1992, which was resumed in May. It was a period of hard bargaining, many trial balloons, efficient Secretariat work to produce background documents and compile proposals, and above all confident leadership by Jean Ripert. It was also a period when many of the negotiators began to understand better the issues at stake, and to develop a sense of the global importance of the undertaking, going beyond national interests.

But it was also a time of doubts and difficult negotiations in capitals to formulate instructions and proposals which could move the negotiations forward. At the time, Sweden was not yet a member of the EU, and we tried to play a mediating role between the European Community and the United States, without taking any major initiatives. In this respect, we were less active than Norway, which took a strong stance on the need to open possibilities for cost-effective solutions to emission reductions, pioneering reflection on such issues as emission trading.

The main problem between the United States and the EC was linked to the question of targets and time-tables for emission reductions. The EC position was that such elements were clearly indispensable in the future climate regime, whereas the United States claimed to reach the same results through unilateral measures, with strong emphasis on technological advances. In the course of the negotiations, various efforts had been made to bridge this gap, most notably in an effort by UK and Japan to develop the concept of "pledge and review", based on unilateral targets which would be monitored internationally. This attempt led to long and difficult negotiations, and it was perceived by the NGO community as a backward step. Ultimately it proved a non-starter, unacceptable both to the US and the EC.

The INC 4 session in a cold and misty Geneva in December 1991 helped to clarify a number of issues, and a single negotiating text existed, but it was full of square brackets, indicating disagreements on central points. In this situation, to my surprise I was approached by the EC Commission with a request to mediate informal discussions between Annex I countries on the question of targets and timetables. The Commission chief negotiator, the Dane Joergen Henningsen, believed that non-committed Sweden could make a contribution in this situation. I accepted, without having a very clear picture of how I could best manage the task. It was clear that many ideas had already been tried and that no panacea existed: my best hope was to keep the dialogue going in the hope that some clever drafting could enable the process to continue and the Convention to be agreed.

Consultations before INC-5, which was due to meet in New York in February, did not lead to any progress, and since agreement on targets and timetables among Annex I countries was so crucial for the whole package, a large part of the New York session was spent in informal Annex I consultations about this issue. This did not mean that progress was blocked on a number of other issues, reflected in the deletion of square brackets, but there was also a sense of frustration among many non-Annex I delegates, who simply had to wait for long hours while we tried to settle our differences. As mediator, I tried a number of formulas without much success, and many delegates made valiant efforts to move the negotiation forward; but at the end I had to report to plenary Working Group I that there was no agreement. Time was really running out on us, since the meeting rooms in UN Headquarters had to be taken over by the last and decisive session of the UNCED Preparatory Committee. These were busy days.

Nevertheless, the session did not end in total gloom. Jean Ripert felt that sufficient progress had been made to warrant a resumed session to finalize the text and to enable signature of the Convention to take place as planned in Rio de Janeiro in June 1992. This session was to start in New York on April 30. Furthermore, he convened a consultation in a small group of key negotiators to be held in Paris in the middle of April. I profited from this invitation to convene an Annex I meeting at OECD Paris Headquarters in conjunction with the Ripert consultation.

My own meeting did not produce a major breakthrough, but it gave good opportunities for testing various compromise formulas. The US Chief negotiator, the witty and imaginative Robert Reinstein, himself originally a scientist, made various suggestions, sometimes in the form of "anonymous" proposals circulated around the table, not necessarily a conference table. (In particular, I recall a productive and delicious dinner at Restaurant Ferrero in Paris.) Some of these proposals actually formed the basis for the language ultimately employed in the central Article 4.2 of the Convention.

Ripert's consultation in Paris, with participation from all major countries and country groups, became decisive. Everybody realized that the draft that had emerged from New York contained too many square brackets to be negotiable, and there was agreement to give Ripert a free hand to produce a Chairman's draft without brackets, and to carry out the necessary consultations to reach agreement at the resumed COP-5.

Now Ripert's personal authority and contacts became decisive. He mobilized the highest level of the French government to support his efforts, he explored his contacts in Washington and elsewhere: generally there was a flurry of high-level contacts at this time, including a visit to Washington by Michael Howard, then UK Secretary of the Environment. Furthermore, Robert Reinstein used his considerable influence in Washington to move the United States to a compromise.

As COP-5 reconvened, Jean Ripert took the process firmly in hand, and negotiated his text in a small but representative group of key delegates. Negotiations were difficult, but ultimately there was agreement, and the Framework Convention on Climate Change could be adopted without reservations, but with some countries indicating that they would not sign the Convention.

Nevertheless, at UNCED in Rio de Janeiro a few weeks later, 153 countries, including the United States, and EC countries, signed the Convention. Ratification processes proceeded smoothly, with the US ratifying already in the autumn of 1992. The requisite number of fifty ratifications was reached in early 1994, and the first Conference of Parties (COP-1) was held in Berlin in March-April 1995.

What were then the main features of the agreement, as seen in the EC/US context?

It is quite clear that the Europeans had to accept a significantly weaker text on quantitative commitments than they had originally intended. In fact, articles 4.2 a) and 4.2 b) contain very convoluted language, with the commitment to stabilize emissions of greenhouse gases at 1990 levels to the year 2000 divided between the two subparagraphs in such a way that no binding compliance rules could be used.[5]

To dissociate the years 1990 and 2000 was obviously in the US interest, and it would seem that the compromise went largely Washington's way. However, it has to be recognized that the United Sattes moved considerably from its initial complete refusal to consider targets and timetables. Furthermore, the original US position was to avoid mentioning carbon dioxide specifically and to include also CFC's in the comprehensive definition of greenhouse gases. The specific mentioning of policies and measures, initially a US position, also gradually came to be acceptable to the European countries. Therefore, I am inclined to see the Framework Convention as a fair compromise between the European and American positions, achieved through intense bargaining, constructive contributions by many different parties, and excellent Chairmanship.

What then about the environmental effects of the Convention? When the agreement had just been concluded, I had a telephone conversation with Bert Bolin, the then Chairman of IPCC and one of the leading climate scientists. Bolin's comment was to the point: "It is of course fantastic that you managed to agree, but of course it is not enough."

This is a fair assessment, and I believe it is shared by most negotiators. The Convention was a starting point: the negotiation could only succeed if it was perceived by all Parties as a good compromise. Among Annex I countries, and in particular in the EU/US context, the Convention had established a fragile equilibrium, a basis for further negotiation. Many of the conflict points from these early days are still with us: it is important to see the continuity of the negotiations on climate change, beyond political conjunctures and controversies, as we move on to consider COP-1 in Berlin and the saga of the Kyoto Protocol.

Just one final remark in this section on the Rio Conference itself: the work on Chapter 9, Atmosphere, of Agenda 21, was clearly linked to the negotiations on the Climate convention, but it was general agreement that the processes should be kept separate. Chapter 9 with its special emphasis on sectors, such as energy and industry, can rather be seen as a contribution to creating enabling conditions for the strengthening of emission reduction commitments. It also serves as a reminder of the fundamental linkages between climate change and other environmental problems in the atmosphere, such as trans-boundary air pollution and the depletion of the ozone layer. The political importance of climate change was underlined in Rio in several general statements and through the impressive line of high-level politicians waiting to sign the Convention in one of the Conference Halls at Riocentro.

Because of the character of the work on Chapter 9 in Rio de Janeiro, the EU/US divide on climate change played only a minor role in the negotiation of the chapter; as has been pointed out in previous chapters of this book, the main controversies were linked to north-south problems, and in particular the specific position of Saudi Arabia and the other oil-producing states.

COP-1, AND THE NEGOTIATION OF
THE BERLIN MANDATE

After the successful conclusion of the negotiations for the Convention, it was decided that the Intergovernmental Negotiating Committee should continue its work until the first Conference of Parties would be held. The first sessions mainly dealt with organizational matters, but as the ratification processes moved at considerable speed, the preparation of COP-1 became the central issue. Three questions were of central importance: first, the position of the financial mechanism, provisionally managed by the Global Environment Facility (GEF), located in the World Bank, but a joint venture of UNDP, UNEP and the Bank, second, the criteria for "joint implementation," and third, the question of the adequacy of the commitments of the Convention.

The issues related to the Financial Mechanism were controversial in the north-south perspective, since G 77 wanted to ensure that the institutions of the Convention itself would have a strong say in GEF policies related to climate change, whereas the north wanted to maintain the integrity of GEF's own institutions. As for Joint Implementation, G 77 feared that such a mechanism would lead the north to seek an "eco-colonial" division of the world's resources: they therefore fought hard, and successfully, to limit this new concept to the Annex I group itself.

If these two issues were mainly part of the north-south relationship, the question of "adequacy of commitments" concerned every party, being central to the implementation of the Convention. The language in Article. 4.2.d)[6] was a compromise reflecting the inability of the negotiators to agree on more precise and long-term commitments beyond the vague language in Article 4.2.a) and b). At one stage, there had been a subparagraph to Article 4.2, which stated ambitions beyond the year 2000, but this proved unacceptable to the US, and was therefore removed.

In looking towards the first Conference of Parties, which was to be held in Berlin March 28 to April 11, 1995, the EU/US relationship entered a new phase, as the Clinton/Gore administration took over the White House in January, 1993. I recall vividly a visit to Washington in December, 1993, as a number of the collaborators to Al Gore, all enthusiastic environmentalists, were moving into their new offices, full of expectations at the new opportunities that were now open to them. Among them was Eileen Claussen, who later became Chief negotiator for climate and who today heads the much respected PEW Center in Washington. In this context, it is also worth mentioning that as Senator, Al Gore had published a very radical book on the environment a couple of years earlier, entitled *Earth in the Balance*.

There is no doubt that this political change opened new possibilities; the large Republican victory in the congressional elections in the autumn of 1994, however, limited the scope of action of the new administration.

This was the situation as we went into the final stages of preparations for COP-1. Jean Ripert had retired, and the jovial and resourceful Argentine diplomat Raúl Estrada had succeeded him. A number of INC meetings could agree on a general position that the commitments in the Convention were not adequate to meet the ultimate objective, as formulated in Article 2. As for action, there was less agreement. The AOSIS Group came forward with a proposal for a Berlin Protocol with substantial emission reductions for Annex I countries, and Germany, as host country, proposed a text with less far-reaching commitments. Not even the EU, however, was ready to consider the adoption of a protocol at the Berlin Conference.

In order to clarify the situation and prepare COP-1, the German Chief negotiator, Cornelia Quennet, convened a small informal group, which had its first meeting in Bonn. This "Berlin Group" managed to outline in quite some detail the prospects for agreements at COP-1, and contributed greatly to the relative success of the conference. In particular, it was now clear that it was unrealistic to expect a serious negotiation on a Berlin Protocol. On the question of adequacy of commitments the meeting should concentrate on a "Berlin Mandate", which would aim at establishing a negotiating process with a view of the adoption of a Protocol at a later Conference of Parties.

As COP-1 opened, this procedure was generally welcomed. The immediate question was how such a mandate should be negotiated. At a reception one of the first evenings of the Conference, the Executive Secretary, Michael Summit Cutajar told me that he had been mandated to ask me if I would be ready to chair this negotiation. I was hesitant, recognizing the difficulty of the task, but answered that I could accept if there would be a consensus around my name.

There was such a consensus, and we started the negotiation with a general discussion in a room which was too small for all the delegations that wanted to participate. I told the Bureau, chaired by the new German Minister of the Environment, Angela Merkel, that quasi-plenary discussions could not lead to an agreement. Merkel, who had just taken over the post from her very experienced predecessor Klaus Töpfer, who had become Minister of Building, promised to consult on the matter; and in a very skilful way she and her collaborators managed to get agreement on a balanced group of around twenty-five countries.

This decision started ten days of very intense negotiations. In parallel, several other issues were successfully negotiated, including Joint Implementation, central budgetary matters, and the location of the Secretariat, which surprisingly went to Bonn, when most people expected Geneva to be chosen. But it was the negotiation of the Berlin Mandate which was in the centre of the session.

In the negotiating group there were many tense moments, but, on the whole, it was a constructive atmosphere. Everybody realized that a concrete decision was necessary as a result of this first Conference of Parties. Nevertheless, there were many obstacles to overcome, and discussion went on far into the night on many occasions.

The developing countries were strongly advocating their position that non-Annex I countries should have no quantitative commitments in the new instrument to be negotiated on the basis of the Mandate.[7] EU countries were ready to accommodate this, but the US took a harder line, foreshadowing later controversies on this issue. The views of the south were defended with particular vigor by the impressive but rigid Chinese delegate, professor Zung. As the G 77 split, under the pressure of the conflict between AOSIS countries and OPEC, the new, so-called Green group, led by T. P. Srinivasan of India, did not change positions, but the atmosphere improved. Nevertheless, compromises were hard to find; on one occasion I had drafted a Chairman's proposal which I showed to the US Chief negotiator Eileen Claussen, who promptly declared that she would leave the negotiation if such a text appeared. I had no choice but to go back to the drawing board.

The EU countries, on the other hand, were much more relaxed on this particular issue, but had strong views on the other central negotiating problem[8]: whether the Mandate should explicitly talk about targets and timetables as objectives for the new instrument to be negotiated. Here was another traditional subject of discord between the EU and the US, and compromises were hard to find.

As we neared the end of the Conference of Parties and Ministers arrived for the conclusion of the COP, negotiations were still going on in the Mandate group. We had, however, made good progress, and ultimately it was only on the two central issues mentioned that we could not agree on the final drafting. But the Group was confident that these problems could be resolved at political level: as I reported to Ministers late in the evening before the last day of the Conference, I gave an account of the different positions and of the various compromise proposals that had been tabled. Angela Merkel then started an efficient and constructive political discussion which led to agreement early the following morning.

THE PREPARATIONS FOR THE THIRD
CONFERENCE OF PARTIES (COP-3) IN KYOTO

The first Conference of Parties had successfully pointed the way forward, as it also agreed on a procedure for the negotiation of a new instrument. A single negotiating structure was established, called the Ad-hoc Group on the Berlin Mandate (AGBM), to be chaired by Raúl Estrada.

At the time, I was called to deal with other environmental negotiations, and I did not participate in the negotiations of the AGBM, coming back to the issue of climate change in early 1997, as the final preparatory negotiations started for COP-3, to be held in Kyoto in November-December, 1997.[9]

In the United States, the environmentalists in the administration had gained in strength, and under the guidance of Senator Tim Wirth, appointed Secretary of Global Affairs in the State Department, US was reassessing some of its positions. In the EU/US relationship, this led to interesting developments. The EU had developed its thinking on policies and measures to an active call for common and coordinated action, which obviously did not tally well with US general reluctance to taxes and fees as instruments for environmental policy. At the same time the Berlin Mandate with its reference to quantified limitation and reduction objectives (in negotiating jargon called "QUELROs") had to be honoured. In his speech to COP-2 in Geneva in July 1996[10] Wirth therefore took up the challenge in stating "...The US recommends that future negotiations focus on an agreement that sets a realistic, verifiable and binding medium-term emissions target....met through maximum flexibility in the selection of implementation measures, including the use of reliable activities implemented jointly, and trading mechanisms around the world."

Obviously the EU welcomed this new US position, but maintained its insistence on common and coordinated policies and measures. Furthermore, EU, which had only recently (January 1, 1995) been enlarged to fifteen member states, with the entry of Austria, Finland and Sweden, now had to consider its own position in more detail, including the question of the compatibility between a common EU target and national targets; and the controversial issue of flexible mechanisms (Joint implementation and emissions trading) which were thoroughly disliked by European environmentalists and several EU governments.

Whereas in the preparations for Berlin, Sweden as a new EU member naturally held a low profile, we were in 1997 deeply involved in EU climate policies, with Anna Lindh as an efficient and enthusiastic Minister of Environment. The negotiations in what was known as the EU Working Party on Climate Change (WPCC), serving as a preparatory group for the Council sessions of Ministers of Environment, were quite complicated, as we set out on the distribution of the national quotas within what became known as the EU "bubble."

At this stage, the EU was fortunate to have the Netherlands assuming the Presidency. The Dutch had a very skilful team of negotiators and a tradition of good contact between the academic world and government services. Their Chief negotiator at the time, Bert Metz, had for a long time been associated with IPCC. The Presidency engaged research in a complicated method to establish criteria for the distribution of national commitments, which would not just be a burden-sharing, but also a form for more objective "equalization of effort." In the absence of any alternative, this method was accepted, and during the Dutch Presidency, the EU established a differentiated scale of national emission reductions, which was later formalized to serve as the basis for ratification by EU member states.[11] This internal distribution meant large reductions, ranging from 12.5 (UK) to 28% (Luxemburg) for countries that were rapidly reducing their dependency on coal; and rather large opportunities to increase emissions in the Mediterranean member states, still in the process of economic development.

The agreed system was supposed to lead to a reduction of emissions for the whole EU area of 10%. In establishing the EU negotiating stance for Kyoto, however, the mood was more ambitious, and the stated objective was 15%. It was then assumed that common EU policies and measures would make up for the missing 5%.

The ambitious EU position was to a large extent due to pressures from environmental NGOs and from green parties, which at this time had become established political actors in many European countries

This situation was also reflected in the EU discussion on emissions trading and the other mechanisms. Several member states, in particular Germany, Denmark and Austria, were very concerned that the mechanisms would sap emission reduction objectives of their content and serve as loopholes which would seriously impair the integrity of any agreement, and they therefore advocated complicated methods to reduce the use of mechanisms. United Kingdom was favorable to the mechanisms, and Sweden took a rather relaxed attitude, feeling that such mechanisms could help engage the corporate sector in combat of climate change.

Another difficult issue as EU prepared for Kyoto related to carbon sinks, based on the fact that soil, and in particular growing forests, absorbs large quantities of coal from the atmosphere. The scientific basis for quantifying these sinks is still shaky and the calculations turned increasingly complicated. Many observers felt that it would have been better never to integrate the sinks in the Convention; but this could not be undone, and the United States, Canada and Australia were insisting on an essential role for sinks. Once again Sweden, with its large forest resources, felt that a well designed regime could help in getting agreement on the Protocol, while we were keen to underline that we did not seek any national advantages through the inclusion of sinks.

So, in preparing for Kyoto, the US had taken a surprisingly forthcoming attitude on the question of emissons reductions (QUELRO'S), and the EU had managed to agree on a reduction target, maintaining that a flat rate of 15% should be the objective for the forthcoming protocol.

But behind these positions there were doubts and uncertainties. Many EU countries felt that the objective was too ambitious, and there were concerns about the stance on mechanisms and sinks. And in the United States, pressure increased as the administration was asked to "respond" to the EU with a specific figure (which later turned out to be stabilization, or 0). In the summer of 1997, the Senate dealt a blow to the administration in adopting the Byrd-Hagel resolution, stating that the US should not accept an agreement that did not include commitments by developing countries. As has been pointed out in Chapter 4, this resolution, adopted 95–0, led to a very negative reaction in G 77.

NEGOTIATIONS IN KYOTO

As negotiations got under way in Kyoto, the EU initially seemed rather isolated, not least with regard to the question of flexible mechanisms.[12] The United States were on many issues supported by Australia, Canada, Japan and New Zealand, as the EU call for a flat rate of reductions had not been well received. The restrictive stance on sinks and mechanisms did not receive much support, even if some members of G 77, in particular the AOSIS countries, appreciated the European insistence on environmental integrity. On the other hand, G 77 did not appreciate EU support for the proposal for voluntary commitments. So the first week passed with its usual mixture of lofty general statements, dreary detailed technical negotiations and small conflicts on most issues, without much progress. The EU was chaired by Luxembourg with the help of the Netherlands and UK, the previous and the forthcoming Presidencies of the Union.

In the beginning of the second week, the United States took the initiative with the intervention of Vice President Gore. He underlined that the US wanted a positive result of the Conference, and stated that he had instructed the US delegation to show flexibility in the negotiations, provided other parties would do the same. This put the onus on the EU, which now had to realize that we had no possibility to stick to the flat rate position, already compromised by our own, differentiated, "bubble, and that we had to move on sinks and on mechanisms.

Ministers had by now arrived, and EU coordination meetings became rather irritated, as the environmentalist stance of politicians like Svend Auken of Denmark clashed with the pragmatism of John Prescott, the UK Vice Premier who increasingly became the point man in negotiating with the US on outstanding issues, in particular on the "QUELRO'S". As we have seen in the previous chapter, Chairman Estrada solved the main north-south issues in the last Plenary. The central controversies between the EU and US were, on the other hand, solved in small informal meetings in Estrada's office, notably the question of targets, though not in a very sophisticated way: the EU opening position was 15%, that of US was 0, and the final outcome was 8% for EU and 7% for US, an almost perfect bargain apparently without much theoretical analysis behind it. It may arguably be said that Japan, with 6%, got the toughest deal. Language on sinks and on the mechanisms papered over diverging views, and it was clear, already in Kyoto, that the Protocol was not complete and that it could not be ratified without further precision on central points.

Nevertheless, the Protocol was adopted, and during 1998 signed by most countries including, the United States and the EU and its member states. Governments had given a strong signal that they were taking climate change seriously, a message that was not lost on the general public and on the corporate sector. It was against that background that EU sharpened its climate policies and that the political controversy around the Kyoto Protocol deepened in the United States.

THE NEGOTIATIONS AFTER KYOTO, LEADING UP TO
THE BONN/MARRAKECH AGREEMENTS IN 2001

COP-4 was held in Buenos Aires in late 1998, and adopted a two-year plan of action designed to fill in the blanks in the Kyoto deal and make the Protocol "ratifiable," an expression minted by the EU negotiators. Green parties were now part of the governments of Germany and France, and they held the posts of Ministers of Environment in both countries. Jürgen Trittin and Dominique Voynet were high profile politicians who wanted to push the climate agenda. With colleagues like Jan Pronk of the Netherlands, John Prescott, Michael Meacher and later Margaret Beckett of the UK, and Svend Auken of Denmark, EU Ministerial meetings became an assembly of colorful people with lively discussions. Sweden's witty and experienced Anna Lindh played an important role in this group; as she became Minister of Foreign Affairs 1998, her successor Kjell Larsson soon took a very active role in the discussions. In writing this, I can still feel the immense sadness at their untimely deaths: Anna Lindh was assassinated in Stockholm in September 2003 and Kjell Larsson died of cancer in December 2002. The disappearance of these brilliant and popular politicians was an immense loss for Swedish politics and for European cooperation.

The Buenos Aires Plan of Action was designed to bring the Kyoto process to completion at COP-6, which was held in the Hague in December. Important agreements were needed on the detailed rules for the calculation of sinks (in the negotiations known as LULUCF – Land use, land use change and forestry), the implementation of the mechanisms, and the rules for the compliance system. These were tall orders, since it was also necessary to manage the north-south issues, so that any deal would be acceptable to the G 77.

The EU struggled with its preparations, but came to the Hague with a rather complete and unified position. France had taken over the Presidency from Portugal on July 1, 2000, and had a well structured preparatory group, linked to the Prime Minister's office, headed by the experienced Michel Mousel. Since Sweden was to succeed France, we were part of the so-called troika, and participated actively in the preparatory meetings, chaired by Jan Pronk, who was to chair the COP in the Hague. We were all reasonably optimistic, even if many issues remained open. At this stage, however, the forthcoming US elections began to overshadow most international events. The climate issue was not a major question in the United States, particularly since Al Gore did not want to push his credentials as a "green" politician, and George W. Bush had not shown any interest.

The Hague Conference started with a week of negotiations at the official level, with reasonable progress on some issues, but generally it was rather disappointing. Jan Pronk now put all emphasis on the "Ministerial segment", starting at the beginning of the second week. It became a strange mixture of acceptable compromises on a number of points and confusing procedures to solve the key issues. The EU/US negotiations ran into many difficulties, not facilitated by the continued uncertainty about the outcome of the American election. Finally it became clear that Bush had won, and that a new administration would take over in a few weeks time.

Internal EU discussions became difficult, as some EU countries, in particular UK and Germany, felt that this was the opportunity to make a deal before the new US administration would come in. The last long night in the Hague revealed open disagreement among EU Ministers, as efforts by John Prescott and some other Ministers to strike an agreement with the US on key issues, in particular on the question of sinks, could not be supported by the EU Presidency. Pronk had to recognize the failure of COP-6 but managed to get an agreement to revert to the negotiations during 2001 for a resumed session.

A public row between John Prescott and Dominique Voynet about the reasons for the breakdown seemed to augur badly for the Union's capacity to deal with this difficult situation, but may also have served to clear the air after the Hague. There was an agreement to try to keep in touch with the outgoing US administration, and an informal meeting of high officials from a number of Annex I parties was held in Ottawa in the middle of December. The United States now clearly wanted a deal, but many of us felt that it was too late. The Ottawa meeting did not reach any results: there was still talk of a possible Ministerial meeting just before Christmas on the invitation of Norway, and a Ministerial telephone conference was held in the margin of the EU Environment Council a week after Ottawa. That consultation, however, could only confirm that further contacts would be meaningless.

As Sweden prepared to take over the Presidency of EU on January 1, 2001, we stated three priorities for the climate work:

- to re-establish the unity and cohesion of the Union;
- to work for an early resumption of COP-6;
- to push EU:s internal climate action, in particular the policies and measures included in the so-called ECCP, European Climate Change Programme.

In this particular framework, I concentrate on the relations with the US, which came to dominate our Presidency as far as climate policies are concerned. As Chairman of the Council Working Party on Climate change, I went to Washington in early February to prepare for a visit by Kjell Larsson, scheduled for early April. At that time, there was, surprisingly enough, some optimism about the intentions of the new administration, with references to some vague statements by Bush candidate. A few weeks later, Christine Whitman, the new Head of the US Environment Protection Agency and a former Governor of New Jersey, made some rather positive remarks about the Kyoto Protocol at a meeting of G-8 Environment Ministers in Trieste.

All the stronger became the impact of President Bush's letter to a number of senators on March 13, when he stated that the United States would not ratify the Kyoto Protocol, because of its negative effects on the US economy and the lack of commitments by developing countries. EU Ministers had stated its strong support for the Kyoto Protocol in the Council the previous week, and the Swedish Minister of Environment, Kjell Larsson, could give an immediate reaction in a Press release a few hours after we had had the news from Washington. The EU was now in the forefront of the battle to save Kyoto.

A few days later, the Swedish Ambassador to Washington, Jan Eliasson, held a lunch with Condoleezza Rice and his EU colleagues. Rice, who was at the time national security adviser to President Bush, made a strongly worded statement where she repeatedly underlined that the Kyoto Protocol was dead: "it was dead upon arrival of this Administration." I wrote a memorandum to Kjell Larsson stating my conviction that the climate hardliners were now firmly in command in Washington and that it was more necessary than ever that the EU would demonstrate its firm will not to accept the US position and to continue to work hard for the conclusion of COP-6 negotiations and the ratification of the Kyoto Protocol. The following week, a previously arranged informal EU summit in Stockholm repeated in a strongly worded declaration the EU position to defend the Kyoto Protocol.

In the beginning of April, an informal meeting of EU environment Ministers in Kiruna in the very north of Sweden agreed on a declaration refuting the allegation that the Kyoto Protocol was dead, stating that EU and its member countries were going to ratify, and that they would do all they could to promote the process leading up to entry into force.[13]

Three days later, Kjell Larsson led an EU delegation to Washington for talks with representatives of the new administration, including the Head of EPA, Christine Whitman, and a number of other officials. The group, which included the other members of the so-called troika, the next Presidency Belgium, represented by its Minister of Environment, Oliver Deleuze, and the Environment Commissioner Margot Wallström, also had talks with Democratic Senators Biden, Kerry, and Liebermann. There was no meeting of minds in the talks with the US administration, but the conversations helped to underline the EU's resolve to go ahead in a situation when many countries might have had doubts that the Kyoto Protocol would ever have a chance, because of the US refusal. On the other hand, the Bush administration had no alternative proposals, and the EU constantly underlined that Kyoto "was the only shop in town," and that the demolition of the Kyoto Protocol would most certainly threaten the Convention itself. In my view, this firm and uncompromising line saved the Kyoto Protocol.

Kjell Larsson and the troika now opted for a rapid travel diplomacy, visiting Moscow, Iran, Beijing and Tokyo in little more than a week. He later had special talks with his Iranian counterpart, Mme Ebthakar, Chair of the Group of 77, and visited Japan once again.. Canada and Australia also received visits of EU representatives at high political level. All this activity served to underline the EU position, and helped Minister Pronk in his preparations for a resumed session of the Conference of Parties. These went through a difficult phase, but the EU support for Kyoto contributed to stabilize the preparatory work and enabled consultations gradually to open prospects for a successful resumed session, which had by now been called for the second half of July, in Bonn.

In this perspective, it was important that the American refusal to ratify the protocol would not lead to active negative action by the United States in the coming negotiations. Therefore, we aimed at consultations with the United States in a spirit of "agree to disagree." One opportunity was the OECD Ministerial Council in early May, where a joint text could be agreed; this became the point of departure for negotiations during the EU/US summit in Göteborg, Sweden, in early June. After very long and complicated negotiations acceptable language was found, which simply repeated the positions of the two parties, and also contained an agreement to establish an EU/US high-level working group on climate.

This working group never became fully operative, but the Göteborg text effectively removed the EU/US controversy from the climate agenda. There has since been a constant concern in Europe that the US would aim at undermining our efforts to make Kyoto a working reality, but on the whole the US has kept a low profile in the multilateral negotiations. No doubt, there has been US activity behind the scenes, notably in offering technological cooperation, but in my view well within the limits of the agreements in 2001.

Even without the constant bickering between EU and US positions, the Bonn resumed COP-6 was not an easy meeting: too much was at stake, and too many issues needed to be addressed in a short time. But Jan Pronk, who had made some tactical mistakes as Chairman in the Hague Conference and initially seemed uncertain about his approach to the resumed session, had by now taken the process firmly in hand. Issues related to the mechanisms, sinks, and compliance, all central aspects of the Buenos Aires Plan of Action, gave rise to protracted and complicated negotiations between Annex I countries, whereas increased financial support for developing countries continued to be a precondition for the acceptance of any deal by the G 77.

A group of industrialized countries with EU, Canada, Japan and Norway as the core group, agreed on a financial package of US$430 million annually as from 2004, an offer which facilitated agreement with the developing countries. There were, nevertheless, important hurdles to be overcome: Japan continued to have problems with the compliance rules, and Russia was not satisfied with the emerging deal on sinks. Saudi Arabia and other OPEC countries continued to press for compensation for potential losses on export markets. EU, now with Belgium in the Presidency, had a number of difficult problems to solve, but there was now an optimistic feeling in the Conference rooms and in the corridors. Finally an agreement emerged, even though a number of details still needed to be hammered out in time for the next regular COP, in Marrakech in November. The deal was greeted with relief, and a certain enthusiasm; the Japanese Minister of Environment, Ms. Kawaguchi received a strong applause after stating that her government accepted the agreement; this was well deserved, since she had had difficult negotiations with her government, notably on the compliance rules. On the contrary, the closing statement of the US representative, Paula Dobriansky from the State Department, got a cool reception.

A drawn-out process like the struggle to make Kyoto ratifiable can sometimes remind you of a steeple-chase race. New obstacles appear constantly. The September 11, 2001, terror attacks in the United States raised questions whether COP-7 could really take place as planned in Marrakech. Closer to the Kyoto Protocol, Russia continued to raise difficulties about the calculation of sinks. It turned out, after all, that the "technical details" to be agreed between Bonn and Marrakech, could still wreck the whole negotiation. The full two weeks of COP-7 were needed to craft the final text, which became known as the Bonn-Marrakech Agreement. The US participated in a muted way, though their delegation was active in north-south issues, and played an important role in the drafting of the so-called Marrakech Declaration, a text which was intended to be a message from Marrakech to the 2002 World Summit on Sustainable Development in Johannesburg.

The dramatic pulse in EU/US relations on climate change, which characterized the Swedish EU Presidency in 2001, subsided in the coming years. But the transatlantic relationship continues to be of central importance for the future of the international climate regime, not least at the time of writing this, after the entry into force of the Kyoto Protocol,[14] the G 8 Summit in Germany in June 2005 and the active preparation for the post-2012 climate regime. I myself retired from active negotiation work after Bonn/ Marrakech, and have since had the leisure to reflect on this uneasy friendship in a more detached way. Some reflections of a more general nature will follow, as the last section of this chapter.

An overall view of EU/US controversies on climate change policies

In the introduction to this chapter, I have presented a brief general background to the differences between Europe and the United States on issues related to climate change. This section aims at structuring this complicated pattern in a way which could provide some clues to the future prospects for the climate regime, to the extent that it will be dependent on the transatlantic relationship.

It is necessary to underline the fundamental differences between these two parties. The United States is now the world's sole superpower with enormous resources and a strong unified executive. The EU is an emerging institution, which struggles to promote integration, going beyond the economic sphere, with an unfinished constitution and a weak command structure. History, and the economic strength of the enlarged European Union, however, means that the United States has to manage its general relations with the European Union in a careful way. It is fair to say that there are strong bonds across the Atlantic. But EU has not (yet?) a real foreign policy to support specific sectors such as climate policy. The Kissinger quip: "What is the telephone number of Europe in an emergency?" still holds true.

Here we are on the borderline between traditional diplomacy and the new diplomacy for sustainable development. The Bush administration policy line on the Kyoto Protocol was based on economic and energy policy considerations. But it slowly became clear that there were deeper motives, which gave a particular virulence to the attacks on the Kyoto Protocol: a general distrust of multilateral cooperation, in particular within the UN framework.[15]

In this same foreign policy perspective, it is instructive to go further back into post-World War II history. The United States was the driving force behind multilateralism, the Marshall Plan, and European cooperation. But as the original six EEC countries became stronger, there was also resentment against the United States, in particular in France: an illuminating episode is General de Gaulle's refusal to admit UK into the EEC in 1963. He claimed that UK was to be a Trojan horse in the community, too linked to the US to be a loyal member. There were echoes of this attitude in the French criticism of UK efforts to make a deal with the US in the dying moments of COP-6 in The Hague in 2000, and of course — far more seriously — in the conflict between France/Germany and the UK on the support for US war in Iraq in 2003.

Constitutional differences also contribute to creating difficulties across the Atlantic. European countries have parliamentary systems, which means that the governments could normally feel rather certain of securing ratification of an international treaty, once it is adopted. In the United States, the administration cannot have full control of Congress; and it can also decide not to submit a treaty to the advice and consent of Congress. In all major international negotiations on environmental treaties, a sizeable Congress representation is normally part of the US delegation.

The Chief of Staff of President George Bush Sr., John Sununu, speaking of the Climate Convention, once said "you do not negotiate about the American way of life." He was heavily criticized in Europe — and some quarters in the US — for this statement, but it certainly also struck a chord with the American public. It is difficult to envisage this kind of blunt statement by a government official in Europe — an illustration of the differences in public attitudes.

There is no reason, however, for Europeans to adopt an attitude of moral rightness when it comes to the question of environmental footprints: it is of course true that the American per capita emissions of CO_2 are double those of Europe, and that Americans consume a very large part of the planet's resources; but also Europeans belong to the world's great consumers, and a real paradigm shift might be quite as difficult to achieve in Europe.

An illustration of this is the multiplicity of views which are presently expressed in the United States about climate policies by entities outside the federal administration. California has already for a long time had very tough standards for automobile emissions, and today several states and cities in the country express their readiness to accept Kyoto targets. Similarly the corporate sector is by no means monolithic in this respect. The administration has to keep a close watch on such developments, which might ultimately have an impact on federal policies.

Flexibility is also a key word with regard to American economic and technological capacity. American corporations have been leading globalization for a long time, with a competitive edge that is based on dominance of financial markets and unsurpassed technological innovative capacity. These are important factors in the design of future climate policies, which might support shifts in American priorities in the multilateral climate negotiations. I will return to these questions in the discussion of the future of the new diplomacy in Chapter 7.

In looking at the long-term developments in the climate negotiations since 1990, the US position has been quite consistent and coherent, reflecting some of the elements that have been mentioned here:

- The United States has more research capacity than any other country in the world; and American climate research is probably of higher quality than anywhere else. Therefore the US also played a leading role in the international scientific effort leading up to the UN decision to establish a negotiating committee for the Framework Convention on Climate Change. American researchers have also played a leading role in IPCC. Furthermore, today it appears that the Bush administration is no longer questioning the science of climate change; since European climate research is presently accelerating, not least in terms of the social sciences, this might open new perspectives for scientific cooperation across the Atlantic.

- The US has consistently opposed common and coordinated policies and measures; a policy instrument favored by the Europeans. This policy line is based on a strong aversion to the use of taxes. On the other hand, the Americans have no problem with nationally decided policies and measures, and regulations are a well-known instrument in environment policy. The EU has had great difficulties finding supporters of binding policies and measures, and it seems that the instrument for the foreseeable future would be limited to the Union itself.

- The US position on targets and timetables has been generally negative over the whole period, whereas the EU has been a strong supporter. It should be recalled, however, that the US has shown flexibility on various occasions, in particular in the preparations for the Kyoto Conference of Parties.

- There is an obvious link between targets and emissions trading: without caps of some kind a trading system cannot work. This is the background to the interest shown by US companies for the European trading system. The United States has constantly supported cost-effective mechanisms, whereas the EU has shown some reluctance in the initial stages. Today, the EU provides a full scale experiment, the EU Emissions Trading Scheme, and no doubt there is a considerable interest in the United States and other parts of the world in following the results.

- From the very beginning of the climate talks, USA has put strong emphasis on the role of technology as a way of tackling the risks of climate change. It is therefore logical that the Bush administration now gives priority to technological development, recently establishing a cooperative pact with Australia, South Korea, Japan, China and India. This technological outreach is no alternative to Kyoto, but it is an example of a coherent American policy, and it would seem desirable for EU to consider similar initiatives. However, new energy technologies cannot avoid the need for societal changes, or modified life-styles. Neither should it be forgotten that targets and timetables are forceful drivers for technological change.

The overview highlights some of the issues which have regularly appeared in this narrative of EU/US negotiations on climate change, an example of an uneasy friendship, but also of the capacity of Europe and the United States to cooperate in moving negotiations forward. The relationship continues to be crucial to the further development of the new diplomacy for sustainable development. As the concerns over global climate change and its consequences have been increasingly sharpened — in particular after the Fourth Assessment Report of the Intergovernmental Panel on Climate Change, published in 2007 — and the negotiation focus shifts to the post-2012 climate regime, the European Union has made climate change a central element of its international stance. The Bush administration continues to hold back, but the pressure from below in the country — including important states as California and the northeastern states, as well as large segments of the corporate sector — led to a more forthcoming position at the G-8 summit in 2007, and can open the way for a radically changed position by the new President to be elected in 2008. Europe would need to be prepared for proposals which would aim at bringing the United States back into the mainstream of the international action to counter global climate change.

Part III
Global Sustainability in the Twenty-First Century

6   The Interface between the National and the International

The Concept of "Enabling Conditions"

The purpose of this chapter is to continue to explore the relationship between national conditions and policies on the one hand, and international negotiations on the other, in order to deepen the analysis of the new diplomacy. In doing this, I hope to create a better basis for thinking on the future of the international negotiations on sustainability issues.

It may be argued that the negotiations I have discussed in Part II do not illustrate very clearly the differences between the new diplomacy and traditional multilateral processes. There is a heavy element of bargaining in these talks, with the customary defense of national positions and interests. The question is how much the existence of absolute global threats such as climate change or deteriorating fisheries influence the behavior of governments as reflected in the way negotiators operate.

The Norwegian sociologist Silje Maria Tellmann has studied the climate negotiations in a recent paper[1], building her analysis on theories about communication in negotiations developed by Thomas Risse and Harald Müller (2001) against the background of works by Jürgen Habermas and Jon Elster. Elster makes a distinction between "arguing" and "bargaining" as two different types of communication in (or "for the purpose of") negotiation, building on Habermas' distinction between *communicative and strategic communication*. "Arguing" is based on a genuine search for the best solution, whereas "bargaining" simply aims at finding a compromise between conflicting interests. Habermas expresses this in his book *The Theory of Communication, Volume 1, Reason and the Rationalization of Society* (Beacon Press, Boston, Mass.), in the following way: "social actions can be distinguished according to whether the participants adopt either a success-oriented attitude or one oriented to reaching understanding" (Habermas 1984: 286).

In *The Theory of Communication, Volume 2, Lifeworld and System: A Critique of Functionalist Reason* Habermas introduces the concept of "lifeworld" as a precondition for real communication: "The lifeworld is, so to speak, the transcendental site where speaker and hearer meet, where they can reciprocally raise claims that their utterances fit the world (objective, social, or subjective) and where they can criticize and confirm those validity claims, settle their disagreements, and arrive at agreements" (Habermas 1987: 126).

These are useful ideas for better understanding why the New diplomacy is still so often bogged down in very traditional bargaining in the final stages of all the Conferences that have been held so far, often in stark contrast to the lofty general declarations made by leading politicians at the start of a session, representing a common "lifeworld." This is also a close parallel to the points made by Owens, referred to in Chapter 1, with the distinction between concepts and conceptions and her explanation of why sustainable development as an idea is so difficult to fill with concrete substance.

However, this common "lifeworld" — accepted as a general idea by most responsible world leaders – is challenged by the political, economic and social pressures generated in the real world. Elections have to be won, unemployment has to be reduced, immediate problems have to be solved — and the long-term issues of human survival, like other matters of principle, are put in the background.

So, the dilemma between the overwhelming long-term importance of certain problems, and the immediate urgency of others is solved through a disconnect between leaders' rhetoric and the actual instructions given to negotiators. Hence, the observation that introductory general statements on sustainable development ("arguing" in Elster's terminology) tend to be replaced with tough bargaining in the final phases of a Conference.

This reality seems to contradict the claim that one aspect of the new diplomacy is the existence of absolute threats (like climate change) which need to be addressed in a different manner than that provided by traditional international practice. However, I believe that experience over the last twenty years or so has shown that the common "lifeworld" of concern about the impact of humans on the earth system is constantly expanding and increasingly influences the way governments behave in the negotiations on sustainable development. But we must also admit that the process is slow and laborious.

My experience from the negotiations, as outlined in Chapters 4 and 5, seems to confirm many of the theoretical assumptions about the different concepts we are addressing here, and their interrelations. The new diplomacy is constantly seeking to expand its scope in a world where traditional conflicts still dominate; this is another aspect of rapid change in our time, and of the need to rethink how things are being done, nationally and internationally. The analysis in this chapter will form the background to a review of the prospects for the various international processes on sustainability issues over the next decades in the final chapter of the book.

THE NATURE OF THE THREATS

Long-term sustainability is certainly not the only global threat facing mankind. The risk of a nuclear war has been with us for the last sixty years;

it has so far been managed successfully, with a combination of statesmanship and good luck. Hopefully, we will be quite as lucky in the future. But the nuclear risks have developed as the ultimate result of a long history of weapons technology, a consequence of the theories of strategic thinkers such as Klausewitz about war as diplomacy pursued with other means; that is, within a traditional mind-set.

On the contrary, the problems we face now are of a different nature, created by the normal, peaceful needs of an increasing world population, where the general pursuit of improved living conditions risks creating disasters that will ultimately affect us all. This is a new situation, never before experienced by mankind. The present generation is the first to possess the capacity to influence the whole world system. In a certain way, one can maintain that we are all on the same side, in this particular struggle for human survival.

As already noted, most world leaders are aware of this predicament, and their public statements confirm it. Since the Rio Conference in 1992, the theme of our global responsibility has been repeated many times. But for the negotiators on the floor, the reality has been different, as their instructions have contained several restrictive points based on national interests and short-term considerations. Why is this so? How is it possible to develop the correct policies for sustainable development when the highest political level does not seem to be able to translate lofty and no doubt genuine statements into concrete policy?

The answer is partly in the character of the threat, partly in the character of democratic policy-making itself.

The threats to the earth system are diffuse and long-term; it is difficult to visualize them in a way that captures people's imagination. In discussing climate change, for instance, the perspective of a warming of the planet over a period of fifty to one hundred years might be considered with a certain equanimity, even if there are appeals for our sense of responsibility for future generations. This is the reason why it is attractive to dwell on climate episodes, such as the heat wave that struck France in 2003, or extraordinary storms, flooding or droughts, as examples of climate change, while the scientists themselves are still reluctant to commit themselves to a firm causality between climate change and such natural disasters.

However, the question of the long-term as discussed above, is more complicated than it may seem, because of the very structures that have an impact on the climate system. Energy production and transports are key sectors; a common characteristic is that they are very dependent on investments with a long life-span, such as power plants and road and railroad infrastructure. Fifty years is a very long time in terms of human life, but today 's key investments with an impact on climate will be decisive for our capacity to manage global warming over three or four decades. These are decisions which to a large extent are made within the private sector, and therefore the increasing commitment and knowledge about the global survival issues among bankers, industrialists and business people is a prerequisite for success. It is they who will have to turn research into reality and provide the technological solutions that will have to go hand in hand with improving the methods of international negotiations within the new diplomacy.

The present time is also characterized by a weakening of the authority of political leaders, in itself a healthy questioning of their motives and policies, which however reduces their capacity to pursue unpopular policies. No doubt this is one reason why governments and different agencies increasingly use sophisticated methods of advocacy to try to influence public opinion. Certainly, the concept of propaganda has been frequently used for a long time, but in a different context. We are talking here about democratic leaders who have a general mandate from a majority of the people, but find great difficulties in pursuing policies which for various reasons are unpopular. A case in point is the level of petrol tax: increases are deeply resented by a majority of people, but they are an important element in policies to combat climate change.

So, even if the awareness of the dangers to the earth system among political leaders is increasing, their capacity to act is limited by the limitations of their own power and by the lack of precision in the perception of the threats. Their power is further circumscribed by the strength of other national actors, such as corporations, trade unions, churches or the media; or in the international arena by regional organizations such as the European Union, trans-national corporations or powerful international NGOs.

Nevertheless, in the international multilateral system, the national state is still the main actor. Furthermore, since we are talking here about global problems that require a global response, it is unavoidable that the new problems discussed here have become a central issue in international negotiations; and that national governments, notwithstanding the limitations treated here, have to deal with them as best as they can. But the character of the threats requires a new approach; and my experience over the last fifteen years seems to confirm that governments increasingly feel that national interest has to be balanced against the long-term interest of the global system, both natural and social.

It is against this background that I now turn to some central elements of the decision-making process in multilateral negotiations on sustainable development.

ENABLING CONDITIONS, AND THE PERCEPTION OF RISKS

As already noted, the negotiator's bottom line is her or his instructions. They can be interpreted in more or less flexible ways, dependent upon the personality, experience and standing of the negotiator[2], as well as the drafting of the instructions; they can be more or less specific. But they represent the position of the government, and they have to be respected. Furthermore, in organizations such as the European Union, important pre-negotiations are taking place, where positions are hammered out with difficulty, and consequently hard to modify.

In the new diplomacy, it is particularly important to focus on the national scene and the environment in which governments define their negotiating positions. Traditional foreign policy has certainly been influenced by domestic situations, but normally it has tended to be seen as something apart from social or economic policy. When we are now discussing how governments should react to global threats of a new nature, the situation is different. Corrective measures of different kinds, be they fiscal or regulatory, will often have a strong impact on living conditions and economic circumstances for individuals and enterprises; therefore the perception of global and long-term risks among the general public as a motivation for imposed changes in life-styles and consumption patterns will be of key importance.

The government position is certainly in the centre, but there are a multitude of other forces, influencing its position. Traditionally, of course, political parties represented in Parliament, as well as the media, are important actors; but when we deal with sustainability issues many other stakeholders appear. As an example, we might consider the transport sector, with its strong polarization of public opinion.

On the one hand, there are environmental movements, which strongly support action to reduce the dependence on the automobile in our societies. Often affiliated to strong international NGO's such as IUCN, WWF or Greenpeace, they militate against the construction of new motorways and are generally in favor of investments in railways and support improved public transport in urban areas. In the political arena, green parties have achieved a strong position in many European countries, defending the same objectives.

On the other hand, important actors in the economy point to the crucial importance of automobile transport for a healthy economy. A slogan used in Sweden can illustrate the point: "Without the car, Sweden will grind to a stop." Since most Swedes own a car, there is no doubt that arguments of this kind have a relatively strong impact. Furthermore, the general importance of the automobile-making industry for the national economy is well anchored in public opinion; and both upstream, among subcontractors, and downstream with the whole network of petrol stations, repair shops etc, the importance of the car is lost on no-one.

Add to this the obvious and growing role of road freight transport, and we all realize that there are no easy and rapid ways in which the dependence on fossil fuels in the transport sector can be quickly reduced, without serious negative impacts on production and jobs. The evolution of air transport adds another dimension to this picture. What was once a high-priced means of transport, reserved for rich people and for professional travel, has turned into a way of mass transport for everyone with the liberalization of the industry and the appearance of low-cost airlines. Almost everybody in Europe can now afford holidays in far-away places, and the tourism industry is growing faster than other economic activities. With the growing concern over climate change, it is now pointed out that air transport has to carry its share of the cost to reduce emissions, which might have important repercussions, impacting on tourism, the evolution of property markets in popular destinations, or social tensions.

These examples show that organizations of stakeholders, and lobbyists, in a field which literally concerns everyone, are ultimately dependent on the judgments of individuals, and their influence will be defined by their capacity to correctly gauge the state of public opinion. In a society of many stakeholders, the government remains the central decision-maker, but it has to base its policy on an evaluation of the various signals it receives from different sectors. Ultimately this process will boil down to an interpretation of the nebulous and volatile concept of public opinion.

Of course, also in traditional foreign relations, public opinion plays a role. However, its real impact is generally reserved for matters of central interest to national security — war and peace. In normal times, foreign policy is not a central issue in the political life of most countries. But in the diplomacy for sustainable development there is a continuous interplay between the ambitions of governments to tackle global environmental — and often long-term — threats, and the consequences for people in terms of new regulations, new taxes, possibly losses of job opportunities. It is a situation which is difficult to handle for political leaders as they face the need for international agreements to counter global threats. They may be personally convinced of the need for bold action, but they are not ready to take measures which might be so unpopular that they lead to certain defeat in the next election.

This is one important reason for the previously observed dichotomy between general declarations of lofty principles at the highest level, and the complicated bargaining about texts as the principles are to be translated into concrete recommendations. Everybody who has seen government decision making at close range has experienced the same frustration as inter-ministerial coordination unfolds within the iron triangle of domestic political ambitions, perception of public opinion, and objectives of international cooperation. The negotiator, as the middleman between the desirable and the achievable, is caught in a complicated web of objectives and goals which very often are — or at least are seen to be — mutually incompatible.

THE SOCIAL SCIENCES AND THE CONCEPT OF ENABLING CONDITIONS

For these various reasons, the notion of enabling conditions is a useful tool. We have found that governmental action on global environmental threats is conditioned by the perception of the state of public opinion, or as Bismarck said: "Politics is the art of the possible." If domestic political risks of a certain line of action in the international arena are deemed to be too high, no action will be taken. If, on the other hand, the government feels that the right enabling conditions exist, international initiatives can be taken and international agreements concluded.

It is clear that in a world of rapid change, enabling conditions are constantly evolving. This means that over time, dependent on events, perceptions, new information and a host of other elements, a "tipping point" is reached which can modify negotiating positions.

In the study of the new diplomacy these close links to the domestic political scene, and to the state of public opinion, mean that careful analysis of what is really happening in our societies becomes a necessary tool to better understand the conditions for successful international action and the structuring of multilateral cooperation in this new world of anthropogenic impact on the whole global system. In this book, it is only possible to develop some basic ideas, but I hope that further research, involving different disciplines of social science, and hopefully also the humanities, will clarify more details and interconnections in a broad societal framework.

An important point of departure for this analysis is the concept of the "risk society," as developed by Ulrich Beck and others. In his book *Ecological Enlightenment*[3] Beck defines risk society as "an epoch in which the dark sides of society increasingly come to dominate social debate." He also states that "the transformation of the unseen side effects of industrial production into global flash points is not an environmental problem, but a flagrant institutional crisis of industrial society, with considerable political content." For our present reflection, it is also important to add that increasingly not only production patterns, but also consumption patterns, i.e., our personal responsibilities in everyday life, have an impact on the pattern of global risks. The Irish researcher Piet Strydom has also spoken about "the erosion of the boundary between society and nature and the recognition of the newly emergent unity of the socio- and biosphere."[4]

In watching developments in the international arena, and particularly in trying to draw conclusions for the evolution of global processes and institutions for coming decades, we have to analyze more carefully what is happening at the domestic scene in different countries. The social sciences provide a number of instruments and methods for such analysis. Dr. Max Steuer of the London School of Economics[5] has used an interesting method in his book "The Scientific Study of Society," which consists of referring to recent research in the five disciplines of anthropology, sociology, social psychology, political science, and economics, using the findings to comment on and clarify a series of topics of interest to society, such as crime, migration, family, and religion. Steuer also refers to "input sister subjects" to the social sciences, namely demography, geography and linguistics.

It is not possible here to go into the details of Steuer's chosen method, but it seems perfectly doable to use a similar approach for an analysis of the various elements influencing the way in which environmental threats are perceived at different levels of society, and consequently impact on international negotiations and the performance of international institutions within the area covered by the new diplomacy. This could well be an interesting field for future academic research. Here, I only wish to give some random comments as an illustration of the potential of the method and as a way to further clarifying my general point that international negotiations on sustainable development are strongly dependent on domestic conditions and processes in society.

Following Steuer, I wish to use the five disciplines of social sciences (in turn economics, political science, sociology, social psychology and anthropology) to comment on the way society perceives and deals with sustainable development, and more particularly with the concept of global threats. However, it is clear, but unavoidable, that the analysis will suffer from the ambiguity of the term sustainable development itself, as was pointed out in Chapter 1.[6]

In conclusion, I will also make some comments on the role of personalities who have been central to the evolution of the new diplomacy, in particular through their capacity to influence both national policies and interational action.

ECONOMICS

In Chapter 2, I have already commented on some aspects of *economics.* That section is mainly dealing with costs; this is logical, since this question inevitably comes up in all discussions about sustainability. In many ways, the economic and environmental components of sustainability are seen to be in constant conflict: at the local level industries are complaining about environmental regulations which threaten profitability or even the very survival of the enterprise; nationally or in the EU the debate on environmental legislation is often based on arguments about international competitiveness; globally there is a strong focus on the risks for economic development and combat of poverty in developing countries.

There are also counter-arguments underlining that environmental regulations, or taxes, serve as an impetus for technological innovation and actually strengthen economies. But if we look at the discussion in the perspective of international negotiations, and the notion of "enabling conditions" there is no doubt that the economic arguments largely lead to a slowing down of global environmental action. With unemployment at historically high levels in many developed countries, risks for job losses are taken very seriously and tend to restrict the latitude for concessions in negotiations. This tendency is strengthened by a fair amount of conservatism in the way most people look at economics: new ideas have difficulty to be generally accepted, and the argument about the enormous costs to tackle global environmental threats is readily accepted.

It can also be argued that neo-classical economic theory is at the present time dominating the political discourse to an extent that makes it difficult for alternative theories to make their way into economic decision-making or economic policy in general. The neo-classical theory is based on the idea of the management of scarce resources, and the cost-benefit analysis becomes a cornerstone of the reasoning. In terms of environmental action, this is not necessarily an obstacle, provided that the thinking includes also environmental resources. However, critics of neo-classicism such as the Swedish economist Peter Söderbaum[7] have pointed out that there is a "monetary reductionism" in the theory, which tends to deal with resource allocation largely in monetary terms. This simplification also extends into the political domain, since it is maintained that policy-makers need simple answers to complicated problems.

Economic theory is certainly not free from fads and fashions, and it may well be that there are undercurrents of thinking among established economists that will ultimately change this pattern, and influence the way in which authorities responsible for macro policies and the world economy will look upon sustainability in economic terms. For the time being ecological economists have a limited impact on policy-making, and on public opinion.

However, the publication of the so-called Stern Review on the Economics of Climate Change in the autumn of 2006, commissioned by the Chancellor of the Exchequer of UK, introduces a new element in this discussion.[8] Sir Nicholas Stern certainly represents mainstream economic thinking: he has been Chief Economist at the World Bank and Chief Economist of the UK Treasury. Therefore the impact of the report will be strongly felt in governments around the world, even if the proposals and the findings of the report do not command unanimous support in the academic community. A central point of departure of the report is that "climate change presents a unique challenge for economics: it is the greatest and widest-ranging market failure ever seen." Against this background, the report argues that climate change may lead to consequences for global economic growth which will be disastrous, and that the benefits of strong early action far outweigh the costs. Furthermore, the transition to a low-carbon economy will bring challenges to competitiveness but also opportunities for growth. Therefore, the reduction of the expected adverse effects of climate change is both highly desirable and feasible. And this policy should be based on three essential elements: carbon pricing, technology policy and removal of barriers to behavioral change.

The Stern review approach, based on traditional economic analysis, thus comes to the conclusion that preventive action is actually the most cost-effective approach. It is an important development of thinking and will no doubt influence the prospects for global agreements on climate change, and ultimately on other negotiations on issues related to global change.

At the micro level, in the corporate sector, thinking has already evolved. Instruments such as Environmental Impact Assessment (EIA), Environmental Impact Statements (EIS), and the standardized Environmental Management Systems (EMS), such as ISO 14000 are generally used by enterprises, and seen as active and important components of the company profile. At the global level, the establishment of the Business Council for Sustainable

Development within the preparations for the Rio Conference reflected a line of thinking among big and influential companies that environment and industry would not be incompatible, a policy which was actively supported by the Secretary-General of the Conference, Maurice Strong. In 1992, the Business Council published a book, "Changing Course," which laid down a global business perspective on development and the environment.[9] In particular the Chapter on *Pricing the Environment: Markets, Costs, and Instruments* contains many useful insights, expressing satisfaction for the triumph of the market system, but also concern over its ability to integrate environmental aspects in its operation. This chapter is prefaced by a quote of Dr. Ernst U. von Weizsäcker of the German Institute for Climate, Environment and Energy, which reflects the same dilemma: *Bureaucratic socialism collapsed because it did not allow prices to tell the economic truth. Market economy may ruin the environment and ultimately itself if prices are not allowed to tell the ecological truth.*

Nowadays, the Business Council has merged with environmental activities of the International Chamber of Commerce to form the World Business Council for Sustainable Development (WBCSD), continuing its advocacy for a responsible business approach to environmental problems and using the notion of eco-efficiency.

It is hard to tell how much influence institutions like the WBCSD carry in the perspective of international negotiations and the formation of national positions. They represent only a part of the business community; we have noted that in particular the US corporate sector over the years has been deeply divided over climate change.

This point brings us back to the direct impact of economics on governments' negotiating positions: the main reason given by President George W. Bush to refuse to ratify the Kyoto Protocol was explicitly referring to its expected negative effect on the US economy. At the time, important sectors of the US economy were also sharing Bush's misgivings. Today, the situation is changing in the US; the majority of big corporations are now supporting a more constructive line in the climate negotiations. Market logic seems to have inspired this development. On the one hand, the large automobile producers have found that Toyota's hybrid cars sell extremely well, also in the United States, and on the other hand they are wary about their exclusion from the Kyoto mechanisms, now that the EU pilot scheme ETS (European Trading System) is in operation.

The Kyoto mechanisms warrant a special comment, because of the interest demonstrated by financial markets. As we were negotiating the mechanisms (The project-based Joint Implementation (JI) and Clean Development Mechanism (CDM), and the system for emissions trading) several negotiators, including myself, were concerned that negotiations would produce schemes that would not be attractive to markets, and consequently without real impact. As we have now seen the increasing investor interest in the CDM and the relatively successful introduction of the EU Emissions Trading Scheme, these concerns seem to have been overstated. In connection with the 2005 Montreal Conference of Parties of the Climate Convention (COP 11), and the first session of the Meeting of the Parties to the Kyoto Protocol (COP/MOP 1), as well as in later meetings, the financial sector has been well represented, seemingly convinced that there is considerable future business opportunities in these schemes.

The insurance sector has for a long time been active in support of action to limit environmental threats; this is quite natural given the enormous costs of disasters that can be directly or indirectly attributed to environmental causes. In some regions, such as part of the Caribbean, insurance can no longer be provided for property. This recalls some of the arguments of Ulrich Beck, namely that in the risk society nuclear, chemical, genetic or environmental mega-hazards abolish the supporting pillars of the calculus of risk and subvert the established risk logic. It is clear that this development can threaten the very foundations of important segments of the insurance industry. Consequently, big corporations, concerned with the stability of the system, might be more active players in supporting strong international action to limit risks which are considered unacceptable.

This brings us back to the question of enabling conditions. Can common action by the corporate sector ultimately be a factor that radically modifies the way in which economics influences international negotiations and structures? This question cannot be answered today . But it lingers in the background and underlines the volatility of the economic arguments, ultimately based on notions of costs, which can easily be modified; one concrete example being the price of oil: if cheap oil will never happen again, other forms of energy will be radically more competitive and attractive for investors. On climate, we are still far away from the experience of the ozone negotiations, when readily available substitutes for CFC's turned producers in the US into strong proponents of the Montreal Protocol. But it could happen, and the previously mentioned Stern Review might turn out to be an important reference point in the future.

One final point on the subject of economics: as tipping points might appear in different sectors, facilitating international environmental agreements, the linkages between negotiations on sustainable development and other areas of economic diplomacy, related to trade or international payments, need to be closely integrated with the New diplomacy. To a certain extent this is already happening, but in the future it will require a more determined and better structured effort. I will revert to this issue in Chapter 7.

POLITICAL SCIENCE

Let us now consider the question of enabling conditions in the light of *political science*. I propose to structure this section in a different way from the previous one, using some specific issues and situations to illustrate my points. In turn, I will deal with Swedish energy policy, the role of green parties in the EU, and the US attitudes to climate change, insofar as these different clusters relate to positions in international negotiations.

Swedish energy policy

Ever since the early 1970s, the question of nuclear power has haunted Swedish energy policy and created divisions in Swedish political life, going beyond the traditional left-right divide. As nuclear energy became an option, Sweden took a generally positive attitude to its peaceful use, started research and prepared for the construction of twelve nuclear reactors. But in the beginning of the 1970s, public opinion became more critical, and one party, the Centre party, with its main support in rural areas, took a strong negative stance. At this time, it seemed possible for parties right of center to break the long period of social-democratic dominance in Swedish politics, and the Centre party dominated the coalition with a popular leader, Torbjörn Fälldin who could well match the charismatic Prime Minister Olof Palme. Fälldin made the opposition to nuclear power a central issue in the election campaign of 1976. This line struck a chord in public opinion, and it contributed to the victory of the coalition, which also included the liberals and the conservatives. These parties did not share the strong opposition to nuclear, and Fälldin had to give up a promise not to start the twelfth reactor. At the time, the social democrats were supportive of the nuclear option, which was attractive in a country with large needs of energy. In fact the twelve nuclear reactors represent almost 50% of Sweden's electricity production.

The Harrisburg accident in 1980 had a strong impact on public opinion in a country which was already before increasingly divided in its attitudes to nuclear energy. Now there were divisions in all the main parties; and the political response was to organize a referendum, an unusual measure in Swedish politics. The voters were faced with three options: (1) to continue with nuclear, (2) to limit nuclear to the existing twelve reactors and decommission them as soon as possible, and (3) to start decommissioning straight away. There was a majority for option 2, and Parliament later decided that nuclear should be completely abolished by 2010.

Rather soon, the realism of this decision was questioned, as the highly energy-dependent Swedish industry (iron and steel, paper and pulp, mechanical engineering) started to worry about the potential absence of alternatives. Then came the Chernobyl disaster in 1986, which for climatic reasons hit Sweden more than any other country in Western Europe. The concern about nuclear grew again, considerable and successful efforts were made to improve energy efficiency, but there was no agreement on measures which would have radically changed the energy mix towards renewables. With nuclear and energy savings, Sweden's emissions of CO_2 were reduced by almost 40 % between 1973 and 1988.

This was the background situation in Sweden when climate negotiations started in 1991: uncertainty in public opinion, parties deeply divided, long-term energy policy fixed to a 2010 goal that could clearly not be achieved; while our general stance was to support reduction of CO_2 emissions in line with a deep concern for the global environment. The "enabling conditions" would only permit generally formulated instructions. To a certain extent it was like flying blind, but the way the Climate Convention finally developed, with only vague, non-binding commitments for 2000 and a reference to action taken before 1990, we had no difficulty signing and ratifying the Convention.

Later in the 1990s, the Social Democrats and the Liberal party managed to agree on a long-term energy policy, which had its main merit in abolishing the 2010 limit to nuclear, while maintaining the long-term goal. The anti-nuclear opinion has been given some satisfaction through a decision by the Social-Democratic Government, back in power since 1996, to decommission two nuclear reactors already by 2004. Recently it seems that opposition to nuclear in the Centre Party has flagged, but public opinion remains divided, as in many other countries.

There is no doubt that the concern about global warming has strengthened the position of those who wish to prolong nuclear as long as possible. As future Swedish governments will have to formulate negotiating instructions for crucial climate negotiations in the preparatory phase for a post-2012 regime a host of concerns on nuclear from political leaders, different stakeholders and the general public will have to be accommodated: economic and social well-being, jobs, risks of nuclear accidents, long-term storage of nuclear waste.

All countries will face the same problem, as the risks of long-term effects of global warming are becoming more precise. The role of nuclear remains one of the most central underlying issues in the climate negotiations; and because of its public opinion impact it is a good example of the linkage between domestic and global concerns.

Green parties in Europe

The nuclear issue has played an important role in the formation of positions also in other European countries and in the stance taken by the European Union in negotiations, reflecting political developments in the various countries, in particular the emergence of green parties as strong partners in coalition governments in Belgium, France, Finland, and Germany, and as active, sometimes influential, political players elsewhere, as in Sweden.

The green parties grew out of popular movements, particularly among young people, following the emergence of environmental concerns in the 1960s, sometimes merging with other radical movements at that time. They wanted to provide an alternative to the established parties and took pride in being different, demonstrating a new political style in speaking, dress codes and parliamentary behavior. In the beginning they were also strongly focused on environmental issues, leaving other political concerns aside. It was not surprising that they had, and continue to have, a strong appeal to young people, not least women, who feel that traditional politics are stuffy and boring, dominated by middle-aged men.

Not surprisingly, with time the green parties have become more like other parties, as they have moved into positions of greater responsibility, and in particular in joining governments.

However, they continue to be an important new element in the political life of European countries, and in the perspective of this analysis of enabling conditions they play an essential role in introducing the notion of global threats to new generations and providing a rallying point for their concerns. In many countries they are also attractive to the ever increasing number of university students, which is of course important for the future.

Green parties were influential in defining the EU stance in global negotiations around the turn of the century, in particular on climate change and the preparations for the World Summit on Sustainable Development 2002. At that time, green parties were holding positions of Ministers of Environment in Belgium, France, Finland, and Germany. They were strong personalities and contributed to make EU Ministerial meetings lively and interesting; Olivier Deleuze of Belgium, Dominique Voynet of France, and Jürgen Trittin of Germany also held their posts during Presidencies of their respective countries. It should be noted that Dominique Voynet was leader of her party.

Trittin was Minister of Environment during the German EU Presidency in 1997, during crucial preparations for the Kyoto Protocol. He was suspicious of trading and the other proposed flexible mechanisms, considered loop-holes in the system: it was largely at his insistence that EU introduced the notion of supplementarity, to ensure that countries would mainly meet their commitments through national action.

As the laborious negotiations on practical implementation of the Kyoto Protocol came to a decisive point at the 2000 Conference of Parties (COP 6) in the Hague, Dominique Voynet led the EU team at Ministerial level, though with mixed success, mainly because the lines of command were unclear between officials of the Prime Ministers office and the Ministry of Environment. Voynet also had difficulties to agree with the UK Deputy Prime Minister John Prescott, who tried to mediate between the EU and the US. The problems of that particular session in the Hague were due to an exceptionally complicated negotiating situation, as outlined in Chapter 5, and the EU unity was relatively easy to restore, first in connection with a Ministerial session later with Voynet in the Chair, and then during the following Swedish Presidency.

It fell to Olivier Deleuze to lead the EU team during the negotiations that ultimately made the Kyoto Protocol "ratifiable" (word minted by Trittin), first in Bonn in July, and finally at COP 7 in Marrakech in December 2001. His informal style and his no-nonsense approach greatly contributed to the success of the negotiations.

At that time, the EU was already deeply involved in the preparations for the World Summit on Sustainable Development (WSSD), to be held in Johannesburg in early autumn 2002. There were still several Ministers from green parties present, and their contribution was important, not least Satu Hassi from Finland, who also held the portfolio of development cooperation.

In summary, it seems probable that the existence of European green parties has contributed significantly to help the articulation between national public opinion and negotiating positions at the EU level, and serve as a bridge between public opinion, particularly representing young people, and the world of global negotiations.

US politics and climate change

I now move across the Atlantic to consider how political developments in the United States have influenced the negotiations on sustainable development, and in particular on climate change, over the last decades. Because of the central position of the United States in the world and in the negotiating rooms, a full study would require a volume of its own. Here I just wish to highlight some main points.

US research has played a major role in the climate issue, and at various points, science has had an impact on the political process. One example was in 1988, when James Hansen, then Chief climate scientist at NASA's Goddard Institute for Space Studies made a stern warning about the risks of climate change at a hearing of the Senate's Energy and Natural Resources Committee. In the same year, there was a disastrous drought in large parts of the United States, and concern about climate change grew. In the UK, Margaret Thatcher delivered a speech at the Royal Society in September, echoing the worries of scientists, widely reported as a "conversion". All this prompted George Bush to make climate an issue in his election campaign, promising to convene an international conference on the subject during his first year in office.

In July 1989, the G 7 held its annual summit in Paris, with the Declaration calling for "common efforts to limit emissions of carbon dioxide" and a "framework or umbrella convention" on the subject.

This was a time of sweeping general statements, the establishment of IPCC, and several international research meetings; but it was also a period of new concerns in governments for the political consequences of an international regulation of matters so close to central policy-making as energy and transport policy. The position of the Bush administration became more restrictive, and when his promised international climate conference was finally held in April 1990 the gulf between the US and Europe became clear. Bush underlined that there was still much scientific uncertainty, and highlighted the costs of action against climate change. The insistence on new technology as a sort of panacea was already there. But the interest of the government in the issue was important enough to bring the US to invite the first negotiating meeting for the Convention to be held in Washington in February 1991.

The story of the negotiation, which led to the Framework Convention on Climate Change with weak concrete commitments, has been told in Chapter 4 and 5. After much hesitation, President Bush decided to attend the Rio Conference in 1992 and sign the Convention there. The US was among the first countries to ratify the Convention, already in the autumn of 1992.

The election campaign that year saw a tired and worn-out President Bush lose to Bill Clinton, with Senator Al Gore as the candidate for the Vice-Presidency. Gore had been in Congress since 1976 and represented Tennessee in the Senate since 1984. He had been an active campaigner on environmental issues, and in 1992 he published the book *Earth in the Balance*, which is a personal testimony and a plea for radical policies on the global environment and on development issues.

In 1992, I spent a large part of the autumn attending the UN General Assembly, and in December I visited Washington and was introduced to some young and enthusiastic members of the Gore team, including Eileen Claussen, later Chief negotiator on Climate and presently Director of the Pew Centre. Among environmentalists around the world, there were now high hopes for what the new administration would bring to the global environmental negotiations. However, once again, we had to realize that "enabling conditions" were not ready for radical measures, and that the new administration would mean a change more in style than in substance. In particular, Congress was a stumbling block, and the disastrous defeat in elections for Congress in 1994, landed the Clinton/Gore administration without any possibility to run a radical environmental agenda.

However, the US continued to play a constructive role in several international negotiations, and they were able to agree on the Berlin Mandate at the first Climate Conference of Parties in 1995. But a cloud was hanging over the US negotiating position, after the so-called Byrd-Hagel resolution in the Senate in the summer of 1997, which stated that the US would not be allowed to undertake any quantified commitments in Kyoto, unless major developing countries would do the same.

Even so, in Kyoto, Al Gore was to play a decisive role. Arriving in the beginning of the second week of a negotiation, which had up till then been rather frustrating, he stated that he was now giving the US negotiators more flexible instructions; hard bargaining continued, but success was achieved. One year later, the US also signed the Protocol.

No doubt, there were early concerns in Washington that Congress would not ratify the Kyoto Protocol, particularly since the booming US economy was making it increasingly doubtful whether the Kyoto target of –7% by 2012 could really be met. Against that background, in the continuing efforts to agree on implementing rules for the Kyoto Protocol, the US negotiators were taking very tough positions on the need for liberal rules on using the Kyoto mechanisms and on the calculation of sinks. As Al Gore became the democratic candidate for the Presidency in the elections in 2000, many foreign observers believed that he would be well placed to mobilize public opinion and somehow achieve a senate majority for ratification.

At the time of the decisive negotiations on implementation of the Kyoto Protocol in The Hague in December 2000, the result of the election was not yet clear. With the ultimate victory of the Bush/Cheney ticket, things did not look good, and as told in Chapter 5, very serious efforts were made to make an eleventh hour deal on the presumption that it would be better to have a firm agreement with the out-going administration.

At the time, I was against such a deal, mainly because I felt that it would not be confirmed by the new administration. Later events have shown that this was a reasonable assumption; the first signals were, however, rather positive, indicating that the Bush administration would be ready to resume COP 6 and to try to make the Kyoto Protocol ratifiable.[10]

Therefore the Bush letter to a number of Senators in March, stating that the US refused to ratify the Kyoto Protocol, had a shock effect; it was of course not wholly unexpected that the US would try to reopen the Kyoto Protocol, but the brutality of the letter surprised.[11] A more sophisticated approach would have seen to be in the US interest, but it was obvious that very strong forces in the administration, not least the Vice President, were adamantly against the Kyoto Protocol, and that the concern of oil interests was a part of this political line. However, as subsequent events show, a very strong driving force was the negative attitude of the Bush administration to the United Nations and to the very notion of binding international commitments.

Developments after September 11, and the Iraq war, have pushed climate, and more generally, environmental issues, down the priority line of the Bush administration. The President has had to concede, however, that global warming is a serious issue, and that US leading scientists do not take any other view. The answer has been to insist on the potential of technology, bringing this issue also to the international arena, with bilateral and multilateral agreements on technological cooperation concluded with a number of developing countries.[12]

Bush and the UK Prime Minister Tony Blair have had a close cooperation on Iraq, and on a number of other issues as well. However, when it comes to environment, and in particular climate, Blair has had a radically different view; so far it has obviously had a limited impact, even if the G-8 meeting in the UK in July 2005 led to a reasonably positive mention of the climate problem in the final communiqué.

In looking towards the future of climate negotiations, particularly in view of the post-2012 regime, the question of "enabling conditions," represented at different levels in the United States, is of greater importance. The federal administration's negative line is less and less reflected in the economically most important states. The northeastern states and California have all introduced legislation aiming at reducing emissions of greenhouse gases, some of them with non-binding targets and timetables. In the corporate sector, important companies have joined pro-environmental associations, and wish to be involved in emissions trading. Strong think-tanks, academia, and environmental NGOs are exerting pressure on the administration.

Nevertheless, most observers would agree that it is very unlikely that the Bush administration would change its climate policy to enable it to even consider joining the Kyoto protocol; furthermore such a step would lead to very complicated negotiations. But domestic pressure would make it possible for preparatory talks related to the post-2012 regime to be reasonably constructive. Furthermore, it is generally assumed that the next President, republican or democrat, would take a different policy line than George W. Bush.

The environmental policy of the United States after 2009 cannot be foreseen with any accuracy. The superpower's line of action will be dependent on strategic interests far outside the environmental realm. But US responsibility with regard to the global environment will be engaged and cannot be relinquished. Domestic "enabling conditions" will change, both with regard to public opinion and to Congress. A repetition of disasters like hurricane Katrina will have their impact on thinking.

There is a lesson for Europe in this uncertainty; the United States has by far the largest and most flexible economy in the world. It has the best research and the best technology. It also has a great potential for energy savings. A new administration might find it attractive to use these assets to reduce dependence on oil, and to act swiftly in the international arena. In that case the rest of the world might be faced with bold US proposals, which would challenge the now traditional role of the European Union as a driving force in global environmental negotiations.

SOCIAL PSYCHOLOGY AND SOCIOLOGY

The previous section has considered the impact of domestic policies on countries' approach to international negotiations, based mainly on tools derived from political science analysis. In trying to dig deeper into the formation of these policies in relation to environmental threats I now propose to consider two other social sciences, *social psychology and sociology*. The purpose is to try to understand better how public opinion is formed in the face of environmental threats, and more particularly survival issues, linked to global change. Ulrich Beck's notion of the risk society is a useful point of departure.

Beck considers that our industrial civilization has created several new categories of risks, but that they have been considered acceptable because of the existence of insurance. He feels that this represents a consensus on progress, which constitutes in reality a sort of "security pact". However, at present this pact is violated in a series of new technological challenges, such as nuclear power, new chemicals or climate change. It is worth quoting Beck on this point "Since the middle of this century (i.e., the 20th century) the social institutions of the industrialized countries have been confronted with the historically unprecedented possibility, brought about by our own decisions, of the destruction of all life of this planet. This distinguishes our epoch not only of the early phases of the Industrial Revolution, but also from all other cultures and social forms, no matter how contradictory."

This statement reflects the same idea as that of the Amsterdam Declaration,[13] that the planet is now in a "no-analogue" situation: we have never been here before. The question is what conclusions are drawn by all of us as individuals and as members of society. In Chapter 1, I have made a comparison with the long period of the cold war, which certainly was a time when the threat of "destruction of all life" looked real enough for large parts of the world's population. But at that time the fragile balance of power between the super-powers was supported by enormously large investments in military capability. The "enabling conditions" for facing the threat existed in the western democracies, since the threat was perceived as concrete and immediate. It was also linked to traditional considerations of national security. Now the threats are long-term and diffuse, and the willingness to accept the costs involved is limited, both in terms of money, and in terms of accepting other types of sacrifices. We come back to the question of the formation of public opinion and the various forms in which citizen's views can be expressed.

One important element in this analysis is the relatively short time in which the concern for global environmental matters has existed. It was not until the publication of Rachel Carson's book *Silent Spring* in 1962, which raised the problem of the impact of pesticides, that the problem became public knowledge. The 1960s created a new awareness, which also had an impact at the political level. In Sweden, a well-known politician and diplomat, Rolf Edberg, wrote a number of books during this time, which had a considerable impact on public opinion. Their strength was not only the skill with which Edberg presented the scientific evidence, but also his literary style[14]; his writings, and those of others, were well received in a turbulent decade when many old values were questioned, including the very notion of economic growth.

On this latter theme, the Club of Rome, which in 1972 published the book *Limits to Growth*, certainly had an impact. The notion of "zero growth" became popular, in particular among many young people in Europe, who at that time were ready to question many old values and ideas in a radical, left-wing way. The lesson one can learn from this is of course that the general mood of the time, or "Zeitgeist," to borrow a German word, can have an important impact on the way environmental matters are perceived.

The wave of radicalism in Europe ebbed out in the seventies, and we have seen how neo-classicism has come back in economic policy. It is proof of the growing strength of pro-environment public opinion that support for environmental action has grown even in this period.

There are several reasons for this. One is that concrete evidence of environmental deterioration and global threats has been strengthened; another is that events in the outside world have brought home the need to rethink features of the functioning of our societies. The oil shocks in the 1970s demonstrated that cheap and abundant oil supplies could not be taken for granted. And after the fall of the Soviet system it became clear that exclusive concentration on production without taking into account environmental consequences could lead to disasters at a large scale.

Does this mean that people in general in the industrial countries are ready to support far-reaching, and costly, action to tackle global environmental threats? The subject merits further study. On anecdotal evidence it seems that we are moving in that direction, but that there is still a long way to go. And the professionals in trendsetting do not seem very sure. Is this an era of individualism which limits the willingness of people to accept changes in consumption-patterns or lifestyles just as an act of solidarity with the planet and future generations? There is no easy answer in a world of rapid change and in the middle of the information and communication revolution. We are furthermore witnessing the widening of generational gaps and increasing inequalities in our societies, social trends which reduce social cohesion, and could make it more difficult for people to take in concerns for global environmental threats.

Elements like these are important as governments try to use information campaigns to broaden the enabling conditions for international and national action on the environment. However, to fine-tune such campaigns to reach real lasting effect seems increasingly difficult in an era when there are so many subjects pressing for attention, not least the enormous quantity of information and entertainment flowing from an ever-present television.

Yes, this is an era of individualism in our western democracies but we also sense a common responsibility to try to understand the global issues threatening the future; and in consequence to create the enabling conditions for action at the international level. This creates a particular responsibility for the educational system. There are many efforts made at present to improve education for sustainable development; but I am not sure that the methods chosen are the right ones. However, this work has to be continued, and go hand in hand with creating a better understanding of the mechanisms that govern the earth system.

In this situation, with uncertain societal trends, and a perceived need for "trend breaks,"[15] which would signal "discontinuity" or "radical change," it is important to analyze the constraints and opportunities for a society that would enable policies and practices, for instance leading to drastic reductions in emissions of greenhouse gases. What makes people change?

I have already pointed to the role that extreme events, disasters of different kinds, can have in this regard. As far as climate change is concerned, scientists have so far been reluctant to make these causal connections, because of very uncertain evidence; but in the public debate the issue appears more and more. I believe we must accept this dilemma and see it as an opportunity to bring home the fact that we are living in the Anthropocene, and with it a new perception of the world. The problematic reminds me of the controversy around the American movie *The Day After Tomorrow*, released in 2004. This story about a break-down of the Gulf Stream leading to a rapid disastrous cooling of Europe and North America was rightly criticized by experts, who explained that such a speedy change as described in the film could simply never happen. But the film was professionally made and appealed to young people; even if the story was not realistic it showed with ample evidence that if immense forces of nature are unleashed through the impact of human activities, modern man with all his technology cannot stop them. And that message may make people more ready to listen to scientists' warnings about the consequences of practices that are detrimental to the global system, and consequently to accept changes in life-styles and consumption patterns. More recently, former Vice President Al Gore has had considerable success with his film on climate change, and it seems that at the general level the public is now really concerned about this issue in most developed countries.

Linkages between global change and consequences for human health are also forceful reminders of consequences which are not only long-term but could be direct enough. The European Regional Office of the United Nations recently took the initiative to publish a major study on the relationship between climate change and human health,[16] recognizing the concern of health authorities on the effects of air pollution, ultraviolet radiation, and climate change on populations in Europe. Since people in other parts of the world are still more vulnerable, the conclusions in this report are of great importance also for developing countries as they take adaptation measures to reduce the effects of global change, and in particular global warming.

In the particular perspective of this chapter, that is the sociological and socio-psychological effects on "enabling conditions", the results of the WHO study confirm the concerns that many people have about health effects of climate change. No doubt there are other dangers of this kind that would have priority at the individual level, but it is probable that vaguely felt dangers of effects of climate change — and their confirmation in specific events — will increasingly weigh on public opinion.

The report puts special emphasis on the effects of extreme events, such as heat-waves and flooding, which might occur much more frequently in a warmer climate in Europe. Over recent years such events have served as strong reminders of these dangers: flooding in Eastern Europe and Switzerland have claimed many lives, and the heat-wave in 2003 in large parts of Europe, in particular France, is deemed to have caused tens of thousands of excess deaths. To a certain extent, better preventive measures and other types of adaptation will reduce the effects, but the psychological impact will remain.

The risks of vector and rodent-borne diseases are also set out clearly in the report. In particular, it is felt that the distribution of dangerous diseases such as tick-borne encephalitis and Lyme borreliosis would continue to change due to a warmer climate and increases in precipitations. In fact, it is already noted in Sweden that the ticks are moving further north, and that the number of encephalitis and borreliosis has increased. More studies are needed with regard to other vector-borne diseases, as well as to food- and water-borne diseases. No doubt continued research will be followed very closely by the public.

These are some examples of how events and concerns will influence the way people look at issues related to global change: are there disastrous consequences that could have a direct impact on me and my family, or the community where I live? This would then create a general sense of understanding for the need of measures to tackle the negative side-effects of global change and make it easier to carry out such measures as increased environmental taxes or new regulations.

But the analysis would need to go beyond the immediate concerns of individuals for their own safety and for that of their families. I feel that as we are discussing issues of general importance for mankind, deep considerations of an ethical, maybe even religious nature will also play a role in the way we as individuals will face the new situation of the Anthropocene. Are those of us who can afford it ready to sense a deeper responsibility and accept to limit our own well-being as a measure of solidarity with people far away or even with future generations? To a certain extent this is of course happening already, with international development cooperation, financed by tax-payers in rich and middle-income countries. So the notion of intra-generational equity is already an established fact, albeit with far too limited resources. But inter-generational equity is another thing, going well beyond established patterns of international cooperation or what has sometimes been called the "charity of nations." Nevertheless, our responsibility for the unborn is being argued and accepted within the framework of the new diplomacy as an established political fact, being part of the standard vocabulary in Ministerial meetings on sustainable development. The concept derives its strength from three sources: first its close association with the medium-term and the risks for environmental disasters threatening ourselves, second the fact that with increasing life-spans, even our grandchildren may well be around by the end of the present century, and third the notion that a concern for matters that will happen long after we are gone adds to deeper strata of our sense of responsibility and therefore to our perception of life itself.[17]

Arguments of this kind no doubt help to build indispensable psychological foundations for societal changes that will serve as enabling conditions for global action on sustainable development. But such feelings also need to be channeled into structures that will have political consequences. The participation of civil society as represented by non-governmental organizations has had a key role in this regard as an integral part of the new diplomacy.

We have already seen how NGOs have become a more and more accepted part of the structures of the international meetings, influencing negotiations in different ways. At the national level their influence has been unequal, dependent on local circumstances and traditions. The work on sustainable development has been supported by international NGOs such as the IUCN (International Union for the Conservation of Nature), or WWF (World Wildlife Fund). Furthermore, Agenda 21, with its strong emphasis on "major groups" and its call for the establishment of local agendas 21 at the municipality level had a strong impact in some countries. In the case of Sweden, local Agenda 21 were agreed in all municipalities; this became the basis for a strong youth movement, Q-2000, which struck an efficient balance between idealism and realism in trying to bring concrete action under the banner "think globally, act locally." Q-2000 managed to have a considerable influence on policies during part of the 1990s, and many of their members became engaged as coordinators for local Agenda 21 action or joined government services to participate in the formation of policies at all levels. But it was a loosely knit network and its effects have gradually petered out. However, this kind of action created a strong sense of the important links between the different scales of local, national, and international action, which brought the government to important initiatives to support investments aimed at improving the environment while at the same time serving as employment schemes.

The Swedish experience shows that it is important to bring personal commitment and ideas to bear on societal action to promote sustainable development and thereby also create the right kind of support for international initiatives. The concept of enabling conditions is a two-way street, needing government support and understanding, but dependent on the personal reflection of many people and the action of organized independent groupings. Enabling conditions cannot be established by government decrees. It is part of a broad democratic process. Sociology and social psychology are useful tools for understanding better these various societal relationships in connection with sustainable development. I believe that these are important subjects for future, more systematic, research.

ANTHROPOLOGY

I only propose to mention anthropology briefly for the sake of completeness. It is clear that the question of ethnic minorities remains a very important element in studying the social phenomena associated with sustainable development. What are the effects of migration? To what extent does a sense of marginalization of different groups make it more difficult to create enabling conditions? Are there specific ways in which the experiences of different ethnic groups with regard to lifestyles and consumption patterns could be brought to bear, in a positive way, on the search for sustainability? With what methods could authorities improve contacts in order to inform ethnic minorities and get them involved in the work on sustainable development?

This is one set of issues, where anthropology is needed. But there is also a completely different set of issues related to the international negotiations. This is linked to the very particular role played by indigenous people in the new diplomacy. Chapter 26 in Agenda 21 is headed "To recognize and strengthen the role of indigenous peoples and their societies". In fact, in the Rio process indigenous peoples were able to play a significant role and have a real impact. This was based on a general perception that the lifestyles of indigenous people were characterized by traditional respect for nature, and that they were therefore symbols for sustainability. At the same time, it was felt that governments in the modern world were not protecting these traditional values; instead modernization and new technology would threaten the very livelihoods of indigenous peoples, and consequently Agenda 21 called upon governments to strengthen the position of indigenous peoples and protect their traditional livelihoods.

In Rio and beyond it was striking that representatives of indigenous peoples could benefit from the sentiment of no longer being small, vulnerable minorities, but peoples who were recognized and could also have a sense of solidarity between each other: Inuits of Canada, Indians of Central America, Samis of Norway, Sweden, Finland, and Russia — they were there together, as part of a global movement. And the movement has carried on, at COP 11 on climate in Montreal in 2005, Inuits were given great attention, as they were presenting the effects of global warming on their economies and their societies; and the world listened. This is also part of an increasing concern for the effects on global warming on the Arctic region.

SOME PERSONAL COMMENTS ON LEADING PERSONALITIES IN THE NEGOTIATIONS

Even looking at global negotiations from the vantage point of political science, which mainly deals with power and governance, and its underlying driving forces, the role of individuals should not be underestimated. Of course negotiators are bound by their instructions, but some are better than others in interpreting them in a constructive and creative way. Many of them also have the standing and ability to influence the national processes that are behind the instructions. And in all these negotiations, leading officials in Secretariats and Chairmen of various processes have been moving negotiations forward, easing the way for ultimate agreements. Looking back at my fifteen years of negotiations on sustainable development I am convinced that the new diplomacy would not have reached its present maturity if it had not been for a number of outstanding personalities, who have managed not only to seek out compromises but also to present negotiators with the reality of global change and engage their responsibility.

Therefore, I feel that some short mention of some of these people I have met would fit well into this analysis, and add some further personal notes to this book which aims at linking theory and practice. Furthermore, as we move into the reflections on the outlook for international processes and institutions in the final chapter of the book, it seems logical to show that structures and rules only provide the framework of action: results are dependent on the capacity of people. I have only included colleagues with whom I have worked directly; it goes without saying that many others have made equally important contributions. The order is mainly chronological.

The new diplomacy started with the Stockholm Conference on the Human Environment in 1972. Sweden took the initiative to convene the Conference, and the driving force for launching the proposal in the United Nations was the then Swedish Permanent Representative to the UN, Ambassador Sverker Åström. Supported by his close collaborator Börje Billner, he managed to overcome initial doubts and rally support for the idea through intense diplomatic work. Åström has had an exceptional diplomatic career; before his UN post he had been Head of the Political Department of the Foreign Ministry, and later he became Under-Secretary of State. He was a very influent adviser to the government, and the fact that someone with his credentials would drive the preparatory process for the Conference certainly made a difference.

The Secretary-General of the Stockholm Conference was Maurice Strong, a Canadian with a background both in the private and the public sector. His appointment brought dynamism and structure to the organization of the Conference, and it was logical that he would continue with its follow-up. One of the principal results of the Stockholm Conference was the establishment of the United Nations Environment Programme (UNEP), with Headquarters in Nairobi, and Strong became its first Director-General, later to be succeeded by Mustafa Tolba, an Egyptian scientist and politician, who stayed long at UNEP and who also made a major contribution to the evolution of environmental diplomacy.

Whereas the Stockholm Conference mainly dealt with national and regional environmental problems, it became increasingly clear in the 1980s that global threats related to such issues as climate, ozone, water, oceans and waste and linked to the development imperative moved into the foreground. Therefore the United Nations established the Brundtland Commission which presented its report "Our common future" in 1987, effectively launching the concept of sustainable development. Somewhat later, Åström and Strong wrote a newspaper article together, suggesting that the twentieth anniversary of the Stockholm Conference should be observed by the UN with a new Conference. The idea was taken up by the Swedish government, and after many discussions in New York, the UN Conference on Environment and Development was convened in Rio de Janeiro in June 1992.

Continuity with 1972 was assured through the re-appointment of Maurice Strong as Secretary-General ("lack of imagination, or simply recycling," as he commented himself); on the Swedish side we had Lars-Göran Engfeldt, a brilliant diplomat, who had also participated in the Stockholm Conference and who now became one of my closest collaborators in my job as Chief negotiator. In 1998, Engfeldt succeeded me and became one of the leading negotiators at the World Summit for Sustainable Development in Johannesburg in 2002, in particular on the institutional issues.

Since Strong came from the north, it was necessary that the G 77 be given the key post of Chairman of the Conference. Ambassador Tommy Koh of Singapore was appointed to the job, and a better choice could not have been made. Koh had both an academic and a diplomatic background; very young he was appointed Ambassador to Washington, he had also served as Permanent Representative to the UN, and he had been chairing the very difficult negotiations for the Treaty on the Law of the Sea.

This background was impressive, but it was still more impressive to see Koh in action, managing this extremely complicated process with great skill, courtesy, humor, and if necessary with considerable toughness. Together with Maurice Strong he formed the perfect team as I — in my capacity as Chairman of Working Group I — could observe in hundreds of morning meetings during the process of preparing and running the Conference. His coordination sessions were brief, efficient and to the point, as Koh did not accept any vague statements.

Both he and Maurice Strong had an enormous capacity to work hard. My own conviction is that it is highly doubtful whether we would ever have seen the central documents of Rio — Rio Declaration and Agenda 21 — emerge, if it had not been for the work of these two leaders.

The preparations for the Rio Conference engaged a new generation of negotiators, who learned the necessary skills of the new diplomacy on the job. They were traditional diplomats and their knowledge of the many complex issues of sustainable development was limited; they had to learn fast, and they did. One of those was Mahmoud El Ghaout of Mauretania, who appeared to be a rather arrogant young man, defending G 77 positions with strong conviction and considerable skill. In the course of the process he gained the respect of his colleagues as a constructive negotiator, as did Ahmed Djoglaf, a young Algerian, who served as rapporteur of the Preparatory Committee. Both later served with me on the Bureau of the Negotiating Committee of the Convention to combat Desertification, and they have continued to contribute to the various negotiations with distinction in the coming years, El Ghaouth in particular in the climate negotiations, and

Djoghlaf as an official of UNEP, serving now as Executive Secretary of the Convention on Biological Diversity.

One of the most skilled of my colleagues was Joke Waller-Hunter of the Netherlands who was often acting Chair of Working Group II of the UNCED Preparatory Committee. After the Conference, she moved to the UN Secretariat and later became Director of Environment at the OECD. She thus had a broad background when she was appointed Executive Secretary of the Climate Convention, where her drive and efficiency greatly contributed to the ultimate entry into force of the Kyoto Protocol. For several years she fought a cancer and finally died in October 2004. Her contribution to the diplomacy for sustainable development was of great importance.

Waller-Hunter's predecessor in the Climate Secretariat was Michael Zammit Cutajar of Malta, who came to climate already in 1991 from the Secretariat of UNCTAD, the UN Conference on Trade and Development. His knowledge of the UN Secretariat and of north-south issues proved to be invaluable as the difficult negotiations proceeded, and as it soon became evident that the climate issue required a rapidly expanding Secretariat, his managerial skills were a great asset. He has continued to deal with climate change as representative of Malta, and is now playing an important role in the negotiations for the post-2012 regime.

The surprising rapidity of the negotiation of the Climate Convention between February 1991 and May 1992 owed much to two senior personalities, the Chairman of the IPCC, the Swede Bert Bolin, and the Chairman of the Negotiating Committee, the Frenchman Jean Ripert. Bolin, a Professor Emeritus of Stockholm University, managed to convey to the negotiators the strong sense of urgency that was reflected in the First Assessment Report of the IPCC (September 1990), and Ripert managed the negotiation with an authority derived from a long and distinguished career in the French administration and a background as Director-General of Economic Affairs in the UN Secretariat. The two of them had no difficulties to establish contacts at the highest level of government or in the academic world. It is probably fair to say that Ripert's authority and imaginative leadership saved the Climate Convention in the difficult negotiations in 1992; and that Bolin's continued leadership of IPCC for a large part of the 1990s was instrumental to keep the process on track.

Looking back at these formative years of the diplomacy for sustainable development it is clear that the indispensable link between what I have called enabling conditions and progress in negotiations is the political level. It is therefore clear that many politicians of different countries and of different political parties have made decisive contributions to the negotiations, from Gro Harlem Brundtland of Norway with her 1987 report "Our Common Future" to Stephane Dion, Minister of Environment of Canada, who in 2005 managed to establish a firm base for the implementation of the Kyoto Protocol.

Among these colorful and interesting personalities that I have had the privilege to work with, two may represent all the others: Klaus Toepfer, German Minister of the Environment at the time of the Rio Conference, and Kjell Larsson, who was Sweden's Minister of Environment during the Swedish Presidency of the European Union in 2001.

When Klaus Toepfer led the German delegation to the Rio Conference in 1992 he was already a well established member of the German cabinet, and he played a very constructive role in the negotiations; in particular he chaired the crucial talks on a first consensus on international forest policy, the Forest Principles. Two years later he chaired the first substantive meeting of the Commission on Sustainable Development (CSD) and introduced a number of innovative features, such as informal dialogues between Ministers, which have since been a regular component of environmental negotiations. Later on he became Minister of Building and was in that capacity responsible for the transfer of the German capital from Bonn to Berlin. Between 1997 and 2006 he has continued to play a major role in environmental diplomacy s Executive director of UNEP.

As Under-Secretary of State in the Prime Minister's office, Kjell Larsson had been a close collaborator of two Swedish Prime Ministers, Olof Palme and Ingvar Carlsson, so he had a deep understanding of the operation of the Swedish government, when he became Minister of Environment in 1998. This became particularly important during the Swedish EU Presidency in 2001, when the European Union had to react quickly to the US refusal to ratify the Kyoto Protocol. He had no difficulty in rallying the Swedish Prime Minister, Göran Persson, and his European colleagues, to a very strong reaction, reaffirming that the Kyoto Protocol was not at all dead, and that the EU would intend to ratify and try to convince others to do the same. Personally, I am convinced that Larsson's strong convictions and intimate knowledge of the political process created confidence and saved the Protocol in a situation when many might have felt that the game was lost. Regrettably, Larsson died of cancer in late 2002, so he would not witness the entry into force of the Protocol in 2005.

CONCLUDING COMMENTS

In the previous pages I have tried to integrate concepts and practice in order to illustrate one particularly important point in my reasoning about the new diplomacy for sustainable development: that efficient international action requires different sets of enabling conditions at the national level, since everybody is affected both by anthropogenic global change and by measures to soften the impact of such change. International negotiations require support in national capitals, both with regard to instructions for the meetings, but also in defining the conditions for carrying out international agreements in the real world.

This chapter has mainly aimed at clarifying elements of domestic processes by looking at them from different angles. No doubt future research will be able to integrate these ideas in a more sophisticated way. At this stage, I have mainly wished to demonstrate that there is a whole network of complicated linkages between on the one hand human, social, economic, and political developments on the ground and on the other the international arena for negotiations on sustainable development. This interface is also part of a rapidly changing reality. All these elements have to be taken into account as we look towards future negotiations and reflect on the prospects for success over the period of the next decades in the final chapter of this book.

7 The New Diplomacy at Work
The Next Decades

The quest for global sustainability is built upon the realization that the world has entered a new era, the Anthropocene. For the first time in history, humans have the capacity to impact on the whole global natural system; and this has led to changed conditions for international relations, the new diplomacy for sustainable development. But we have also seen that the instruments and processes for international relations, in terms of both bilateral and multilateral diplomacy, basically remain the same. This is not surprising in itself, since diplomacy, based on the notion of state sovereignty, is a conservative trade. However, the previously observed mismatch between sweeping general statements and the tiresome haggling over detailed texts is widened by the absence of bold thinking at the global level.[1]

As we look towards the perspectives of the new diplomacy for the next decades, stretching to 2025 and beyond, there are a number of general aspects which are fundamental to the understanding of the potential for change, and consequently for the prospects of success in the many difficult negotiations that lie ahead. Our approach needs to be guided by some background ideas, which I will set out initially. I will then discuss the present situation and the medium to long term perspectives in some of the key areas of negotiation, both with regard to the normative work of the United Nations and in relation to the Rio Conventions. No doubt important progress will be needed, and will also happen. But it is doubtful whether gradual change will be sufficient in international institutions and processes; more radical reforms will probably be necessary. These will be reviewed in the concluding section of the chapter.

SOME BACKGROUND IDEAS

My thinking on these issues is of course guided by my own experiences as a negotiator. I realize that we are dealing with heavy systems, which are not easy to change. Therefore it is important to be *realistic* and try to avoid formulas or reform suggestions which are clearly outside the realm of the politically possible. With regard to the United Nations, most observers seem to agree that any suggestion that would lead to amending the Charter, would be unrealistic. Recent discussions about a reform of the composition of the Security Council seem to confirm this. However, realism clearly contains an element of timing. Things that were impossible yesterday might seem perfectly feasible tomorrow.

Therefore, I believe that we need a *realistic* and gradual approach. It is necessary to have a clear picture of where we want to go, both in negotiations and in crafting proposals for reforms of the system. But circumstances are changing, and there is no single blueprint that would lead to the desired result. Experience has shown that a staged approach is often helpful, setting clearly defined goals for specific target dates. We must also aim at a high degree of rationality and make sure that ideas can be turned into reality.

We also need to be *coherent*: the international system is very complicated, and ill conceived solutions in different areas might end up neutralizing instead of supporting each other.

These points are warning signals to would-be reformers: don't dream up ideas that would not have a chance to work in the real world. But they are not a call for avoiding *boldness*. We are dealing with new types of problems, and they may not be possible to solve in the old way. That is why I believe that the concepts I have discussed in previous chapters could serve as a background for efforts to create new frameworks for international cooperation which would permit negotiations to be run in a different spirit than in traditional diplomacy, and to negotiate in a different atmosphere. Visions can turn into reality, and the global and long-term character of the challenges facing us should make us all open to new ideas and approaches. But we must not underestimate the obstacles, the strength of established ideas, and the continuing importance of classical security policy in relations between states, or the new concerns related to terrorism. All this captures the front pages of our newspapers and makes it more difficult to rally support for the long-term and the global, even if those issues relate to something as important as the long term survival of our species.

These remarks reflect the dilemma of a negotiator turned academic, who tries to merge his own experience with the many theories around the various subjects touched upon in this book. The field of study is immense; and I have become more and more convinced that we need to look at the problems of global sustainability both from the angle of theory and in the perspective of practice, and practicability. Therefore, we should all welcome the present efforts to bring academia and policy-making together, sometimes referred to as the science/policy interface. I can foresee vast fields of study in this direction over the next decades; and it is in this spirit that I have written this book, hoping that it can stimulate more detailed and sophisticated analysis of the problematic I have described.

THE NORMATIVE WORK IN THE UN: THE MILLENNIUM
GOALS AND THE JOHANNESBURG FOLLOW-UP

For the United Nations, the normative work is an essential task. The General Assembly has an important role not only as a forum for discussion, but also for deciding on important principles, which will serve as norms for policies of governments. The resolutions and decisions by the General Assembly are not legally binding, and are not submitted to national parliaments for ratification. But they represent a body of international consensus that influences the policies of governments and helps modifying national enabling conditions. United Nations Associations in different countries helps spreading UN influence at the grass-root level.

In the perspective of the new diplomacy, the 1972 Stockholm Conference on the Human Environment launched new thinking and had a considerable impact on policies in capitals both domestically and in the international arena, as previous chapters have shown. Within the UN system, it led to the creation of UNEP, the United Nations Environment Programme. The 1992 Rio Conference on Environment and Development had a broader scope and gave substance to the notion of sustainable development. Nevertheless, many developing countries still had misgivings about the concept, and this was reflected in the UN, when the then Secretary-General, Boutros Boutros Ghali, launched an Agenda for Development, even though the Rio Conference had agreed on Agenda 21, an Agenda for Sustainable Development.

This divide has been bridged by now, but there are still some remnants, illustrating that the combat of poverty, and issues related to development are traditional UN issues, very much a part of multilateral diplomacy, whereas global environmental threats are still from time to time seen as something apart.

The first years of the twenty-first century were a period of intense activity in the normative work of the United Nations. In 2000, a special high-level session of the General Assembly was held in New York. It was a splendid occasion with a great number of heads of state and government assembled to issue a Millennium Declaration and to decide on the UN Millennium Development Goals (MDG). All member countries of the UN pledged to meet these goals by 2015; even if progress is uneven, this major effort of giving substance to UN normative work will play an important role during the first decades of the century. It is worth recalling the Millennium Development Goals:

1. *Eradicate extreme hunger and poverty.* There should be a reduction by half the proportion of people who live on less than one dollar a day; and a similar reduction by the proportion of people who suffer from hunger.
2. *Achieve universal primary education.* All boys and girls should complete a full course of primary schooling.

3. *Promote gender equality and empower women.* Gender disparity in primary and secondary education should be eliminated preferably by 2005 and at all levels by 2015.
4. *Reduce child mortality.* The mortality rate among children under five should be reduced by two thirds.
5. *Improve maternal health.* The maternal mortality ratio should be reduced by three quarters.
6. *Combat HIV/AIDS, malaria and other diseases.* The spread of HIV/AIDS as well as the incidence of malaria and other major diseases should be halted and reversed.
7. *Ensure environmental sustainability.* The principles of sustainable development into country policies and programs should be integrated, and the loss of environmental resources should be reversed. There should be a reduction by half of the proportion of people without sustainable access to drinking water. Furthermore there should be a significant improvement in the lives of at least 100 million slum dwellers by 2020.[2]
8. *Develop a global partnership for development.* The components of this goal refer to the need for an open and rule-based trading and financial system, the problems of least developed countries, the special needs of land-locked and small island developing states, the debt problems of developing countries, employment of young people, access to affordable essential drugs in developing countries, and transfer of technology.

As the Special Session of the General Assembly was held in September 2000, preparations for a decision to hold a World Summit on Sustainable Development (WSSD) in Johannesburg in September 2002, were already under way.[3] In the preparatory work for WSSD it was made clear that the Conference would not try to renegotiate Agenda 21, but aim at improving its implementation. With the adoption of the Millennium Development Goals, another important objective became the completion of the MDGs with the inclusion of more precise goals of an environmental nature. Several of these were controversial in a north-south perspective, but developments in the crucial fields of trade and finance outside the preparatory process were helpful: in 2001 a new round of trade negotiations with special attention to developing countries was launched in Doha, and in 2002 the Monterrey consensus on financial issues was adopted.[4]

Even so the Johannesburg, negotiations were not easy, in particular with regard to many subjects related to gender and women's rights. However, there was progress on a number of environmental issues:

- measures should be taken within the framework of integrated water resource management, with a planning target of 2005;
- new measures to ensure the implementation of the Convention on Biological Diversity and reduce losses of biodiversity until 2010;

- supplement the prescriptions on water in MDG with an effort to reduce by half the proportion of people without sustainable sanitation by 2015;
- restoration of threatened fish stocks, if possible by 2015;
- action to ensure that environment and health effects of the production and use of chemicals will be minimized by 2020.

The Johannesburg Conference also adopted a political declaration, which was rather pale in comparison with the Rio Declaration or the introductory part of Agenda 21. The institutional section, on the contrary, was substantial; in particular it opened the way for important change in the functioning of the Commission on Sustainable Development (CSD). I will revert to institutional questions in the concluding part of this chapter.

I believe that the results of WSSD were relatively satisfactory in the light of the international situation at the time. No doubt, September 11, 2001, and the war on terrorism had created a new tension in world politics, further accentuated by the negative attitude to multilateral cooperation of the US administration. This contrasted rather sharply with the mood in Rio de Janeiro in 1992. Personally, I do not think that it would have been possible to negotiate such a detailed and forward-looking document as Agenda 21 in 2002.

Under all circumstances, the WSSD allowed UN action on sustainable development to continue; and it meant a strengthening of the concept of environmental sustainability in relation to the vague wording of Millennium Development Goal nr 7. Nevertheless, discussions around these issues as heads of state and government reconvened in New York in September 2005 to consider issues related to UN reform, showed that the effective merger of the three components of sustainable development was not yet assured.

In fact, the Secretary-General's High-Level Panel on Threats, Challenges and Change, chaired by the former Prime Minister of Thailand, Anand Panyarachun, which gave an important input to the process leading up to the 2005 Summit, concentrated on traditional security issues, such as use of force, peace-building and prevention. In addition it raised central issues of UN reform, in particular on the composition of the Security Council. However, it underlined the links between the various threats and provided "a bold new vision of collective security for the twenty-first century. We live in a world of new and evolving threats, threats that could not have been anticipated when the UN was founded in 1945 — threats like nuclear terrorism, and State collapse from the witch's brew of poverty, disease and civil war."[5] But it would have been logical to include environmental disaster in the witch's brew.

The Secretary-General's own report to the General Assembly, largely based on the High-Level Panel's report, published in March 2005, gave more place to the environmental threats, but these references were weakened in the long-drawn preparatory negotiations for the summit. These were tense and difficult, not least because of north-south conflicts, but also due to the generally negative attitude of the United States to the UN in this particular period. Questions of UN reform came to the forefront, mainly because of the very controversial issue of an enlargement of the Security Council. A few days before the Summit, it seemed possible that it would end in total failure.

However, as is normally the case, the dynamics of a negotiation of this kind, particularly when it involves 160 heads of state and government — the largest summit gathering in the history of the United Nations — led to an outcome which was reasonably successful, though this one could only be achieved through a postponement of any decision on the Security Council. But there were other important reforms, notably the creation of a new Peace-building Commission and a Human Rights Council. Furthermore important progress was made on disaster relief financing, on special support for Africa, and on the confirmation of the Millennium Development Goals.[6] Ambassador Jan Eliasson of Sweden, the Chairman of the General Assembly 2005–2006 and later to become Foreign Minister of Sweden, has stated that "it was a miracle that we could achieve so much,"[7] though on the same occasion he recognized that the UN is in a rather difficult phase.

Obviously, he referred to the many crises of different kinds which have affected the confidence in the United Nations in recent years, particularly the Iraq Oil for food program. It is somewhat surprising in this situation that the UN advances so cautiously on issues related to global environmental change, and more generally in areas which are part of the new diplomacy, since an increasing number of people recognize that these eminently global problems can only be tackled successfully in a truly global framework, namely the United Nations. One can only conclude that traditional diplomatic thinking still prevails in governments and in particular in Ministries of Foreign Affairs.

The 2005 World Summit Outcome certainly mentions sustainability issues, but in a rather convoluted way, as in the initial section on "Values and Principles," which states in paragraph 10: "We reaffirm that development is a central goal in itself and that sustainable development in its economic, social and environmental aspects constitutes a key element of the overarching framework of United Nations activities," followed by paragraph 11: "We acknowledge that good governance and the rule of law at the national and international levels are essential for sustained economic growth, sustainable development and the eradication of poverty and hunger."

It is true that the section on "Global partnership for development" contains an opening paragraph 20, which states "We reaffirm our commitment to the global partnership for development set out in the Millennium Declaration, the Monterrey Consensus and the Johannesburg Plan of Implementation." And later on comes a section entirely devoted to "Sustainable development: managing and protecting our common environment," which reaffirms the commitment to achieve the goal of sustainable development, referring to the implementation of Agenda 21 and the Johannesburg Plan of Implementation. But the contents of the section are mainly a list of the issues treated in various negotiations on the subject of sustainable development without any new ideas or proposals. The only subject given a more extensive treatment is climate change, but here the US refusal to ratify the Kyoto Protocol is reflected in language like "We emphasize the need to meet all the commitments and obligations we have undertaken in the United Nations Framework Convention on Climate Change and other relevant international agreements, including, for many of us, the Kyoto Protocol. The Convention is the appropriate framework for addressing future action on climate change at the global level." Since 157 countries and the European Union have now ratified the Kyoto Protocol (not just "many of us) and continuing negotiations will have to be based both on the Convention and the Kyoto Protocol, this rather awkward language reflects heavy US pressure and, possibly, a certain lack of climate experts in the negotiation.

These examples show that global sustainability remains outside the traditional concerns of the central political institutions of the United Nations. On the contrary, several of the specialized agencies and programs are increasingly influenced by the notion of world-wide sustainable development. And in the centre, the Commission on Sustainable Development (CSD), which was created by the Rio Conference, tries to develop more efficient methods of work and structural improvements, based on recommendations of the Johannesburg Conference to strengthen the position of the CSD. In particular, new efforts have been made to promote efficient discussion at the ministerial level and to create new forms for participation of corporate actors. Most importantly, the CSD now works with central clusters of problems on a bi-annual basis: year one the Commission holds general discussions on the cluster, and year two, practical conclusions are drawn for continuing work in the UN structure. The first bi-annual subject was water and sanitation, which led to some practical recommendations; and a second cluster — beginning in 2006 — deals with energy and climate. Successful results of this central discussion will certainly enhance the standing of the CSD; and may contribute to make it a central institution for global sustainability in the UN. However, it formally remains a subsidiary body of the ECOSOC, and we are far from the proposals of the so-called Carlsson-Ramphal Commission, which in its 1995 report[8] suggested that the Trusteeship Council, one of the original main bodies of the United Nations, should be given the new task of trusteeship for the global commons.

BETWEEN NORMS AND PRACTICE: UNITED NATIONS ENVIRONMENT PROGRAMME (UNEP)

One of the main results of the 1972 Stockholm Conference on the Human Environment was the establishment of UNEP, with Headquarters in

Nairobi, and with Maurice Strong as its first Director-General, later to be succeeded by Mustafa Tolba. According to its mandate, UNEP would be the Environment Protection Agency of the world, with a broad mandate but with rather limited funds at its disposal. The general idea was that UNEP should be a catalyst, promote international cooperation and propose environmental policies. It should also coordinate UN action on environment and monitor implementation; in this context follow the evolution of the world's environment and take initiatives for action by governments. Particular attention should be given to international scientific developments and to the support of developing countries.

On the whole, it seems that UNEP has lived up to its mandate rather well, but its limited resources and its location in Nairobi has made it difficult for the program to effectively perform its coordination role in the United Nations. Nevertheless, important initiatives have originated in UNEP: the severe Sahel drought in the 1970s led Tolba to launch the Plan of Action against desertification; and he also played an essential role in the negotiation of the Vienna Convention and the Montreal Protocol on ozone depleting substances. He was also instrumental in setting up the IPCC as a joint initiative between UNEP and the World Meteorological Organization (WMO).

The Rio Conference and the creation of CSD changed the institutional position of UNEP in the UN system, and it took some time for the program to find its place in the new landscape. Tolba's successor, Elizabeth Dowdeswell of Canada, had a rather ungrateful task of adapting to this new situation, but she managed it well, and with the former German Environment Minister Klaus Töpfer as Executive Director, UNEP created a new platform as the main international defender of the environment component of sustainable development. The program has played an instrumental role in launching negotiations on chemicals, which has led to the adoption of the Stockholm Convention on persistent organic pollutants (POPs) in 2001 and important work on an international chemicals strategy. Similarly, UNEP plays a leading role in informing about the world's environmental situation, in promoting cooperation with NGO's, and in mobilizing public opinion, not least in environmental and human disasters, such as the devastating Tsunami in 2004. Building on an initiative already launched by Tolba, Klaus Töpfer has also firmly established the Global Ministerial Environment Forum as an essential venue for Ministers of Environment to discuss policies in an informal way.

Various efforts have been made to strengthen the coordinating role of UNEP within the UN system, but these have had very limited results: the resources of UNEP are too small to play that role in a complicated system with several strong actors such as the FAO, the WTO, the Bretton Woods institutions (IMF, World Bank), or the new Convention Secretariats. There have therefore been proposals (among others by France) to upgrade UNEP to a specialized agency, a World Environment Organization. These initiatives have not led to concrete results, and at least for the next decade or so it seems doubtful whether such a change would occur: it makes no sense just to change the name, and therefore a meaningful strengthening of UNEP's coordinating capacity could only be part of a more general overhaul of UN environmental activities. However, the discussion continues.

LEGALLY BINDING AGREEMENTS: THE RIO CONVENTIONS

Strictly speaking, the Rio Conventions are just three: the Framework Convention on Climate Change, the Convention on Biological Diversity, and the Convention to combat Desertification. The first two were negotiated in parallel with Agenda 21, and the third one was launched in Agenda 21 and concluded two years after the Rio Conference. Closely linked to these Conventions is the Vienna Convention for the Protection of the Ozone Layer (1985), with the Montreal Protocol on Substances that deplete the Ozone Layer (1987). These instruments are also tackling global problems and may in many ways be seen as precursors of the Rio Conventions. There are, of course, a number of other important environmental agreements, which are of a global nature; in this chapter I will briefly refer to them, but the main attention will be given to the Rio Conventions, and in particular to the Convention on Climate Change. The main reason for this is that in looking towards the next decades, climate change raises so many central questions about the capacity of international cooperation to effectively tackle a global survival issue. Furthermore, climate change will influence other global environmental issues, such as desertification, water and forestry, as well as the future of our societies. It is the arch-type of a global environmental threat.

Two further general comments need to be made on the Conventions. One relates to the notion of "legally binding": it is true that the Conventions are legally binding in the sense that they must be compatible with national legislation in the countries Parties to the instrument. Therefore they generally need to obtain the consent of Parliaments before they are ratified. However, the Rio Conventions are to a large extent to be considered "process conventions," with a limited number of precise commitments but with procedures and institutions designed to strengthen the instruments in the future. Therefore the analysis of the prospects for coming years becomes so important for the Parties, and it underlines the need for close contacts between researchers and policy agents.

The background to the second general comment is my view that the normative work of the UN on sustainable development within the General Assembly framework will have limited concrete results over the next ten to twenty years. On the contrary, it seems that progress in the Conventions may well be substantial, certainly not in all respects, but in some key areas.

If this happens, there will be spill-over effects of different kinds, also of a more general nature. Therefore, I see the legally binding instruments as the most important arena for the new diplomacy in the short to medium term.

THE CLIMATE ISSUE

The background

Global change has many components, one of them being climate change. But there is no more pervasive concept of global change than the impact of humans on climate. Emissions of greenhouse gases go straight into a common atmosphere without borders. And this atmosphere can be observed from space and distinguishes the earth from other planets. Anyone who sees those first images of our planet that were taken by astronauts from the vicinity of the moon cannot avoid being impressed and moved: this is our home in space, and "it is small and blue and beautiful" as one of the first men on the moon stated. It was not surprising that these images had a forceful impact on all of us at the time and helped shape a new way of looking at things: the first landing on the moon took place in 1969, and influenced the radical generation of the late sixties. The world was definitely different, floating in dark space with its thin layer of blue atmosphere as the precondition for life. Environmental movements certainly gained strength from these photographs.

However, this was not yet the time of climate politics: global warming was not on the political agenda, even if some scientists had started to worry about the problem. It was not an issue at the Stockholm Conference in 1972. But the first oil shock just a few months later with the rise in oil prices, and the concern about supplies, brought home to the western world the vulnerability of a civilization addicted to oil. It was a time of restrictions in driving automobiles, of energy-saving and of search for new sources of energy. Even in the United States smaller cars started to appear on the market. In Paris, the North-South Dialogue saw a new spirit of accommodation among Western negotiators with Henry Kissinger in the lead.

But the wave of fear subsided as oil distribution systems became more efficient, as OPEC solidarity wavered, and as new oil fields came into production. A new price hike in the early eighties did not change the overall attitudes; and then came the "reverse oil shock" in 1986, when the price of oil collapsed, changing the economic situation of OPEC countries and opening an era of non-inflationary growth in the western world. Twenty years later, with climate change a major concern, we may regret that promising developments on renewables were crushed by cheap oil.

Today, the political concerns about oil supplies remain, and the price has risen to new levels; but the debate has a different tone. It has become more directed towards the long term: the question of oil production peak-ing in one or two decades has opened a lively discussion about possible substitutes; and the question of climate change has definitely entered world politics through the main door. A new sense of urgency is felt in the discussion. New scientific evidence seems to confirm the risks of global warming, images of melting glaciers and disastrous droughts and storms increase the concern that human impact on the global climate system can have serious consequences. The voices that question the existence of global warming are becoming weaker; and the Stern Review, published in November 2006, has opened a new discussion about the economic rationality of action to counter climate change.

The risks connected to climate change are now definitely on the national and international political agendas. At this time, the negotiations on climate change constitute the strongest driving force in the new diplomacy for sustainable development; and they respond to all the criteria outlined in Chapter 3. The process of climate negotiations that started in Westlands outside Washington in February 1991 reached a new platform with the entry into force of the Kyoto Protocol on February 16, 2005 and the adoption of its rules of implementation at the first Conference of the Parties of the Convention serving as the meeting of the Parties of the Protocol (COP/MOP 1) in Montreal in December 2005. Furthermore, that Conference of Parties effectively launched intergovernmental talks on the future of the Climate Convention, including commitments after 2012, when the first commitment period of the Kyoto Protocol expires. Intensive talks are now going on at different levels to tackle the many intricate problems that have to be solved to launch real negotiations for a new climate regime. At the time of writing, it seems clearly possible that COP 13 in Indonesia in December 2007, would agree on a road map for this process. The post-Kyoto system will have to lead to very substantive reductions of global emissions over the next decades, while at the same time supporting considerable needs for adaptation measures and disaster management, in particular in the developing countries. A new phase begins for the new diplomacy; and events in the climate negotiations will have impacts elsewhere in the system.

In fact, climate change politics illustrate well both the different components of the diplomacy for sustainable development, and its relationship to traditional diplomacy. I will therefore comment in some detail on the perspectives for these negotiations, bearing in mind that there is still genuine uncertainty about the course of events over the next years. This is a time when governments, researchers, and other stakeholders need to show imagination and flexibility in laying out the road map for future negotiations. Here I wish to concentrate on the central features in discussing the future of climate change politics and policies, recognizing the risk of being corrected by events.

The strengthening evidence of climate change has created a near unanimity among political leaders that the problem has to be taken seriously. The year 2005 saw the Group of the eight most industrialized countries bring the issue to their Summit in Gleneagles in Scotland, with UK Prime

Minister Tony Blair as a leading force. Certainly, he did not bring his US colleague George W. Bush to change his views on the climate issues, but at least he came around to recognize the problem. At the G-8 Summit in Germany in June 2007, President Bush went further, agreeing to participate in concrete talks about the post-2012 regime. And leaders of China, India and South Africa were also invited to part of the meeting in Scotland to discuss the future of climate negotiations. The results of the Montreal Conference of Parties showed that there is now a consensus to move forward with preparatory talks on the post-2012 regime: this means that the period up to 2009–2012 will be decisive for developments in the crucial next decades. They are crucial, because the earlier real reductions of greenhouse gases begin, the better are the prospects for achieving by 2050 to 2100 the objective of Article 2 of the Convention, which is to stabilize "greenhouse gas concentrations at a level that would prevent dangerous anthropogenic interference with the climate system."

It should be noted that the European Union has agreed to define that level of temperature increase at 2 degrees Celsius by the end of this century, taking the year 1900 as a point of reference. The EU discussion has led to diverging views about the concentration of greenhouse gases, measured in CO_2 equivalents that would correspond to the 2 degrees target. The present calculation is that 550 parts per million (ppm) CO_2 equivalents would be acceptable, but many would maintain that this is too much, and that 450 ppm would be a minimum. (The present level of CO_2 alone is 380 ppm.)

Given the fact that developing countries, in particular the fast-growing economies of China, India and Brazil, are now beginning to be big emitters of greenhouse gases, but according to the principle of common but differentiated responsibilities cannot be expected to take on similar commitments as present Annex I countries, the long-term targets for today's developed countries have to be very ambitious. In the EU discussion, the reduction levels by 2050 have been set at 60–80%, compared to 1990. It has also been pointed out that significant reductions should be made early in the process, for the EU a minimum of 20% by 2020.

It is at present extremely difficult to forecast what new data will emerge, as this combination of a political and scientific discussion continues, and many different new ideas emerge. The IPCC Fourth Assessment Report, issued in 2007, is bound to strongly influence the negotiations for the post-2012 regime.

The broad outline for the preparation of these negotiations was agreed in Montreal. This result was rightly welcomed; but progress on substance was limited. As the process moves on, it is a race with time; and we do not know how much time there is, since we are up against so many unknown factors in the incredibly large global climate system. However, both in the meeting rooms and in the corridors of the Palais des Congrès in Montreal there was a sense of new urgency among delegates and observers. Science is becoming more precise, the public is beginning to be genuinely worried.

In this spirit, there was rather easy agreement on the final implementation of the Kyoto Protocol, which entered into force on February 16, 2005. Only four years earlier, in the spring of 2001, the Protocol seemed moribund, as negotiations for detailed implementation rules had broken down in COP 6 in the Hague in late 2000, and as the new Bush administration in the US had stated that they would not ratify the Protocol: since one of the requirements for entry into force was that developed countries representing at least 55% of Annex I CO_2 emissions in 1990 would have ratified and that the United States at that time represented 36.1% of the total, the margin was very small. High-level representatives of the US government declared without hesitation that the Kyoto Protocol was dead. But the European Union stated unambiguously that the EU countries would ratify, and that they would do everything possible to convince other Annex I countries to ratify as well.

This was a tough challenge, but many countries accepted the EU argument that the Kyoto Protocol was "the only shop in town" and that a breakdown of the Protocol would threaten the Convention itself. Intense travel diplomacy was immediately initiated by the Swedish EU Presidency, and a first success was the decision of Japan to ratify; several other countries, including Canada, Norway and Switzerland, also followed the EU lead. But Russia wavered, and without Russia (17.4% of total Annex I emissions in 1990) the Protocol could not enter into force. Finally, President Putin took the decision in the autumn of 2004; the Protocol was saved.

In the meantime, the rest of the world had acted on the principle "as if": negotiations continued as if there was certainty that the Protocol would become a reality. Already in the summer of 2001 a resumed session of COP 6 had led to a basic agreement on implementation rules for the Protocol, and this was put into legal form at COP 7 in Marrakech in December 2001. However, everything was put on hold pending the entry into force of the Protocol, and therefore the formal decisions in Montreal were so important.

The road is now open for all the different provisions of the Kyoto Protocol to be implemented fully. Everybody recognizes that the commitments of the Protocol are not enough to stop global warming; but there is now a solid legal ground for action. This is the most concrete example so far of the capacity of the new diplomacy to tackle a major global problem through precise legally binding rules. Therefore, development within the Kyoto Protocol will have a major impact on the capacity of the international community to move forward on the major issue of climate change. The legal framework is in order; now it is up to governments to demonstrate that they can use it in a loyal and efficient way.

This is not a case of brilliant action in the limelight. The Parties will have to live up to detailed provisions on reporting and go through many dreary sessions at home and internationally on how to calculate forest sinks, how to manage the details of the Clean Development Mechanism, or to support the accounting details of emissions trading. And many questions will be asked about the capacity of the system to reconcile the logic of the market with the logic of government policy making. But it is in this day-to-day work that the fundaments of the climate regime for the next two or three decades will be crafted.

We will see a slow and laborious birth of the climate regime that after 2012 will help the world develop the forceful response measures that will enable mankind to meet a global threat of a new kind, and to adapt to the inevitable consequences of already occurring climate change. This will be "a twilight struggle" like the one President Kennedy once referred to in a different context, which will be carried out in a world which will continue to be torn by all the other conflicts, economic, social, religious, and political, that exist in our truly globalized system. And, above all, it will have to be waged in parallel with the combat of poverty, the continuous battle for human dignity and justice.

THE LONG-TERM CLIMATE REGIME

The procedure of preparations for the future regime laid out in Montreal in 2005 is not a very detailed or easily readable proposal. It is a process which reflects traditional and strongly held concerns by governments, as they try to reconcile their national positions with the overriding ambition to tackle climate change.

Since both the US government and the governments of major developing countries have strongly held positions on this future regime, an effort has had to be made to launch methods of negotiation which would give time for careful informal consultations and avoid accelerations that would risk a breakdown of the process. At the same time, ideas for the contents of the future regime will have to accommodate the various concerns of all involved.

In Montreal, decisions were taken on the process, which started in the spring of 2006. Annex I Parties will negotiate within the framework of Article 3.9 of the Kyoto Protocol, in an open-ended ad-hoc group. The United States, being outside the Kyoto Protocol, is not part of any Article 3.9 process, and therefore a broader-based structure has been envisaged for a more general discussion of post-2012, based mainly on the Framework Convention itself. The dialogue will take place in work-shops with two co-chairmen, one from the north and one from the south. The Conference of Parties in the autumn of 2007, to be held in Indonesia, will continue the preparatory work and hopefully establish timetable and modalities for negotiations. However already COP 12 in Nairobi in 2006 could agree on a procedure based on Article 9 of the Kyoto Protocol, dealing with a review of the Protocol, that could have great importance for the future regime. This issue will probably be a major item on the agenda of COP 14 in late 2008. So the procedure is launched, but in order to tackle the many difficult political and economic issues related to the future regime, informal consultations at many levels will multiply over the coming years.

The academic community and the NGOs have already for quite some time made suggestions on the contents of the new regime. The overriding concern is that it has to be universal; no major countries can be outside, since climate change is a truly global issue. With the positions taken by on the one hand the United States, and on the other major developing countries like China and India, most of the ideas turn around some kind of regime with differentiated commitments. In the following section personal suggestions are outlined as an illustration of what this regime, carrying us well into the 2020s, could look like.

There has to be both continuity and innovation. Continuity, because all actors, not least in the business sector, have to see that existing mechanisms, such as emissions trading, and the Clean Development Mechanism, are stable and offer long-term security. Innovation, because the existing regime is not flexible enough to accommodate all the different interests involved. However, if one opts for a differentiated approach, there also has to be a central structure, providing coordination and political cohesion.

This central structure would provide both for political support, possibly in the form of a joint declaration or statement by the Parties, and a common basis for institutions, procedures, reporting, capacity-building, and compliance rules. The exact form for these functions would obviously have to be decided as a result of negotiations.

As for the operative parts of the regime, many observers, including the author, would suggest that the following building blocks be included:

- a "Kyoto bis" component, for present and future Annex I Parties:
- a scheme for "new style commitments/objectives," designed for developing countries;
- an agreement on adaptation measures; and possibly,
- an investment, and technology, facilitation scheme.

The "Kyoto bis" structure would build on present Annex I commitments, covering a period up to 2020, with indicative numbers for a longer time span. An important issue is the choice of base year; it is certainly open to discussion how long 1990 could serve as the base year for commitments stretching quite far into the future. In my view, the United States must be part of this scheme, on an equal footing with other Annex I participants, otherwise no agreement would be credible. Obviously, the quantified commitments must be differentiated, as in present Annex B. Also, present rules on the mechanisms and on sinks would have to be carried forward, duly amended and improved as more experience has been gained. Furthermore, sectors presently exempt from reduction targets, such as aviation or shipping, need to be included.

The market-based mechanisms (joint implementation, the clean development mechanism and emissions-trading) are essential components of the new climate regime. Producing companies with their technological ability, the whole service sector, and not least the world of finance, needs to be fully engaged in the effort to reduce emissions. Governments alone can only create the global framework; action will never be efficient enough without the participation of the corporate sector. And increasingly we can now see that major companies in all sectors are facing up to their responsibilities in this respect.

The "new style objectives/commitments" will be an essential but controversial building block in the edifice. Here, negotiators will have to deal with the so far absolute refusal of major countries in the south, with China and India as the leaders, to even consider any quantified commitments. On the other hand, these giants, covering more than a third of the world population, are very big emitters of greenhouse gases, and even applying theories like the contraction/convergence scheme it would seem very unlikely that a deal could be struck not involving some kind of numerical indicators for China, India, Brazil, and possibly other fast-growing economies. In exploratory talks various ideas for such objectives/commitments have to be discussed: ideas on intensity targets (decoupling of energy use from economic growth), sector targets (energy, transports), relative targets (relative to economic growth) all have been mentioned in the literature. It would not be surprising if this part of the negotiation would be the most difficult and divisive.

Since climate change is already happening, adaptation is gaining increasing attention, both in developed and developing countries. However, it is in relation to the least developed countries and to small island states that the problems seem particularly urgent. It is also on this particular issue that the linkages to the other Rio Conventions are the most important. Both with regard to desertification and biological diversity, climate change will lead to specific consequences, which need to be tackled in an integrated and efficient way. Furthermore, the limited resources of these affected countries will mean that increased international funding will have to be an important part of any deal: expressions of solidarity are necessary if a post-2012 agreement would live up to reasonable requirements of fairness and justice. Disaster prevention and rapid action would also need to be part of the joint effort on adaptation. The discussion is still undecided in what form adaptation would be included in the post-2012 regime; ideas are floating around about a possible adaptation instrument or other form of specific agreement.

Finally, it is clear that technological development is the key to the future of climate change mitigation, particularly in the energy and transport sectors. Politically, the United States has maintained a constant position that more effort should go into technology cooperation, and even be an alternative to the Kyoto Protocol; at present the US has initiated technology cooperation in a multilateral form with a number of countries in Asia. It seems probable that a special global effort to facilitate technology development, transfer and management, hopefully supported by important funding for developing countries, would facilitate the conclusion of a long-term regime for climate change mitigation and adaptation. And once again, it is the corporate sector that will be drivers of necessary technological innovation.

CONCLUDING COMMENTS ON THE CLIMATE REGIME

The regime outlined here would ideally cover the period up to 2020, hopefully even longer. If the agreement would be good enough, it would mean that crucial decades of transition would enable the world to move into a more hopeful trajectory of greenhouse gas emissions. There are many "ifs" and question-marks as we reflect on the prospects for success in these endeavors. But it can hardly be questioned that climate change now is a central concern and an essential component in the overall international reaction to global change. Furthermore, it is linked to present concerns that world oil production might peak in the next decade or decades, and that oil supplies will wane later in the century. I have therefore felt that it was important to give particular attention to the climate issues facing us now and for the coming decades. A number of other important problems will now be reviewed.

DEPLETION OF THE OZONE LAYER, DESERTIFICATION AND BIOLOGICAL DIVERSITY

Many observers would agree that the Montreal Protocol on Substances that Deplete the Ozone Layer is a very important document and that in some respects it paved the way for the Rio Conventions. Furthermore, the particularly essential role of science in alerting the international community to a serious new threat has set a standard for other agreements. It is also a well documented negotiation,[9] and some scholars, such as Scott Barrett, consider the Montreal Protocol one of the best environmental treaties. It was also a document which clearly illustrated the role of the corporate sector: only as DuPont and other major producers of carbon fluorocarbons (CFCs) managed to develop substitute products could the negotiation really get under way.

The ozone depletion issue has of course also captured the imagination of the general public, with the concern about the regularly appearing "ozone hole" across polar regions and the corresponding need for protection against ultra-violet radiation. It has also brought home the tremendous inertia of the large atmospheric systems, with extremely long-term perspectives for a very slow recovery of the ozone layer. Neither in political nor economic terms, the implementation of the Montreal Protocol is seen as a major problem today. Obviously this does not mean that there are no difficulties in implementing the Protocol, not least related to north-south issues, but it seems that procedures are fairly well established.

There are also linkages to other problems related to the atmosphere. Researchers have shown that the depletion of the ozone layer has a tendency to increase global warming through its effects on clouds at very high altitudes. This is an example of the need for more research on the atmosphere from a systemic viewpoint. While it can be expected that the implementation of the Montreal Protocol will continue without major upheavals, the need for integration of various phenomena will remain a serious concern both for scientists and policy-makers. No doubt also linkages between long-range air pollution — an increasingly important problem world-wide — and climate, will need further consideration.

The issues related to the thin layer of the common global atmosphere are all linked to emissions control. As we turn our attention to *desertification* and *biological diversity* against the background of climate change we are faced with the effects of climate change on terrestrial ecosystems. It is the other side of the climate issue: the importance of adaptation to a global climate that is already changing. At the same time, climate change is just one of several factors influencing the situation of the dry-lands, or the perspectives for safeguarding biological diversity. But as we consider the prospects for the future of the Convention on Biological Diversity, and the Convention to combat Desertification, we should keep in mind the central role of climate and the need for an integrated understanding of these various phenomena.

The safeguard of *biological diversity* has been one of the central issues in environmental policy for a long time, and it is likely to remain so. Rachel Carson's *Silent Spring* (1962) in many ways launched the modern environmental movement through its impact on public opinion, raising the concern of losses of species with incalculable consequences. NGOs have been able to raise protests against all sorts of interventions in nature as different species of birds, animals or plants would be threatened. Natural parks have been established to protect biodiversity. Nobody questions the need to take measures to avoid the disappearance of rare species; however doubts are sometimes raised about the need to protect *all* species: where should one draw the line?

For all these good reasons, it was natural that biological diversity would play an essential role in the Rio process, not only in terms of a special Chapter of Agenda 21 but also in the negotiation of the Convention on Biological Diversity (CBD). At the same time, some might have felt that these issues were part of a traditional way of looking at sustainability, with the central focus on the environment. It was not surprising that UNEP took a special responsibility for managing the negotiation and still provides secretariat services for the Convention Many people also felt that the Convention became too focused on principles and generalities, and that it lacked in precision and firm commitments.

However, there were also opposite trends arising out of the questions related to biotechnology, demonstrating that biodiversity was very much part of globalization, and that impacts could be more immediate than in the case of climate change. In particular, national rights of developing countries to benefit from their biological and genetic resources led to very difficult negotiations, and ultimately brought the United States to the point when they decided not to sign the Convention in Rio de Janeiro in 1992, whereas all other OECD countries joined the treaty, bringing the total number of signatories to 153.

Later developments showed that new research, and the increasing importance of the pharmaceutical industry world-wide, brought the issue of biodiversity to the forefront of trade policy attention. Negotiations were difficult, but progress was made, and in 2000 a new instrument was added to the Convention, the Cartagena Protocol on Biological Safety which has taken a number of practical initiatives.

As the relationship between environmental and trade policy is gaining more and more attention, the CBD and the Cartagena Protocol have increased in importance. The question of genetic resources has contributed to this, and guidelines for the management of genetic resources and the defense of the interests of developing countries have been adopted under the umbrella of the CBD. It is also noticeable that the WIPO (World Immaterial and Patents Organization) has established special processes on genetic resources.

The Convention on Biological Diversity is now a well established instrument, and the issues it deals with are high on the agenda both of governments and the corporate sector. Important economic interests are at stake, and several political-economic problems are raised in the negotiations; the United States has still not joined the Convention. No doubt, these issues will continue to be central to government concerns, and it is difficult to see exactly when and where particular sticking points will appear. It would seem a fair guess, however, that the safeguard of biological diversity as a global problem will be politically sensible and the subject of much attention by environmental NGOs over the next decades.

Desertification, and more generally the vast dry zones of the planet, has been treated very differently in the global negotiations. At the time of the Rio Conference, a UNEP-based Plan of Action had been in force since the 1970's, when it was launched to alleviate the effects of the disastrous drought in the Sahel, which had caused enormous human suffering. The Plan was an ambitious project, but its results were very limited; in Rio, the affected countries felt abandoned by the world community, and they accused the developed countries of failing to provide necessary financial resources.

The story of the Convention to combat Desertification has been told extensively in previous chapters. There have been many setbacks and difficulties, and several African countries have complained about what they perceive as flagging interest and commitment on the part of the industrialized countries. Nevertheless, since the first Conference of Parties in 1997 it is fair to say that progress has also been made. Through hard work by the Executive Secretary and his staff, the Secretariat has promoted the adoption of eighty-one national programs and the diffusion of several success stories, and a Committee of implementation — CRIC — has been established. The 2005 World Summit made a call for providing adequate and predictable financial resources for addressing desertification and land degradation. But the outcome of the 2005 Conference of Parties held after the summit, was disappointing. There is little confidence in the Secretariat among donors and distrust between north and south.

This was the situation, as 2006 was proclaimed the International Year of Deserts and Desertification. There are many reasons to be wary about the many international years or decades held over a long period of time. In my view, many of them have not changed much in the real world. But it is important that all efforts are made to take the opportunity offered by this particular manifestation: the struggle against poverty has been recognized as an overriding concern for the international community; food security needs to be assured; the situation of the least developed countries is given special attention; a number of international meetings in 2005 have recognized that the situation in Africa warrants particular concern in terms of financial support.

In the context of the Rio negotiations it was sometimes said that ozone, climate change, and biodiversity are "true" global problems, whereas desertification is more to be seen as "a problem of global significance." The distinction has merit, but the discussion about adaptation to climate change shows that, also in this context, regional or national circumstances are important. One particular feature of the Convention to combat desertification is the existence of regional implementation annexes, which are integral parts of the Convention. They cover Africa (the most detailed and elaborated one), Asia, Latin America, the northern Mediterranean, and East Europe. It is possible that a future instrument on adaptation to climate change could adopt some of this methodology to recognize the important differences between countries. Another aspect of the linkages between climate and desertification is more substantial however: according to climate research there are clear indications that global warming will generally lead to less precipitation in many of the regions which are already suffering from insufficient rainfall. This means that the problems that the Convention to combat desertification has set out to tackle will be magnified by climate change.

This exploration of synergies between the Rio Conventions may well turn out to be a significant part of the effort to tackle global change over the next decades. It would also hopefully open new avenues for the UNCCD, demonstrating that this Convention with its legally binding prescriptions may support the normative work of the General Assembly and special high-level meetings, as well as strengthening the work of FAO and WFP to ensure food security. There is an untapped potential here, waiting to be used, and the International Year of Deserts and Desertification should be used as a point of departure.

However, this is clearly a very difficult task. It will require a conscious and long-term effort to rebuild trust between the Parties to the Convention, and to explore the new situation within the other Rio Conventions, in particular climate change, to revitalize the UNCCD. Will the Conference of Parties be able to rise above the present difficulties and take a long-term view? At present a review group is at work to prepare proposals for reforms that would make the Convention more efficient in tackling future problems. I recognize that I have a special relationship to this Convention and that I may overestimate this potential. But I believe that it would be unwise not to try to explore the possibilities.

One important development in recent years has been the new international agreements on chemicals at the global and European levels. A number of chemicals that accumulate in humans and animals, the so-called persistent organic pollutants (POPs), including DDT, have been subject to special negotiations within the UNEP framework. This led to the adoption in 2001 of the Stockholm Convention, which has since entered into force. This was a major step forward, and it has been supplemented with the adoption of a special global strategy on chemicals. At the European level, the EU has adopted a special far-reaching program (REACH) for the control of a large number of chemicals, putting new obligations on producers with regard to proof of the non-toxicity of chemical products.

There are of course a number of other treaties that are of high relevance for global sustainability. Just to list a few not previously mentioned:

- International Convention for the regulation of Whaling: signed 1946, entered into force 1948;
- Antarctic Treaty, signed in 1959, entered into force 1961;
- Convention on Wetlands of International Importance, especially as Waterfowl Habitat, (RAMSAR), signed 1971, entered into force 1975;
- Convention on the Prevention of Marine Pollution by the Dumping of Wastes and Other Matter (London Dumping Convention), signed 1972, entered into force 1975;
- Convention on International Trade in Endangered Species (CITES), signed 1973, entered into force 1975;
- International Convention for the Prevention of Pollution from Ships (MARPOL), signed 1973, entered into force 1983;
- Convention on Long Range Transboundary Air Pollution (LRTAP) (Economic Commission of Europe), signed 1979, entered into force 1983;
- United Nations Convention on the Law of the Sea (UNCLOS), signed 1982, entered into force 1994;
- Convention on the Control of Transboundary Movements of Hazardous Wastes and their Disposal (Basel Convention), signed 1989, entered into force 1992.

This sample shows that the question of global sustainability has been on the agenda for a long time, even though the issue only came to the forefront in connection with the Stockholm Conference on the Human Environment in 1972. Since then, hundreds of agreements have been concluded at the regional level in various parts of the world, which together form a new body of law, and a subject for the new diplomacy.

As we look towards the future, it is striking that there are some central global issues for which global legally binding agreements have not been established. I refer to freshwater and forests, crucial areas for the survival of the human species, and closely linked to most of the other subjects and problems mentioned in this book; off and on there have been efforts made to fill this void, but they have never come very far.[10] And in my view, it is highly doubtful whether such instruments would be very productive, since there are already a number of established processes and structures which ensure that these broad areas are kept on the international agenda. The ever present risk of excessive bureaucratization at the international level could also militate against the negotiation of such treaties.

Thus, we can foresee that the existing International Forum on Forests within the UN framework will continue to play a central and increasingly important role in the continuing international discussions on the world's forest resources, and that the rules on carbon sinks in the Convention on Climate Change will give rise to many discussions about general aspects of forest management. Specialized regular Conferences on forestry will continue to link scientific and policy action, and the role of forests for livelihoods will be part of the increasing interest in the combat of poverty, linking environmental and social aspects.

These linkages are still more important in the case of water and sanitation: among the Millennium Development Goals the ambition of halving the number of people living in poverty, and the halving of the number of people without adequate water and sanitation, both in the perspective of 2015, are central to the success of the whole UN project. Over the next decade, therefore, the water issue will be high on the agenda for sustainable development. But the international community will have to make renewed efforts to explore the many linkages that exist between poverty, water, desertification, and climate. These different strands of approach come together in the many efforts that are now made to explore more in depth the concepts of resilience and vulnerability, which are central to our understanding of how social and environmental factors interact. It is also an area where research and policy-making need to develop closer interaction and a better understanding. Important developments are taking place in the many conferences on water that are now taking place very frequently, including the regular World Water Forums, and the annual Stockholm Water Week.

At the same time, it is essential to recognize that the international efforts on all these issues closely related to poverty can only create a framework: real improvements in the real world can only come about as a result of the efforts of the affected populations. The role of the international community is to provide these people with the tools and the right conditions for positive action at the local level. It is not surprising that the most recent World Water Forum, in Mexico City in March 2006, brought its main attention to local action. This approach can only be fully efficient, however, if the international community will be ready to support local schemes with finance and know-how without resorting to excessive control schemes requiring heavy bureaucratic support to be effective. In this context, it was significant that the great promoter of micro-finance schemes, Mohammed Younus of Bangladesh, was awarded the Nobel Prize for Peace in 2006.

- - - - - - - - - - - - - - -

The existence of the various legal instruments reviewed in this section represents an ever stronger framework of international law that supports the new diplomacy. The scope and the risks of the Anthropocene era is now generally recognized. I have no doubt that these legal instruments will continue to grow stronger, that they will be supplemented by others, and that their impact on international affairs will grow significantly over the next decades.

BOUNDARY CONDITIONS IN A GLOBALIZING WORLD: PERSPECTIVES ON TRADE AND FINANCE

In a previous chapter, I have commented on the importance of the economic and social structures created by the establishment of institutions to support increasing trade and financial flows in a global market economy in the post World War II period. There are signs that this system is coming under increasing strains as new actors appear on the stage and as the systems are becoming increasingly complex. Furthermore, the new concerns related to global environmental change and the corresponding developments of the new diplomacy tend to create new tensions in the operation of structures which were designed long before humanly induced global change became a political issue.

At the same time, problems related to trade and finance are of decisive importance for the functioning of the closely integrated global system. Over the coming decade(s) the tensions in these fields will therefore be an essential feature of international discussions. The Doha Round of trade negotiations in the WTO and the increasing pressure for reform of the Bretton Woods institutions — World Bank and IMF — demonstrate that institutional business as usual is not a viable option.

In the trade field, there is no future for traditional subsidies for agricultural production in developed countries, and there is already an agreement in principle that they should be scaled down. But the difficulties of the Doha Round show that that the timing of change is still controversial; and that domestic political pressures in many countries slow down the process.

Similarly, the question of competitiveness becomes a burning issue in many developed countries as rapidly industrializing low-cost countries such as India or China make rapid advances in production and services on world markets: particularly in European economies questions related to job loss and employment are now major political issues. And they will remain so for the foreseeable future.

The best answers to these dilemmas are still those of classical international economics with the theory of comparative advantage. As the emerging economies will benefit from the international division of labour, living standards will rise, demand will increase, and new equilibriums will appear in the international market place. But in a complicated real world with many time lags, structural imperfections, and glaring inequalities, political realities tend to obscure the rationality of trade theory.

The tremendous growth of the world's financial and monetary system has also created a new situation in the control mechanisms created after the Second World War through the Bretton Woods institutions. Today immense capital movements take place every day, and the capacity of the International Monetary Fund and major governments to manage the world financial system has been reduced. The volume of transactions means that the great financial centers have limited possibilities of reducing instabilities. The world has gone from a fixed rate exchange system to floating currencies and free capital flows. The Governor of the Bank of England, Mervyn King, has argued that as private capital flows now dwarf IMF resources and as Asian countries have built up huge foreign exchange reserves, the role of the Fund as lender of last resort has been diminished. Radical reform would therefore be called for.

Other observers have different views, and it seems unlikely that much would happen over the next years, but for coming decades it is difficult to see how IMF structures and priorities could remain untouched. Above all, the fundamental question of the role and influence of emerging powers such as China, India and Brazil, has to be addressed. In the IMF and the World Bank this means that the dominating position of the United States will be questioned.

A GLOBAL REFORM AGENDA

The remarks about reform of the monetary system beg the question of a broader reform agenda for an international system that was established sixty years ago in a radically different world: the five permanent members of the Security Council were the uncontested masters of the system, reconstruction after the devastating war was the main priority, a large part of the South was still under colonial rule, and the human impact on the earth system was not yet apparent. In concluding this book, I wish to briefly review and resume some of the central points that I find particularly relevant to our efforts of creating structures that reflect present and future realities. These are personal views, and they are a contribution to a discussion which I hope will ultimately lead to concrete results. The present world situation is not conducive to radical change in international institutions; and incremental reforms may be all that can be achieved in the short term. But I have no doubts that global environmental change and globalization will ultimately lead to the establishment of a more adequate multilateral system.

GLOBAL GOVERNANCE

As we move further into the twenty-first century, the United Nations continues to be the centerpiece of the world's multilateral governance structure. There is at present important discussions going on about reforming the UN, but the Summit in 2005 demonstrated the rather narrow limits to governments' willingness to consider radical reform. The proposed enlargement of the Security Council is a case in point. Here the suggestions of the Secretary-General aimed at achieving a balanced enlargement, permitting important states like Germany, Japan, India and Brazil, to gain permanent seats on the Council. However, this met with stubborn resistance on the part of the present permanent members of the Council. This is indeed a reflection of what has happened in discussions on IMF reform, or in recognizing the position of the emerging countries in the World Trade Organization. An unbiased observer must conclude, however, that the position of the traditionalists is impossible to defend in the longer run, if the UN, or other concerned institutions, would maintain their legitimacy and influence.

Previously, I have referred to the reform proposals of the Commission on Global Governance, co-chaired by Ingvar Carlsson, former Prime Minister of Sweden, and Sridath Ramphal, former Secretary-General of the Commonwealth. This commission presented its report, "Our Global Neighbourhood," in 1995, and many of the proposals before the 2005 UN Summit had their origins in this document. However, there were some proposals that never received proper attention, which continue to be of high relevance.[11]

In the perspective of global change and of the role of the new diplomacy, it seems necessary to strengthen the normative work of the United Nations on global sustainability issues. It is true that decisions at the World Summit on Sustainable Development in Johannesburg in 2002 and its follow-up, have improved the functioning of the Commission on Sustainable Development with thematic bi-annual work programs; but the requirements of the Anthropocene Era impose a higher political profile for these survival issues.

The Carlsson-Ramphal Commission proposed a totally new role for the Trusteeship Council, one of the UN's principal organs, namely a trusteeship for the global commons. In this role, the Trusteeship Council would obviously also exercise a trusteeship for unborn generations. The United

Nations would then have a new prestigious instrument for all these issues of global significance, to support the various conventions that deal with the subjects.

This proposed solution would not seem to be viable any longer. But the need for a high-level regular treatment of the normative issues of global change and environment will not go away. Can the Commission on Sustainable Development be further improved? This is open to doubt, since its formal status is just that of a subcommittee to ECOSOC, which is also one of the original principal organs of the UN. Carlsson-Ramphal proposed that the ECOSOC be abolished in its present form; this was a rational proposal, since there is at present a clear duplication of work between ECOSOC and the second and third Committees of the General Assembly. One possible solution could be to agree on a new mandate for ECOSOC and give it an enhanced role as the guardian of the global commons and future generations.

The increased role of civil society has been recognized as a special feature of the new diplomacy; the Carlsson-Ramphal Commission proposed that an annual Forum of Civil Society should be established. However, experience from the Rio process and the various Convention negotiations show that active NGO participation has developed in a constructive way within the boundaries of existing rules,[12] and it seems that this practice could be extended to ECOSOC in its new role. The need for a Forum of Civil Society could be further explored against the background of that experience.

Present discussions and negotiations on a UN reform package are anchored in the General Assembly, with the President of the Assembly playing a key role. Reform of the Secretariat is an important point on the agenda. But it has to be recognized that it is the political positions of member states that will ultimately decide whether the world will have a United Nations organization that can deliver the ambitions of the Charter. And in the perspective of this author there is no doubt that this effort will not succeed if it does not incorporate the concerns of the new diplomacy. The challenges of global change can only be met in the multilateral framework provided for by the United Nations. This point was strongly underlined by the former Secretary-General of the United Nations, Kofi Annan, in speeches before his departure from the UN at the end of 2006.

Natural disaster preparedness and management

Over recent years, the world's attention has increasingly been brought to the risks for natural disasters. Quite logically, the devastating tsunami in late 2004 and the earthquake in Pakistan in 2005 have been in focus, but also weather-related events have made public opinion aware of a risk profile that might be changing. In particular, the 2005 hurricane Katrina that struck New Orleans with tremendous effect, captured imagination.

The United Nations and its various agencies and programs play a central role in providing practical and humanitarian assistance; and they perform an admirable work. But even if climate change experts are still very careful in linking global warming to single events, such as Katrina, they admit that human impact on the global weather system leading to a warmer atmosphere and warmer oceans are likely to lead to stronger tropical storms and other disturbances in the sensitive system. Seen together with the likelihood for regularly occurring earthquakes along the planet's many fault lines where continental plates meet, the present international system for disaster preparedness and management does not seem adequate. A particular weakness seems to be the lack of coordination and control during the first two or three days of a major disaster, which are also the most murderous.

We have all seen on our television screens the unbearable images of scared and suffering men, women, and children waiting for relief. We are also aware of the waves of solidarity that accompany this situation, the funding, the voluntary helpers, the deliveries of food and other needed provisions. But we have also seen the confusion and uncertainties: lack of leadership, weak national and local administrations frantically trying to cope, and international institutions scrambling to help without sufficient coordination.

In many countries today there exist national structures for rapid, and coordinated, action in emergency situations. Imagine the impact of a similar arrangement in the United Nations: a global disaster coordinator with the power to mobilize within three to four hours an international help action that would serve as the immediate focus for everything that would follow; helping national governments to coordinate all the aid flows and taking on whatever tasks that would be necessary in the first crucial seventy-two hours. This can be done if such a system is trained through regular maneuvers and practice. The objective would be to have a disaster coordinator who would push a button and thereby set in motion without delay a well-oiled international machine.

Of course, there are objections: the present system does not function too badly, a structure of this kind would be too costly, where should the rapid intervention force be located?, etc. But what could be a better symbol of the capacity of organized mankind to deal with crises in an efficient way than images of a UN emergency force that operates swiftly and professionally to save lives in the immediate aftermath of a disaster and to prepare for the long-term reconstruction in a coordinated way, together with national governments? In the globalized world of today, the impact would be strong and create greater support for the United Nations also in other activities, such as peace-keeping operations or long-term development support.

Action supported by research

To a large extent, the new diplomacy has been driven by the natural sciences, as illustrated by the Rio Conventions. We also realize that the social sciences are needed to facilitate public support for environmental action, and more generally explain what will be the impact on our societies of different ways to cope with global change. Global problems require global research efforts, and we can see a tremendous increase in networking between researchers in different parts of the world, a development which is also strongly facilitated by the phenomenal growth of new information and communication technologies. For anyone familiar with the many aspects of climate change research, it is astonishing to see how new international initiatives are mushrooming at a time when the administrators and politicians are preparing for the post-2012 climate regime.

This underlines the importance of research as an essential component of the new diplomacy. Increasing efforts are made to ensure more contacts between researchers and the policy process. However, the new global research environment is still rather confused and unclear, characterized by a multitude of national and international initiatives. In Europe, the successive Framework Programmes for research command important resources in a manner which many Universities and Institutes find overly bureaucratic. On the whole, research funding is considered by many scholars as too complicated, forcing researchers to spend a large part of their time preparing bids for funding and working on reports how the resources are used.

No doubt, these tendencies are to a certain extent unavoidable in a world where research is expanding enormously and the number of people who receive higher education has increased in an astonishing way. This development is one of the central characteristics of the early twenty-first century, and all over the world governments are trying to cope with the requirements of this rapidly changing reality. It is also an environment characterized by hardening competition and questioning of old traditions in an academic world that is under rapid change.

Developing countries have for long been at a disadvantage in terms of higher education and research. The lack of resources has made it difficult to establish really good universities, even though development cooperation in many cases has enabled very fruitful exchange between academia in south and north. However, the natural career path for many scholars in the south has been to use scholarships to attend universities in Europe or North America, with the well-known corresponding risks for brain drain and a further weakening of the research environment in the south. In recent years, economic development in many Asian and Latin American countries have enabled radical improvement in the quality of university teaching and research, which means that in particular countries like India, China, and Brazil offer new opportunities, both with regard to research and to career perspectives.

Even so, however, the research agenda is heavily tilted in favor of the north, and in international discussions and negotiations, representatives of G 77 constantly underline the need for increasing participation in common research efforts related to global sustainability.

One example of this is IPCC, the Intergovernmental Panel on Climate Change, which includes more than 2000 scientists and government representatives, the large majority coming from the industrialized countries. Therefore, the appointment of Dr. R.K. Pachauri of India to chair the Panel has been an important signal, and a recognition of the problem.

Since we are dealing with eminently global problems here, it is natural that the issue of developing country participation in research must be given high attention. But the more general problem of the organization of research to have a maximum impact on policy processes is also a priority issue. We know that the success of our efforts to agree on global policies that will avert dangers of unknown dimensions may be a precondition for long-term survival of the species. We know that these efforts need to be based on solid foundations of knowledge. What models and methods should be used to reach the desired results?

IPCC has undoubtedly been a successful model with its efforts to integrate different disciplines, as well as natural sciences and social sciences, even if the main impact has been reached within the natural science domain. The Panel does not carry out research of its own; its over 2000 members evaluate research from all over the world and assess its relevance. The four assessments reports presented so far have all had a significant effect on the negotiations: in this respect the main tool has been the summary for policy-makers, normally presented by the IPCC Chairman at a session of the Conference of Parties. Between the assessment reports, the ongoing preparatory work serves to keep a continued interest in the issues discussed.

In my view, the climate negotiations would not have advanced the way they have, were it not for the work of IPCC. The political process needs this kind of input from the research community. A logical conclusion would be to ask whether also other negotiating processes could benefit from a similar scientific structure. All the other Rio conventions have some kind of scientific input in the form of subsidiary bodies to the Conferences of Parties. These are normally composed of government experts. I believe that the performance of these bodies is relatively uneven, but it is difficult to see the need for such further measures as the creation of an IPCC structure.

If there is one survival issue that has the same broad character as climate, it is *water and sanitation*. These problems are linked to a great number of natural and social sciences, and they are an integral part of the combat of poverty, as recognized in the Millennium Development Goals. There is no single institution dealing with them, but a significant number of organizations at all scales, both intergovernmental and nongovernmental. The concerns related to water range from the dry-lands of Sahel to the bustling metropolitan areas in Asia or Latin America. An important economic-political discussion about privatization and pricing of water resources leads to heated debates. Questions related to integrated water resource management and cooperation around international rivers are high on political agendas. On the scientific side, theories and practice on the movement of water in soils and rivers — the green water/blue water approach[13] — have led to a better understanding of the functioning of watersheds. There still needs to be a better understanding of irrigation practices, and more generally, the most economical use of water for agriculture. All questions related to water quality, and the role of healthy sanitation, are central to the quality of life for the hundreds of millions of people on the planet who are without these essential facilities and essential to global food security.

Against this background, I believe that it would be worth while to consider the arguments pro and con some kind of Intergovernmental Panel on Water, with a broad, but well defined mandate. Its role would be to review current research on the central issues related to water and present it to policy-makers in different fora, where water resources are discussed. Because of the complexity of the water problem, it is necessary to take time for a serious feasibility study. Such a study could be financed by national governments, or by the European Union, or by an intergovernmental organization. If there would be agreement to establish a Panel, I believe that it would best be linked directly to the United Nations. (IPCC was established by UNEP and WMO).

Information to the Public

Rational policies on global change are difficult to establish without the support of a well-informed public; in this book I have emphasized the importance for international negotiations of the enabling conditions at the national level. These conditions determine the boundaries of what can be achieved in the international arena; and they also determine the limits to implementation of international agreements on sustainable development.

However, in our information society with its fantastic stream of sensations, news and comments in the newspapers, on radio and television, on the web, available at any hour, it is not easy for information about long-term global change to reach the level of attention needed. Public discussion is limited to small, but rather active and highly motivated groups, often around Universities. And I do not see any great changes on the horizon, even if extraordinary events such as hurricane Katrina raise the awareness of the general public, and even if climate change has been given increasing attention over the last few years.

Our open and dynamic societies with their efficient market economy are essentially rather short-term in their way of looking at the world. I do not believe that this can be changed in a few years, and I am wary about public information campaigns. This is a long-term effort that has to begin with children at school, giving them a sense about the planet's limitations and our common responsibility for future generations, without alarmism, giving an understanding that the task is difficult but far from impossible. Such an approach should be linked to an effort to craft the tools for people to understand better the many different cooperation processes that exist in the world of today, thereby reducing the risks for alienation and passivism.

Public service media would have to carry their responsibility in promoting this approach and give more people the possibility to really understand the challenges we are facing. Once issues such as climate change appear more regularly in the media they will most probably remain there, increasing the possibilities for an enlightened political and public discussion about future action. To a certain degree this is already happening, but I hope that studies in journalism would from now on underline the importance of global survival issues, so that readers, listeners and viewers would have the opportunity to form their own opinion, and ultimately, require and support farsighted political action. These are also subjects that would seem to call for increased interest by others in the public eye, such as actors, musicians or writers. Ultimately, we are talking of issues that are not just cross-disciplinary between natural and social sciences. They also involve deep existential and ethical considerations, close to the humanities, to theology and, more generally, to culture. At the same time, the media must realize that there has to be increased, high-quality attention, based on serious and well-understood data, avoiding unnecessary scare-mongering.

SOME CLOSING COMMENTS

Our world today is an insecure place. Far from being the "end of history," the breakdown of the precarious and risky world order of the bipolar cold war, also meant the end of a logic that, paradoxically, tilted towards global security stability. The present situation with its single hegemon, increasingly challenged by new types of threats — the spread of nuclear capability, risks of terrorism, clashes of religious fundamentalisms — has a tilt towards global security instability.

The forces of democracy are stronger than ever, and new technology offers new opportunities for improvement of human conditions. More people than ever can aspire to a life in relative comfort. But these gains and potentialities often seem to lose in the race against forces that tend to increase inequalities, limit personal freedoms, and reduce the scope for civilized dialogue.

Traditional security thinking and traditional diplomacy, with its roots in the Westphalian tradition,[14] now struggles to adapt to a new and rapidly changing world. Strong new actors appear on the world scene and the role of national governments is limited by the emergence of world-wide corporations. In Europe, the European Union has created a new and positive relationship between countries, limiting the scope of sovereignty. It is in this situation that governments and individuals have to try to adapt to the requirements of the Anthropocene era with the emergence of global threats of a totally new character. As was pointed out in the Amsterdam Declaration of 2001, "the earth is currently operating in a no-analogue state." Mankind has never been here before.[15]

Does the existence of new global threats change the conditions for crisis management in the world, since all nations are in fact facing these new threats together? Can the new diplomacy contribute to lay the bases for a better working multilateral system? Can it craft the institutional structure that will permit us, and new generations, to effectively meet these new challenges? Long-term survival of the species may be in the balance. There will be pressures of a new kind in this process at all levels. For me it is quite obvious that we need to encourage and maintain a strong sense of fairness and justice, a culture of commonly shared burdens, if nations and the international community would be able to solve the problems facing us at this time.

As a practitioner of the new diplomacy, I believe it can be done; and that the next decades may well be decisive. But success will require far-sighted political leadership, and a firm trust in the capacity of people, of everybody, to understand the nature of the challenge. And ultimately, it can only be done within a well-functioning global multilateral system. After more than forty years of work in the world of multilateral institutions, I firmly believe that future historians will consider the evolution of the multilateral system as one of the great achievements of the twentieth century, and its adaptation to the new challenges of global change as a major sign of progress in the twenty-first century.

Notes

CHAPTER 1

1. The quotation is from an unpublished paper, referred to by the author in a personal conversation.

CHAPTER 2

1. It is worth noting that the Club of Rome with the report, "Limits to Growth," written by Donella H. Meadows, Dennis L. Meadows, Jorgen Randers and William W. Behrens III, already in 1972 made an extensive presentation of these problems. The world model set up by these researchers was built to investigate five major trends of global concern: accelerating industrialization, rapid population growth, widespread malnutrition, depletion of non-renewable resources, and a deteriorating environment. At the time, the Report was given a lot of attention, but as predictions with regard to non-renewable natural resources did not seem to materialize, the value of the whole exercise was questioned. However, a closer reading today shows that the main conclusions are still very pertinent today: "If the present growth trends in world population, industrialization, pollution, food production and resource depletion continue unchanged, the limits to growth on this planet will be reached sometime within the next one hundred years. The most probable result will be a rather sudden and uncontrollable decline in both population and industrial capacity." It is noteworthy that the Report talks about the "next one hundred years." We have still two-thirds of this period ahead of us. But the report also offers hope, in terms which also recall to-day's discussion, e.g., the recommendations of the Stern report on climate change: "It is possible to alter these growth trends and to establish a condition of ecological and economic stability that is sustainable far into the future....If the world's people decide to strive for this second outcome rather than the first, the sooner they begin working to attain it, the greater will be their chances of success."
2. "Stern Review: The Economics of Climate Change," 2006, Her Majesty's Treasury, London, http://www.hm-treasury.gov.uk.

CHAPTER 3

1. These principles were partly repeated in the Rio Declaration, one of the main documents of the 1992 Conference. To show that there has been a considerable continuity in the basic ideas behind the new diplomacy, I quote here the first point in the preamble to the Principles: "Man is both creature and moulder of the environment, which gives him physical sustenance and afford him the opportunity for intellectual, moral, social and spiritual growth. In the long and tortuous evolution of the human race on this planet a stage has been reached when, through the rapid acceleration of science and technology, man has acquired the power to transform his environment in countless ways and on an unprecedented scale. Both aspects of man's environment, the natural and the manmade, are essential to his well-being and to the enjoyment of basic human rights and the right to life itself."

CHAPTER 4

1. The participating countries were Algeria, Argentina, Australia, Brazil, Cameroon, Canada, Egyptian Arab Republic, EEC, India, Indonesia, Iraq, Iran, Jamaica, Japan, Mexico, Nigeria, Pakistan, Peru, Saudi Arabia, Spain, Sweden, Switzerland, United States, Venezuela, Yugoslavia, Zaire, Zambia. The reports are available in a 1977 document, entitled "Conference on International Economic Co-operation".
2. Morissey, O, Osei, R, Capital Flows to Developing Countries: Trends, Volatility and Policy Implications. *IDS Bulletin January 2004*, Institute of Development Studies, Sussex 2004.
3. For these reflections, I am indebted to an article in the review *Bridges* (published by ICTSD (Geneva), Year 10 No 7, November 2006, by Aaron Cosby, Associate and Senior Adviser, International Institute for Sustainable Development, Winnipeg).
4. The text of the foot-note certainly did not reflect the drama of its drafting:
5. As Chairman of the negotiating group in Berlin, I tend to agree with G 77 on this point. Furthermore, as an ironic footnote to the Byrd-Hagel resolution, Senators told me in the spring of 2001, after the Bush "no" to Kyoto, that by that time a Senate vote on such a text would probably have given a much smaller majority. Obviously, this question also played a role in the struggle between Republicans and Democrats on the ratification of Kyoto, since the United States, and in particular Vice President Al Gore, had agreed in Kyoto that developing country commitments were in fact strong enough and that US could sign the Kyoto Protocol, which they did in 1998.
6. Together with the brilliant Iranian diplomat Mohammed Salamat I chaired the negotiations between 1998 and 2000 on the question of the effects of actions to combat climate change (Articles 2.3 and 3.14 of the Kyoto Protocol), which raised several of the problems related to the OPEC position. We tried several formulas to achieve agreement, including a compromise package in the Hague COP-6 in November 2000, which could not be adopted there. In the Bonn COP-6 bis, however, a very similar text was agreed.
7. It remains to be seen if this long text will have much impact. It goes further than Article 4.1 of the Convention and it contains a number of ideas, which could promote positive action on such issues as energy and transport, adaptation and spatial planning. The article is of an enabling rather than a prescriptive nature, and its ultimate fate will no doubt depend on the general political atmosphere in which the Protocol will be implemented.

CHAPTER 5

1. The "soft" windows of the multilateral development banks provide funding for development purposes on concessional terms with grace periods and low interest rates, often close to grants. Since this erodes the capital base available, resources have to be replenished, normally for a period of three or four years. The negotiations are drawn-out affairs over a couple of years, with short meetings followed by long periods of informal consultations. It is generally an efficient method to raise substantial sums of money.
2. For this section, I am indebted to an extensive description of events during these important years leading up to the climate negotiations in M. Paterson, *Global Warming and Global Politics*, Routledge, London and New York, 1996.
3 The original proposal was made by Malta.
4. In the SEI publication *Negotiating Climate Change*, I.M. Mintzer and J.A. Leonard (eds.) 1994, Cambridge University Press, Cambridge.
5. The key text in Article 4.2.a) should be read in conjunction with Article. 4.2.b):
   Art. 4.2.a): "........These policies and measures will demonstrate that developed countries are taking the lead in modifying longer-term trends in anthropogenic emissions consistent with the objective of the Convention, recognizing that the return BY THE END OF THE PRESENT DECADE to earlier levels of anthropogenic emissions of carbon dioxide and other greenhouse gases not controlled by the Montreal Protocol would contribute to such modification......."
   Article 4.2.b) (Mainly dealing with reporting): "In order to promote progress to this end, each of these Parties shall communicate........detailed information on its policies and measures referred to in subparagraph a) above, as well as on its resulting projected anthropogenic emissions by sources and removals by sinks of greenhouse gases not controlled by the Montreal Protocol for the period referred to in subparagraph a), with the aim of returning individually or jointly TO THEIR 1990 LEVELS these anthropogenic emissions of carbon dioxide and other greenhouse gases not controlled by the Montreal Protocol........"
   (Texts in capitals marked by the author).
6. Since this subparagraph continues to have an impact on negotiations, it is worth quoting in full:

   The Conference of Parties shall, at its first session, review the adequacy of subparagraphs a) and b) above. Such review shall be carried out in the light of the best available scientific information and assessment on climate change and its impacts, as well as relevant technical, social and economic information. Based on this review, the Conference of the Parties shall take appropriate action, which may include the adoption of amendments to the commitments in subparagraphs a) and b) above. The Conference of Parties, at its first session, shall also take decisions regarding criteria for joint implementation as indicated in subparagraph a) above, A second review of subparagraphs a) and b) shall take place not later than 31 December 1998, and thereafter at regular intervals, until the objective of the Convention is met.

7. The text of the Mandate on these issues is contained in paragraph 2,a) and b). Relevant parts are reproduced here:
   "The process will, inter alia,

a) Aim, as the priority in the process of strengthening the commitments in Article 4.2 a) and b) of the Convention, for developed country/other Parties included in Annex I, both

- to elaborate policies and measures, as well as
- to set quantified limitation and reduction objectives within specified time-frames, such as 2005, 2010 and 2020, for their anthropogenic emissions by sources and removals by sinks of greenhouse gases not controlled by the Montreal Protocol taking into account the differences in starting points and approaches, economic structures and resource bases, the need to maintain strong and sustainable economic growth....

b) Not introduce any new commitments for Parties not included in Annex I, but reaffirm existing commitments in Article 4.1 and continue to advance the implementation of these commitments in order to achieve sustainable development...."

8. See second bullet point under a) above.
9. A detailed account of this period, as well as an analysis of the Kyoto Protocol itself, is to be found in the commentary by Michael Grubb with Christiaan Vrolijk and Duncan Brack, *The Kyoto Protocol. A Guide and Assessment*, The Royal Institute of International Affairs and Earthscan, London, 1999.
10. Held after the publication of IPCC's Second Assessment Report, which for the first time stated the conclusion that there was now an anthropogenic impact on the global climate.
11. The Swedish case could serve as an example how the Dutch method worked: In the period 1973–1988, Swedish emissions of carbon dioxide were reduced by almost 40 % (largely because of the development of nuclear, but also as a result of increased energy efficiency). Given the use of 1990 as a base year, Sweden was granted the right to increase its emissions under the Kyoto Protocol with 4%. For domestic political reasons, however, Sweden has decided not to use this facility, opting instead for a reduction of 4%.
12. On the general question of the status of mechanisms, the EU had to accept vague language saying that mechanisms should be supplemental to domestic action: in the following years the EU spent many hours trying to define what supplementarity really meant.
13. This was a bold statement, since the construction of the conditions for entry into force of the protocol contains a double criterion: a total of 55 ratifications, *and* the participation of Annex I countries representing at least 55% of Annex I CO2 emissions in 1990. As the United States then accounted for 36.1% of these emissions, it is easy to see that the margin was extremely narrow and that the ratification of Russia with its 1990 emissions of 17.4% of the total was a necessary condition for success.
14. After long hesitations, Russia finally decided to ratify the Protocol, which entered into force on February 16, 2005.
15. It is against this background that I feel that there were never any prospects for a last-minute deal with the US in The Hague in December 2000 to be accepted and honoured by the Bush administration.

CHAPTER 6

1. Tellmann, S.M., *Fra argumentasjon til kjøpslåing*, (From arguing to barganing) 2005, Institutt for sociologi og samfunnsgeografi, Oslo University, Oslo.

2. The hierarchical position of the negotiator is an important factor: senior officials have more latitude in interpreting their instructions. This is also the reason for the ever more frequent participation of Ministers in the final stages of negotiation. Experience shows, however, that political level negotiations can only be really efficient if the issues to be negotiated are few and clearly defined.
3. Beck, U., 1995, *Ecological enlightenment: Essays on the politics of the Risk Society*, Humanity Books, New York; original 1991, *Politik in der Risikogesellschaft, Sihrkamp*, Verlag, Frankfurt am Main.
4. Strydom, P, 2002, *Risk, Environment and Society*, Open University Press, Buckingham, UK.
5. Steuer, M, 2003, *The Scientific Study of Society*, Kluwer Academic Publishers, Boston.
6. Sustainable development is now generally considered to include economic, social and environmental sustainability. However, the first two components have been objectives of governments' policies for a long time, whereas the environment, and in particular the global environment, has appeared only over the last decades.
7. Söderbaum, P, 2000, *Ecological Economics*, Earthscan, London.
8. http://www.hm-treasury.gov.uk
9. Schmidheiny, S., with the Business Council for Sustainable Development, 1992, Changing course. A global business perspective on development and the environment, MIT Press, Cambridge, Mass.
10. It had originally been planned to have a resumed session of the COP in May, but the United States asked for more time to prepare, and other parties agreed to postpone the session until July; I met a rather optimistic tone, even in environmentalist circles, when visiting Washington in February, representing EU; and the Head of EPA, Christine Whitman made encouraging noises at a G 7 meeting of Ministers of Environment in February.
11. For a detailed account of the EU reaction and the ensuing negotiations, see Chapter 5.
12. At the time of writing, the most important of these agreements is the one with Australia, Japan, Korea, China and India, concluded in the summer of 2005. However, it is yet unclear what would be its real impact.
13 See Chapter 2, p. 15.
14. A typical example is "Letter to Columbus" (1973), in which Edberg has a dialogue with Columbus that ends on the following note: "What we do, or not do, to-day, may decide whether we have any future at all. Much will be different from what we hope or fear. But it just does not happen. Our action is dependent on our view of the future. And our view of the future may within certain limits shape the future. If we accept that a disaster is inevitable, this may become a self-fulfilling prophesy. But utopias can also become reality, if they are allowed to determine our action. It is late in the world, Senor Almirante. But not too late, if we decide to live on the conditions imposed by the planet. So easy — and therefore so difficult!"
15 This expression is coined by the Dutch researcher H.J.M. de Vries in an article in "The Environment: Towards a Sustainable Future," Kluwer, Dordrecht 1994, quoted in Marcel Kok et al. , eds. 2002, *Global Warming and Social Innovation*, Earthscan, London.
16. Menne B., Ebi KL (ed.) 2006, *Climate Change and Adaptation for Human Health*, Steinkopff Verlag, Darmstadt.
17. The famous French writer Antoine de Saint-Exupéry has formulated this feeling in an excellent way in his book *Terre des Hommes* (1939), in English, *Wind, Sand and Stars: What makes us human is our sense of responsibility.*

It is being ashamed of something beyond our direct control. It is to be proud of the achievement of our friends. It is to realize that when we place our stone, we help building the world.

CHAPTER 7

1. At the European level, the original idea for European integration by Jean Monnet and Robert Schumann was an example of adapting notions of sovereignty and multilateral processes to a new reality, aimed at strengthening the notion of a European identity. In practice, this was manifest in the independent position of the European Commission and in rules for majority voting in the Council.
2. It is notable that the two concrete goals included here strictly speaking are more part of the combat of poverty than of environmental improvement.
3. The role of the WSSD in the overall follow-up to the 1992 Rio Conference on Environment and Development is described in Chapter 3.
4. For more details, see chapter 4.
5. Secretary-General's High-Level Panel , 2004, United Nations, New York: Executive Summary.
6. General Assembly Resolution 60/1; 2005 World Summit Outcome.
7. Lecture at Uppsala University, Sweden, January 26, 2006.
8. Commission on Global Governance, 1995, *Our Global Neighbourhood*, Oxford University Press, New York.
9. The Chief Negotiator of the United States in this negotiation, Ambassador Richard Benedick, has given an important contribution to the understanding of the particular problems of the New diplomacy in his book *Ozone Diplomacy.*
10. It should be mentioned, however, that an international agreement on tropical timber (ITTA) has been concluded within the FAO. Also, on water, there is an international convention on the non-navigational use of international waterways.
11. In fact, Ingvar Carlsson, in his autobiography *Så tänkte jag* (*This is how I thought*) (Hjalmarson och Högberg Bokförlag, Stockholm, 2003) has stated that the cool reception of some of these proposals was among the worst disappointments he had experienced in a long and successful political career.
12. Decision 1/1 by the Preparatory Committee for the Rio Conference gave NGOs the right to participate in all meetings of the various bodies with the consent of the Chairman and the members of the committee concerned; this decision has governed practice in all related negotiations. In practice, NGOs have been present in most meetings with the exception of particularly sensitive negotiations.
13. Elaborated by the prominent Swedish researcher, Professor Malin Falkenmark.
14. It was the Peace of Westphalia in 1648 that established a European security system, based on established national states.
15. The Amsterdam Declaration was adopted by the Global Change Open Science Conference on July 13, 2001. This Conference was sponsored by the scientific communities of four international global change programmes (IGBP, IHDP, WCRP, DIVERSITAS). The full quote of the text follows: "In terms of some key environmental parameters, the Earth System has moved well outside the range of the natural variability exhibited over the last half million years at least. The *nature* of changes now occurring *simultaneously* in the Earth System, their *magnitudes* and *rates of change* are unprecedented. The Earth is currently operating in a *no-analogue state.*"

Bibliography

Acot, Pascal, 2003, *Histoire du Climat*. Paris : Editions Perrin..

Beck, U., 1999, *World Risk Society*. Cambridge: Cambridge Polity Press.

Benedick, Richard Elliot, 1991, *Ozone Diplomacy. New Directions in Safeguarding the Planet*. Cambridge, Mass.:Harvard University Press,

Biel A., Hansson B., and Martensson, M. (eds.), 2003, *Individual and Structural Determinants of Environmental Practice*. Aldershot: Ashgate Publishing Ltd.

Brennan A., 2005. Globalisation and the Environment: Endgame or a New Renaissance? In *Environmental Values in a globalising World*, J. Paavola J. and I. Lowe (eds.). Oxon and New York: Routledge.

Chase-Dunn, C., 1992, *Global Formation: Structures of the World Economy*. Cambridge, Mass.: Blackwell.

Chasek, Pamela, S., 2001, *Earth Negotiations, Analyzing Thirty Years of Environmental Diplomacy*, United Nations University Press, Tokyo.

Clark, W. C., Crutzen, P. J., and Schellnhuber, H.J., 2005, *Science for Global Sustainability, towards a New Paradigm....* In Schelluhuler et al. eds. Earth System Analysis for Sustainability. Cambridge, Mass.: MIT Press.

Corell, E. 1999. *The Negotiable Desert*, Linkoping, Sweden: Linkoping University.

Cox, R. W., 1996, A Perspective on Globalization. In *Globalization. Critical Reflections*, J. H. Mittelman (ed.). Boulder, Colo: Lynn Rienner Publishers.

Commission on Global Governance (co-chairmen Carlsson, I. and Ramphal, S., 1995), *Our global neighbourhood*. Oxford: Oxford University Press.

Dasgupta, C., 1994, The Climate Change Negotiations, in *Negotiating Climate Change, The Inside Story of the Rio Convention*. Cambridge: Cambridge University Press and Stockholm Environment Institute,

Ebbesson, J., 1996, *Compatibility of International and National Environmental Law*. Uppsala: Justus Publishing Company.

Elliot, Lorraine, 1998, *The Global Politics of the Environment*. London: MacMillan Press.

Final Text of Agreements negotiated by Governments at the UN Conference on Environment and Development (UNCED) 3–14 June 1992, Rio de Janeiro, Brazil. 1992. New York: UN Publications, Sales number E 93.1.11.

Friedman, T. L., 2000, *The Lexus and the Olive Tree*. New York: Anchor Books.

Gilpin, R., 1987, *The Political Economy of International Relations*. Princeton, N.J.: Princeton University Press.

Grubb, Michael, et al., 1999, *The Kyoto Protocol. A Guide and Assessment*, London: Royal Institute of International Affairs.

Hobshawn, E., 1994, *The Age of Extremes: A History of the World 1914–1991*. New York: Pantheon.

Hurrel, Andrew, 1993, International Political Theory and the Global Environment. In *International Relations Theory Today*, (ed.) K. Booth and S. Smith (eds.), University Park: The Pennsylvania State University Press.

International Labour Organization, 2004, Press release issued February 24, 2004 (ILO/04/07), Geneva.

Jakobsen, Susanne, 1999, International Relations and Global Environmental Change: Review of the Burgeoning Literature on the Environment. *Cooperation and Conflict*, 34 (2), 205–236.

Keohane, Robert, 1996, *Internationalization and Domestic Politics*. New York: Cambridge University Press.

Kjellén, B., 1993, Lessons to be drawn for the Future, in *International Environmental Negotiations*, Swedish Council for Planning and Coordination of Research (FRN) Stockholm/Uddevalla.

———, 1994, A personal assessment, in *Negotiating Climate Change. The Inside Story of the Rio Convention*. Cambridge: Cambridge University Press and Stockholm Environment Institute.

———, 1999, Acceptance address, *Pace Environmental Law Review*. New York: Vol. 17.1.

———, 2001, Climate Negotiations at a crucial stage. *Natural Resources Forum* 25 (2001), 173–184. New York: United Nations/Elsevier Science Ltd.

———, 2005, Diplomacy and governance for sustainability in a partially globalised world, in *Environmental Values in a Globalising World*, J. Paavola and I. Lowe (Eds.). London: Routledge.

Kok, M., Vermeulen W., Faaij A., and de Jager D. (eds.), 2002, *Global Warming and Social Innovation. The Challenge of a Climate-Neutral Society*, Kluwer, Dordrecht.

Lewis, W. A., 1978, *The Evolution of the International Economic Order*. Princeton, N.J.: Princeton University Press.

Lipschutz, R.D., and Conea, K. (eds), 1993, *State and the Social Power in Global Environmental Politics*. New York: Columbia University Press.

Litfin, Karen, 1999, Environmental Security in the Coming Century, in *International Order and the Future of World Politics*, (ed.) T.V. Paul, T V and J. H. Hall (eds.), Cambridge: Cambridge University Press.

Mittelman, J. H., 1996, The dynamics of Globalization, in *Globalization. Critical Reflections*, (ed.) J.H. Mittelman (ed.), Boulder Colo.:Lynn Rienner Publications.

Mwandosya, M.J., 2000, *Survival Emissions, A perspective from the South on Global Climate Change Negotiations*, DUP Limited, University of Dar es Salaam.

Myers, Norman, 1993, *Ultimate Security: The Environmental Basis of Political Stability*. New York:WW Norton.

Myrdal, G., 1978, Institutional Economics, in *Journal of Economic Issues*.

O'Riordan, T., and Jaeger, J. (eds.), 1996, *Politics of Climate change: The European Perspective*, London: Routledge.

O'Riordan, T., and Stoll-Kleemann, S. (eds.), 2002, *Biodiversity, Sustainability and Human Communities*. Cambridge: Cambridge University Press.

Paterson, Matthew, 1996, *Global Warming and Global Politics*. London/New York:Routledge.

Raskin, P., Banuri, T., et al., 2002, *Great Transition, The Promise and Lure of the Times Ahead*. Boston: Stockholm Environment Institute

Rassool, N. 1999, *Literacy for Sustainable Development in the Age of Information*. Clevedon UK: Multilingual Matters Ltd.

Riggs, J. A. (ed.), 2004, *A Climate Policy Framework: Balancing Policy and Ppolitics. A Report of an Aspen Institute Policy Gialogue November 14-17, 2003.* Washington, DC: The Aspen Institute.

Sachs W., 1995, *Global Ecology: A new Arena of Political Conflict.* London: Zed Books.

Sánchez, V., and Juma, C., 1994, *Biodiplomacy. Genetic Resources and International Diplomacy.* Nairobi:African Centre for Technology Studies.

Soderbaum, P., 2000, *Ecological Economics.* London:Earthscan.

Steger, M.B., 2003, *Globalization. A Very Short Introduction.* Oxford: Oxford University Press.

Steuer, M., 2003, *The Scientific Study of Society.* Amsterdam: Kluwer.

Stokke, O.S., Hovi, J., and Ulfstein, G., 2005, *Implementing the Climate Regime: International Compliance.* London: Earthscan.

Stripple, J., 2001, *Climate Change and International Relations.* Lund: University of Kalmar, Sweden, KFS AB.

———, 2005, *Climate Change after the International.* Lund: Lund University.

Strydom, P., 2002 *Risk, Environment and Society.* Buckingham: Open University Press.

Susskind, Lawrence E., 1994, *Environmental Diplomacy. Negotiating more effective global agreements.* Oxford: Oxford University Press.

Thurow, Lester, 1992, *Head to Head. The Coming Economic Battle among Japan, Europe, and America.* New York: William Morrow and Company, Inc.

Urquhart, B., and Childers, E., 1996, *A World in need of Leadership: Tomorrows United Nations.* Uppsala: Dag Hammarskjold Foundation.

World Bank, 2003, *World Development Report 2003: Sustainable Development in a Dynamic World.* Washington, DC: World Bank and Oxford University Press.

World Commission on Environment and Development (Chair Brundtland G H), 1987, *Our Common Future.* Oxford: Oxford University Press.

Yamin Farhana, and Depledge Joanna, 2004, *The International climate change regime: a guide to rules, institutions and procedures.* New York: Cambridge University Press.

Young, Oran, 2002, *The Institutional Dimensions of Environmental Change.* Cambridge, Mass.: MIT Press.

Index

184 *Index*